Sent as a Gift

Sent as a Gift

Eight Correspondences
from the Eighteenth Century

EDITED BY

Alan T. McKenzie

The University of Georgia Press

ATHENS & LONDON

© 1993 by the University of Georgia Press
Athens, Georgia 30602
All rights reserved

Designed by Kathi L. Dailey
Set in Garamond No. 3 by Tseng Information Systems, Inc.
Printed and bound by Thomson-Shore, Inc.
The paper in this book meets the guidelines for permanence and
durability of the Committee on Production Guidelines for Book
Longevity of the Council on Library Resources.

Printed in the United States of America

97 96 95 94 93   C 5 4 3 2 1

Library of Congress Cataloging in Publication Data

Sent as a gift : eight correspondences from the eighteenth century /
edited by Alan T. McKenzie.
        p.   cm.
    Includes index.
    ISBN 0-8203-1466-8 (alk. paper)
        1. English letters—History and criticism.   2. Authors,
English—18th century—Correspondence—History and criticism.
3. English prose literature—18th century—History and criticism.
4. Great Britain—Civilization—18th century—Historiography.
5. Eighteenth century.   I. McKenzie, Alan T.
PR915.S46   1993
826'.509—dc20   92-6568
                                                          CIP

British Library Cataloging in Publication Data available

CONTENTS

PREFACE

This volume originated in a discussion session on correspondence at the American Society for Eighteenth-Century Studies meeting in Minneapolis in 1990. The session was organized and chaired by the editor, and versions of four of the chapters (on Burney, Diderot, Dodsley, and Johnson) were presented. Several of the other contributors participated in the spirited discussion that followed. Subsequent correspondence has availed itself of the post offices of several countries, various parcel services, the fax machine, electronic mail, and the telephone. One of several satisfactions in editing this volume has been corresponding by these various technological means with those who give considerable thought to the letters they write as well as the letters they study. Jill Quirk, the secretary of the Graduate English Office at Purdue, has seen to the comings and goings of this correspondence with her customary cheerful efficiency. My wife, Ann, as always, has provided careful proofreading, good sense, and general encouragement.

THE LETTERS from *Jane Austen's Letters to Her Sister Cassandra and Others*, ed. R. W. Chapman, 2 vols. (1932); *The Letters of Dr Charles Burney*, vol. 1, *1751–1784,* ed. Alvaro Ribeiro, S.J. (1991); and *The Letters of Daniel Defoe*, ed. George H. Healey (1955), are quoted by permission of Oxford University Press. Methuen London, which incorporated Eyre & Spottis-woode, has granted permission to include three letters from *The Letters of Philip Dormer Stanhope, 4th Earl of Chesterfield*, ed. Bonamy Dobrée, 6 vols. (1932). The letters from the National Edition of Diderot, *Correspondance*, ed. Georges Roth and Jean Varloot, 16 vols. (1955–70), are published with the permission of the editors. Letters by Robert Dodsley published in *The*

Correspondence of Robert Dodsley, 1733–1764, ed. James E. Tierney (1989), are reproduced by permission of the Syndics of Cambridge University Press. The two letters reprinted here from *The Letters of Samuel Johnson*, ed. Bruce Redford, 5 vols. planned (1992–), © 1992 and 1993 by Princeton University Press, are used by permission of Princeton University Press, Oxford University Press, and the editor. Southern Illinois University Press has granted permission to use the texts of two letters from *The Annotated Letters of Christopher Smart*, ed. Betty Rizzo and Robert Mahony (1991).

Sent as a Gift

Introduction

Alan T. McKenzie

In the essays that follow, eight scholars discuss two letters apiece, drawn from eight different, important, and absorbing correspondences. The idea is to enable scholars who know an entire correspondence well to write for readers who may not have read all, or indeed any, of that correspondence but who want more than summaries, generalizations, or a ransacking for biographical or critical details. Each of us has selected letters fraught with the excellences, complexities, and considerations that figure throughout the correspondence from which they have been drawn.

Writing for readers we know have these letters in hand, and thus clearly and freshly in mind, has allowed us to elaborate on aspects and materials that have not been dealt with sufficiently in the past. We have allowed the letters we have chosen to combine with our own critical and scholarly backgrounds to dictate our methods. The essays thus offer instructive selections from important correspondences as well as an assortment of critical approaches committed to the inspection of texts rather than the discussion of method. Defoe's letters demand far more attention to local historical detail than to niceties of style, while Chesterfield's deep polish invites comment on the craft of courtliness. The letters of Smart require some discussion of attitudes toward insanity in the period, while the ethical concerns in Johnson's letters admit a surprisingly effective application of Kierkegaard. The letters of Burney and Dodsley provide contrasting lessons in civility—the former deploying it in deference, the latter in retaliation. And while Jane Austen's letters submit rather elegantly to a concern with empowerment, it would be pointless to indict the fatherly tone that Diderot adopts toward a young actress as "patriarchal" at the expense of his concern for her filial duties toward her mother. The afterword draws illuminating parallels of its own and suggests ways in which these gifts might well be construed as commodities.

While we have sought primarily to make more and better readers of these eight correspondences, we hope also to create better readers of all correspondences and perhaps of eighteenth-century literature and history as well. The correspondences of this period throw fresh and stimulating light on aspects of the period important to every genre written during it, from domestic and commercial arrangements to local and international politics. Readers of this volume will gain insight not only into the ways letters were written, sealed, sent, and received but also into the places where they were written and read and the various purposes, private and public, explicit and implicit, for which they originally changed hands. Not all epistolary windows open into the bosom. Those following look in on, among other things, the irregularities of regional electoral practices, the difficulties of selling books by subscription, a music lesson, the politics of getting a play produced, the wisdom of age imposing itself on the young (three remarkably different examples), and an endless, but highly significant, series of comings and goings by coach and carriage. Whatever they look in on is likely to be instructive, and the windows themselves are entitled to more inspection than they have received.

As Bolingbroke and Pope wrote to Swift in a frequently cited joint letter: "When we read them [the letters of Cicero], we pry into a Secret which was intended to be kept from us, that is a pleasure. We see Cato, and Brutus, and Pompey and others such as they really were, and not such as the gaping Multitude of their own Age took them to be, or as Historians and Poets have represented them to ours, that is another pleasure" (Pope 3: 102). Correspondence is an important genre in its own right and is entitled to its own readings and its own informed discussion, of manner as well as content.

We have not sought to generate anything so elaborate as a "poetics" or a "hermeneutics" of correspondence. Nonetheless, we trust that readers of the following essays will turn to the remaining letters in these and other correspondences with a better understanding of the numerous considerations that ought to be brought to such intriguing texts. For years we have all been learning and teaching how to read the poetry, fiction, plays, and essays of this period, yet we have few ways to read its many superb correspondences.[1]

The Letter as a Document

A strong sense of occasion, audience, and author—a sense reiterated explicitly in almost every letter ever written—sets one letter apart from another and any letter apart from many other texts that attract critical attention. Each of the essays below sets forth the controlling particulars of each letter, particulars of origin, purpose, content, and destination. In working with a genre so steeped in historical, biographical, and textual circumstance, we are especially fortunate to have contributions by the editors of four correspondences (those of Burney, Diderot, Dodsley, and Smart) and the biographer of a fifth correspondant (Defoe). The other contributors are similarly responsive to the actual documents and their various contexts.

The letters included here of Burney, Diderot, and Dodsley, as well as the second letter of Smart, were intended primarily, and probably exclusively, for an audience of one—the addressee (though Diderot may have had an eye on posterity). Other letters, as different as the political letters of Defoe, the diplomatic letters of Chesterfield, and the domestic letters of Jane Austen, expected a slightly larger readership to be drawn from and into the recipient's circle. Swift acknowledges this widened, but still select, circle of readers in a letter to Lord Bathurst: "When I receive a letter from you, I summon a few very particular friends, who have a good taste, and invite them to it, as I would do if you had sent me a haunch of venison" (4: 410). That haunch of venison acknowledges the generosity and skill of the landowning letter writer at the same time that it compliments the taste and establishes the size of the circle that will enjoy the letter. It also, I might add, confirms the title of the present volume.

Some letter writers, of course, wrote with publication and posterity very much in mind. Pope is the most notorious example, but Johnson certainly knew that a letter from him was an event and that Boswell would share all sorts of intimacies with his innumerable acquaintances. Even the reticent William Shenstone and the intermittently diffident Anna Seward seem to have hoped for eventual publication of their "private" letters, while Elizabeth and Richard Griffith publicized their courtship and subsidized their marriage with a correspondence that contributed to the former and maintained the latter.[2] The distinction between letters written for publication, like those of Pliny, Seneca, and Voiture, and those, like Cicero's, written with only the recipient in mind, was made early and often, invariably to the advantage of the latter. As Bolingbroke says in the joint letter already quoted: "I seek no Epistolary fame, but am a good deal pleased to think that it will be known hereafter that you and I lived in the most friendly intimacy tog[e]ther.—Pliny writ his letters for the Publick, so did Seneca, so did Balzac, Voiture &c. Tully did not, and therefore these give us more pleasure than any which have come down to us from Antiquity" (Pope 3: 102).

However small or large the circle of original readers the letter writer had in mind, not even the essayist, who comes closest to the letter writer in this regard, can have as clear and confined an idea of, or as much control over, who will read the text as the person who signs his or her name at the bottom of a letter. The letter writer's certainty of original audience, however, often works to the disadvantage of the modern reader, who will almost always need some assistance to enter the coterie and follow the continuing discussion.

At the same time they invoke and extol their own occasion and particularities, most letters develop and extend a correspondence already under way—a record of a friendship, a family narrative, or a history of a business or a political transaction. This element is in some danger of being overlooked by those who read only the two letters from each correspondence on which we concentrate. It ought to serve as an incentive to turn to the several correspondences in their entirety.

The fact that each letter in a continuing correspondence was separated from other letters in that correspondence by several weeks, months, or years may well be lost on those who read straight through one of the multivolume sets in which most correspondences now reach their readers. This foreshortening is inevitable but distorting, as one of the burdens a letter carries is that of contracting or accounting for the interval between it and its predecessor. The letters included here from early and late in the friendship between Johnson and Boswell illuminate the continuity and development of one correspondence, while those from Jane Austen, written within three days of one another, compress this immediacy into continuity as well as intimacy. The sense of domestic urgency and the closeness of the correspondents are reflected in the nearness of the dates. This precise, and actual, sense of time complements the strong sense of place in most letters. Not only the moment at which they were written, but also the interval between that and the moment they will be read, or the interval between the moment one was being written and the moment another was written before it, will often figure in the text itself, as a conceit, a consideration, or a worry.

The written word will always be more formal than the spoken and more intimate than the printed. Every letter brings to the hand that holds it not only the words of the hand that wrote it but, in the writing in which those words are embodied, also the character, authority, and person of the writer. Harley's wound at the hand of Guiscard, we are told in the first essay, showed up in the penmanship of his letters, and Cassandra Austen would have the evidence of her sister's struggles with her pen ("as my pen seems inclined to write large I will put my lines very close together"; November 3, 1813) right in front of her. (She would also encounter her sister's comments on her own, i.e., Cassandra's "pretty hand . . . so small & so neat" later in the same letter.) The heaviness of Chesterfield's fatherly hand must frequently have been felt by his son in the very ink on the page, while the single sheets of Smart have an eloquence of their own. The price subsequent readers pay for legibility, consistency, and annotation is that of estrangement from the hand, and inevitably also from the mind, of the author.[3]

The form of the letter, as a separate, handwritten sheet conveyed across some distance, a tangible, legible "gift" from the writer to a specific intended reader (in the literal and philosophical sense), is the most important of all these considerations and the one most likely to be suppressed by the modern printed format. Obscured by collecting, editing, typesetting, and footnoting, the original sheets that passed, eventually and only after considerable effort, from under the writer's hand into the reader's should always be somewhere in the mind of subsequent readers. Frequent references to torn sheets, half sheets, runny ink, and previous letters remind us that the sense of recipient, occasion, and author will, of necessity, be stronger in this genre than any other.[4]

Other components of the letter follow from these of time and text and deserve attention in turn. A strong sense of place, for example, is to be expected in a text composed in one place and read in another, especially when its author has both places very much in mind and wants to bring the same places and their separation into the mind of the reader. Thus Chesterfield makes much of the dullness of The Hague, Defoe of the dangers of Edinburgh, and Burney of the remoteness of Norfolk, while Jane Austen writes of the excellent fire in her own (borrowed) room and Smart celebrates

his situation "ad marginem Oceani." Occasionally the difficulties of trans-
mitting the text between these two places will come under discussion, but
most letters, like those included here from Paris to Warsaw or one part of
London to another, assume that they will be delivered.

This confidence was not misplaced. Chartered in 1660, reestablished on
a sounder footing in 1711, the British Post Office was made much more
efficient and reliable after 1720 by Ralph Allen, who was well rewarded for
his contributions. Defoe celebrated the efficiency of the Penny Post, which
delivered letters throughout London: "The Penny Post, a modern Contriv-
ance of a private Person, one William Dockraw, is now made a Branch of
the general Revenue of the Post Office; and though for a time it was subject
to Miscarriages and Mistakes, yet now it is come also into so exquisite a
Management, that nothing can be more exact, and 'tis with the utmost
Safety and Dispatch, that Letters are delivered at the remotest Corners of
the Town, almost as soon as they can be sent by a Messenger, and that
Four, Five, Six to Eight Times a Day, according as the Distance of the
Place makes it practicable."[5] Defoe goes on to boast that there is no service
like this in Paris, Amsterdam, Hamburg, "or any other City." Most of the
letters included in this volume would have gone through the Inland Office;
those of Dodsley went through the Penny Post. Chesterfield's letters were
handled, in several senses of the word, by the Foreign (Post) Office, a separate division. Only the letters of Jane Austen would have taken advantage
of the next major improvement of the age, the mail coach, which entered
service on August 2, 1784 (Robinson 137–39).

Considerations of space and time fuse in occasional ballistic (and New-
tonian) figures in letters of the period. Pope uses one in a letter to Gay, just
back from Hanover: "During your Journeys I knew not whither to aim a
letter after you, that was a sort of shooting flying." Chesterfield launches
weightier missiles over greater distances: "I received a letter from him [Lord
Huntingdon] by the last post, but by his account of his intended motions
they were to be too rapid for me to take any good aim at him."[6]

William Cowper invokes this spatial consideration in a more peaceable
figure that, like the trajectory metaphor and Swift's haunch of venison,
draws the reader of this century back into the one in which it was written: "A letter is Written, as a Conversation is maintained, or a Journey
perform'd, not by preconcerted, or premeditated Means, by a New Con-
trivance, or an Invention never heard of before, but merely by maintaining

a Progress, and resolving as a Postillion does, having once Set out, never to Stop 'till we reach the appointed End" (1: 374).

Implicit in these analogies and in most of the letters reproduced below, is the realization that only the letter can transcend the long and difficult distances between sender and recipient and that for many months or years the letter in hand will often have to take the place of the person who wrote it. This is sometimes, but not always, a matter of regret. Walpole and Mann, for example, exchanged 1,800 letters in the forty-five years after they first met in Florence, but they never met again. As Pope wrote to Lady Mary, letters remove "those punctillious Restrictions and Decorums, that oftentimes in nearer Conversation prejudice Truth to save Good breeding."[7] Swift, on the other hand, consoled himself for his banishment to Dublin with long and frequent letters—a consolation that has extended itself, and his self, into later ages.

It is sometimes a matter of regret for later readers when distance does not necessitate a correspondence. Many have wished, for example, that Cicero had not been just across Rome from Atticus at crucial junctures or that Fielding had been out of London longer and had had more leisure and inclination for letter writing.

The distance to be covered by a letter is sometimes more social than geographic. Burney's first letter to Johnson in this volume exploits its remote Norfolk origins to render the social distance visible, but negotiable, while the one to Mrs. Thrale maintains the distance of an employee, though an employee who is also a teacher. This dimension of status and power was carefully measured in the eighteenth century (and one or two others), and a good letter acknowledged this distance at the same time that it crossed it. All of the letters below are good, and all of them, in one way or another, acknowledge the social as well as the geographic distances they have crossed. In most cases both crossings could then have been managed only in an epistolary vehicle.

When a good letter reached the right recipient, it could effect something not often available even in personal encounters. Johnson wrote to Mrs. Thrale what he probably could not have said to her in person: "I know, dearest Lady, that in the perusal of this such is the consanguinity of our intellects, you will be touched as I am touched."[8] A long series of good letters prolonged the intimacy, as Shenstone wrote to one friend about another who had taken his gifts too lightly: "I considered them [his own letters] as the records of a *friendship* that will be always *dear* to me, and as the *history* of my *mind* for these twenty years last past."[9] Some gifts cannot be presented in person but last longer because of it.

The resolve that enabled a postillion to cover the necessary ground in the appointed time would, as Cowper said, have been even more essential to those who wrote the letters he carried. It took a fair amount of resolution to produce a letter worth sending and worth receiving and much more to produce a whole correspondence worth editing, publishing, and studying. The word *resolution* itself sometimes appears in a letter, while the state of mind it designates is always implicit. Johnson speaks of it in his first letter to Boswell reproduced here ("but it is not without a considerable effort of resolution that I prevail upon myself to write"), while Jane Austen mentions how "fatiguing" it is to write a whole long letter in a single day. Keith Stewart reminds us that the "degree of resolution required" to carry on a correspondence must be greater than that to carry on a conversation (180). We must all, I think, be grateful that so many resolute correspondents so often made the effort to produce results of such lasting value.

The Genre

Most eighteenth-century letter writers, and certainly all those whose letters appear in this volume, knew they were participating in, and competing with, a long tradition. Allusions to Cicero, Voiture, and Madame de Sévigné abound, with little trace of anxiety of influence. In letters as in so much else, Cicero is both a polished practitioner and a compiler of the practices and theories of his predecessors. His incidental comments on genre and decorum were often repeated, together with his comment, in a letter of his own, that a letter is either a dialogue or a substitute for one.[10] His lofty position and numerous disappointments, personal and professional, made Cicero's letters absorbing reading, but they are too personal and particular to serve as models for subsequent correspondences. Those eighteenth-century letter writers who managed to project an air of magnanimity in their letters did not learn to do so from the *letters* of Cicero.

After Cicero, the major classical letter writers were the sententious and "perpetually entertaining" Seneca, and Pliny the Younger—a student of Quintilian, a retailer of anecdotes, and a maker of conceits.[11] Various classical texts recommend that letters should be cast as dialogues or conversations and convey glimpses of character, traces of friendship, advice, or proverbs. They mention concision, clarity, charm, and spontaneity as desirable features of style. The classical letter, however, has never received the critical attention given to more public forms of discourse.[12] Rhetoricians have always shown some interest in letters but have seldom made them central to their systems. Sophists, we are told, "quite regularly occupied the position of *ab epistulis* in chanceries" (Malherbe 3), but early handbooks merely sort letters into kinds, discuss style, and provide models.

The early, probably Egyptian (and eminently Ciceronian) handbook of Demetrius, "On Style," was written sometime between 200 B.C. and A.D. 300. It says that the "letter should be a little more studied than the dialogue, since the latter reproduces an extemporary utterance, while the former is committed to writing and is (in a way) *sent as a gift*." Sentences in a letter should have fewer "breaks" than those in a conversation, but the document should provide just as many glimpses of character. It should be short, graceful, and plain, but it may rely on proverbs and a little logic. And letters written to "States or royal personages . . . must be composed in a slightly heightened tone."[13] While it is unlikely that any of the letter writers studied here felt the need to consult this handbook before they took up their quills, it is perhaps worth mentioning that Demetrius was inflicted on both Milton and Coleridge at school.[14]

The letter was an essential tool of the early humanists, given their separation, their commitment to texts, and (frequently) their offices as secretaries to the Renaissance state. Erasmus transmitted the theory and practice of the classical letter writers, especially Cicero, to posterity in an unfinished treatise and a vast number of letters of his own—"two wagon loads," as he put it.[15] Several collections of his letters were published during his lifetime. Erasmus burned these publications whenever he could, but some 1,600 of his letters still survive. It is difficult to calculate their influence in the eighteenth century, but it would be easy to exaggerate it. Nonetheless, there is no question but that Erasmus gave epistolary substance to the idea of a "man of letters."

Incidentally, the early humanists could by no means be certain that their letters would be delivered. Letters to and from Erasmus wandered all over Europe, and some of them never reached their addressee (Binns 56–57). On the other hand, the exchange of letters throughout the Roman empire was much more manageable, as it was effected by slaves maintained by important households solely for this purpose (Ogilvie 56).

Letter writing has always been a device for conducting education as well as displaying it, and it may well have been part of the curriculum in Greek and Latin schools, taught by both grammarians and rhetoricians, and perhaps also by civil servants (Malherbe 6–7). A naughty, demotic letter from Theon, an Egyptian schoolboy of the second or third century, to his father survives, and most of the letter writers of the eighteenth century (including those examined in the essays to come) left evidence of their precocity.[16] Early handbooks put classical models in the hands of schoolchildren: Charles Hoole's *A Century of Epistles English and Latine . . . By imitating of which, children may readily get a proper style for writing Letters* (1660), is one example (see Winn 45–46). More pertinent to our purposes is *The Preceptor: Containing a General Course of Education* (London, 1748). This very popular and pragmatic handbook was compiled by one of the letter writers studied here (Dodsley) and contributed to substantially by another (Johnson), while a third (Chesterfield, just before he resigned as secretary of state) granted the copyright.[17]

The preface, probably by Johnson, recommends that "this great Art should be diligently taught, the rather, because of those Letters which are most useful, and by which the general Business of Life is transacted, there are no *Examples* easily to be found" (xvii). It suggests that it is much more important that "young Persons should be taught to think justly, and write clearly, neatly, and succinctly" than to give orations of condolence or panegyric (xvii–xviii).

The brief introduction to the section of *The Preceptor* "On Writing Letters" quotes Locke on the importance of letters to education and includes the sensible statement that "the Truth is, a fine Letter does not consist in saying fine things, but in expressing ordinary ones in an uncommon manner. It is the *proprie communia dicere,* the Art of giving Grace and Elegance to familiar Occurrences, that constitutes the Merit of this kind of Writing" (84). The handbook laments the lack of English models and then supplies examples by Temple, Pope, Gay, Cicero, Pliny, Voiture, and Balzac. The last example, an anonymous letter "To a young Gentleman at School," recommends a plan "which rises like a well-contrived Building, beautiful, uniform, and regular"; attention; practice; complete freedom of subjects; brevity; and a familiar, but not a mean, style: "A Letter should wear an honest, chearful Countenance, like one who truly esteems, and is glad to see his Friend; and not look like a Fop admiring his own Dress, and seemingly pleased with nothing but himself" (107–8).

As the models supplied by Dodsley suggest, the great early French letter writers were enormously influential. It was they, rather than the humanists, who were published, translated, and mentioned repeatedly in the correspondences of the eighteenth century, especially the formal Jean-Louis Guez de Balzac and the lively and elaborate Vincent Voiture, who eclipsed him. Voiture perfected the art of compliment, a component evident in most of the letters in this volume and at least implicit in every effective letter ever written.[18]

It might be argued that a letter in itself constitutes a compliment to its addressee. Most good letters extend that compliment in one way or another, while trying not to escalate it into flattery. Even letters of scolding and abuse draw on this convention. Johnson's celebrated and indignant letter to Chesterfield is but the most extravagant example (*Letters*, no. 61). The two letters by Dodsley reproduced here could hardly be taken as compliments, but they rely on that convention for their force.

Madame de Sévigné, perhaps the most cited and imitated letter writer of all time, exerted her spell primarily on letters written to convey or dispose of leisure—a form of gift not as well represented in this volume as it is in most of the correspondences of the period. Here is Walpole, her most devoted disciple, extolling the glitter he so admired in her letters and enumerating the elements he expected, and supplied, in a good informal letter: occasion, wit, air, allusions, locations, style, techniques, and content.

> Madame de Sévigné shines both in grief and gaiety. There is too much of sorrow for her daughter's absence; yet it is always expressed by new turns, new images, and often by wit, whose tenderness has a melancholy air. When she forgets her concern, and returns to her natural disposition, gaiety, every paragraph has novelty: her allusions, her applications are the happiest possible. She has the art of making you acquainted with all her acquaintance, and attaches you even to the spots she inhabited. Her language is correct, though unstudied; and, when her mind is full of any great event, she interests you with the warmth of a dramatic writer, not with the chilling impartiality of an historian. Pray read her accounts of the death of Turenne, and of the arrival of King James in France, and tell me whether you do not know their persons as if you had lived at the time.[19]

While the correspondences discussed in the essays that follow all give rise to some very instructive readings, not all of them are among the best known of the period, nor do they by any means represent all the correspondences available, published or unpublished. Dozens of other correspondences have already been well edited and await critical and theoretical readings. *The New Cambridge Bibliography of English Literature* includes nearly a thousand citations of primary and secondary sources (1569–1600). A *Dictionary of British and American Women Writers, 1660–1800* mentions many more correspondences, published and unpublished (esp. 15–16), and the on-line version of the *Eighteenth-Century Short Title Catalogue* offers what looks to be an inexhaustible assortment of gifts that have not been opened for two hundred years.

The Critics

While it is certainly true that the practice of letter writing has outstripped the criticism of it, I do not wish to suggest that nothing has been done since Cicero and Demetrius. I have drawn heavily on my list of works cited throughout this introduction, and the other contributors have cited a good many additional sources. Nonetheless, most of the attention letters have received has been from editors and scholars rather than critics. The reasons are not far to seek.

Most of the reasons that letters enjoyed the neglect of formalism and have yet to receive the interrogations of more recent criticism are implicit in what has just been said about the form and content of the letter. Some years ago Irvin Ehrenpreis complained of the neglect of the letter by formalists: "To the extent that we bound our thinking by the so-called imaginative genres canonized in nineteenth-century criticism, we are cut off from a proper judgment of the so-called nonimaginative masterpieces. We neglect Gibbon for Goldsmith. Not our taste but our narrow critical method has sealed us in; and many who must be academic critics condemn themselves to the minute examination of tedious novels, motionless tragedies, icy pentameters, and frivolous essays sooner than confront the fascination of a Walpole or a Hume." [20]

That passage serves as the epigraph to *The Converse of the Pen*, one book that goes a long way to removing this neglect. Bruce Redford disregards the looseness of the form and treats six major correspondences—those of Montagu, Cowper, Gray, Walpole, Boswell, and Johnson—as "verbal construct[s]," unfolding their intricacies, intimacies, and delicate allusions with sensitivity and tact. Generally, however, the controlling pressures on a letter are those of character and occasion rather than form, and the strong historical and documentary aspects of many letters, especially those in this volume, are of little interest to the formalist.

Brief quotations from letters have always, of course, served the purposes of biographers and historians, literary and cultural. Swift's letter to Pope on "animal rationis capax" (September 29, 1725) is known to every reader of *Gulliver's Travels*, and Johnson's famous letter to Chesterfield is a central text in literary history. Jane Austen's "little bit (two Inches wide) of Ivory" (December 16, 1816) is a critical chestnut, while Cowper's correspondence, to name but one example, opens his troubled bosom to all manner of scrutiny. But the many fine correspondences of the eighteenth century deserve better than the neglect of formalism or the selective ransacking of history and biography. It is not yet clear whether they will get it from any of the current critical camps.

In the first place, letters were both referential and self-reflexive *avant la lettre*. Every one relies and insists on such documentary features as author, date, addressee, and purpose. All of them make frequent reference to events and persons that are manifestly "outside the text" and known to be there by both author and recipient. All these features render the letter inconvenient for those critics who want to assimilate everything into "discourse." The conventions they exploit and the cargo of content they deliver make letters so manifestly "socially constructed" that it cannot be very profitable to deconstruct them. Nor can a document that relies so transparently on preceding texts and an expected reply contribute much to the reputation for ingenuity of someone who explores "textuality."

Substantial portions of a genre that from its beginnings has incorporated what Demetrius called "glimpses" of "character" will elude those critics who prefer to work with fragments of "identity."[21] The men and women who wrote and received the letters in this volume and thousands of others like them may, of course, have been mistaken, but they thought their letters were records of actualities—actual events, actual sentiments, actual insights, actual friendships. They seem to have sent them as tributes to humanity, their own and that of those they sent them to. They trusted the language they put on paper to convey their experiences, ideas, and sentiments to distant others who would be glad (usually) to receive word from them. They sent, in other words, gifts. We need not call them "literature," as long as in reading them we remain attentive to genre, form, style, character, and content. And if we must call them "texts," we ought to remain susceptible to their meanings and charitable to their values.

Several central concerns of postmodernism, especially desire and narra-
tivity, figure in a few genuine correspondences, but these concerns soon
drive critical attention to epistolary novels. Elizabeth J. MacArthur, for example, shows how dependent the fictional letter is on the "groping present"
(24).[22] She then tries to show "the essential similarity of the two forms
[actual and fictional correspondences], in both of which narrative drives
forward to an open future instead of looking back over a completed past"
(32). It seems to me, however, that most of the letters in the following
essays rely on the immediate (and therefore pretty certain) past and the
manageable (and therefore highly probable) future. This makes them, I
suppose, decidedly premodern.

A concern with desire, traceable to Roland Barthes's *Fragments d'un discours amoureux*, draws Linda S. Kaufman to review the genre of the amorous
epistle from the *Heroides* to *The Three Marias: New Portuguese Letters*.[23] Desire
certainly figures at the heart of every epistolary novel (Rousset calls them
cardiogrammes [78]; Versini, *des romanciers qui brûlent le papier* [100]) and less
centrally in some proportion of actual letters. But Redford demonstrates
convincingly that Lady Mary Wortley Montagu's mature style depended
on her having disciplined her desire by a close reading of Epictetus (24–
28), and I suggest that some such detachment is evident in the writing
of even the most urgent of the letters in these essays. The sending of
them presupposes a stronger centrifugal force than most theorists attribute
to desire, and the form modifies that passion in ways too complex to be
considered here.

These and other critics rely extensively on the work of Janet Gurkin Altman, whose *Epistolarity* sets forth many complex techniques that have some
application to documentary texts. That work employed *epistolarity* to mean
"the use of the letter's formal properties to create meaning" (4), whereas
the documents treated here may be thought to contain and convey meaning
within the "formal qualities" of an actual document. It is by doing this
that they become the gifts they were composed to be. Altman's thoughtful
and provoking afterword to the present volume reads the letters that come
between it and this introduction as actual documents.

More could be said of the differences between actual correspondences
and the epistolary novels, in both of which the eighteenth century ex-
celled, but it will be more to the point to indicate some of the ways critical
techniques developed for the epistolary novel might usefully be applied to
actual documents. A genre of some five hundred works, including *Clarissa*

and *Les Liaisons dangereuses*, will not want for strong criticism. Techniques for understanding the *romans par lettres* are considerably more numerous, more sophisticated, and more complicated than those for understanding actual letters. Readers of actual correspondences can probably manage without Genette's intra- and extradiegetic narratees (265–66) and Jost's "kinetic polylogues" (155–59), intriguing though these may be.[24] A few other terms and techniques offer better possibilities for insight and analogy.

For example, the attention to the moments of writing and the interval between these and the time the letter will be read becomes an even more intricate "temporal polyvalence" in Altman's *Epistolarity* (129–34), and the time and space between epistles reproduce the fragmentation that discourse loves to feed upon. Some of the attendant subtleties accorded this feature carry over to actual letters, but most of them derive from the interval between the supposed reading by the fictive reader and repeatedly perceptive rereadings by an actual, and highly trained, critical reader.

Similarly, the distinction between an internal and an external reader is essential to epistolarity, and the "epistolary reader is empowered to intervene, to correct style, to give shape to the story, often to become an agent and narrator in his own right" (Altman 91). Readers of the letters in these essays will want to be no less subtle, critical, or highly trained, but they will, I hope, use these qualities to diminish the disparity between their understandings and those of the original readers. They can never, of course, become "internal readers," but the more they "intervene," the more they risk spoiling something of value.

The critical intricacies necessitated by the epistolary novel may well be adapted to make the reading of actual correspondences more subtle. But the two branches of postmodernism I would expect to be especially useful to reading these works are the ones that might find themselves either challenged or modified by these complex and intriguing texts. First, Habermas's widely employed idea of "public space" is brought to bear, to very good effect, in the first essay and in the afterword. Letters, as I have tried to show, measure space precisely and transcend it resolutely, but with care. These documents render the difference between public and private space less distinguishable and should probably be invoked to adjust this convenient sociological generalization.

In addition, those critics who concern themselves overmuch with the ascription and distrust of power might do well to consider how minutely this entity is measured, and how subtly wielded or deflected, in every letter, indeed in every paragraph in every letter treated here. The might of the pen must have made a strong impression on the original recipients of each of these letters. But these are projects for another occasion.

It is time for the reader to take the letters in hand and, having done so, to begin, with the help of the essays that discuss them, to improve his or her own ways of reading them. Those who wrote them had their own ideas and experiences, and they took pains to express them well (and usually in their own handwriting) for friends or acquaintances, to whom they then sent them, as gifts. Once worth sending and receiving, these well-crafted emanations from good and copious minds will still repay careful, informed reading.

NOTES

1. Excellent work has been done by Anderson, Daghlian, and Ehrenpreis; Irving; Winn; and, especially and most recently, Redford. For a survey of the period's own precepts on letter writing, see Stewart; for some ruminations rooted in letters themselves, especially the letters of Swift and Cowper, see Spacks; for some theoretical speculations on the genre, see Fruman. French correspondence has been well studied in *Men/Women of Letters*; see especially Janet Gurkin Altman, "The Letter Book as a Literary Institution, 1539–1789: Toward a Cultural History of Published Correspondences in France," 17–62. John W. Howland's *The Letter Form and the French Enlightenment: The Epistolary Paradox* (New York: Peter Lang, 1991) appeared too late for us to use.

2. For Pope, see his *Correspondence* and Winn; for Shenstone and Seward, see Irving 261, 324–25; for the Griffiths, see Betty Rizzo's entry on Elizabeth in *A Dictionary of British and American Women Writers, 1660–1800*. Even Pope, who was most willing to see his letters in print, had only about one-tenth of the letters now available published in his lifetime.

3. The recent edition of *The Letters of Charles and Mary Anne Lamb*, ed. Edwin W. Marrs, Jr. (Ithaca, N.Y.: Cornell UP, 1975), conveys "locutions written larger than those near them" by printing them "in boldface or, when underscored, in boldface italic" (1: xciv); the typography does not bring the reader closer to hands of the authors. Nonetheless, half an hour with the recent facsimile edition of Jane Austen's letters will reconcile even the most devoted reader to the convenience of type: see *Jane Austen's Manuscript Letters in Facsimile*, ed. Jo Modert (Carbondale: Southern Illinois UP, 1990). See also the discussion of Defoe's difficult hand in Paula R. Backscheider's essay, in this volume.

4. See, for example, Chesterfield's letter of May 22, 1749 (no. 1641), or Lady Mary's closing to her daughter: "I am at the end of my paper, which shortens the

Sermon of, Dear Child, your most affectionate Mother." *The Complete Letters of Lady Mary Wortley Montagu*, ed. Robert Halsband, 3 vols. (Oxford: Clarendon, 1966), 2: 477.

5. Daniel Defoe, *A Tour Thro' the Whole Island of Great Britain* (London: 1727), 1: 343–44; quoted in Robinson 85–86. In 1750 it took a coach ten days to reach London from Edinburgh and a day and a half to get from London to Oxford. The pressures were greater between London and Bath, and thus both the roads and the service were better; by 1780 the 120-mile trip, which had taken two days in 1750, could be accomplished in sixteen or seventeen hours (Robinson 128–30). Until John Palmer introduced the mail coach in 1784, most letters and passengers traveled by the same slow coach; the letters, presumably, were less susceptible to the discomforts and dangers.

As for Allen, "under the guise of a contractor of the by and cross post letters, he was the prime mover in extending the postal service to all parts of the country, setting up numerous new branches, and effecting nation-wide increases in the number of posts per week" (Robinson 106; see also 100–111). For some evidence of the shortcomings and intrusions of the British Post Office, see Molitor; for the history of the French Post Office, see Charles A. Porter's foreword to *Men/Women of Letters* 9–11 and the sources cited there.

6. Pope 1: 254. Chesterfield 2179, no. 1971; cf. no. 1885.

7. Pope 1: 354; see also Stewart 180–81. For Walpole and Mann, see Wilmarth Sheldon Lewis, *Horace Walpole* (New York: Pantheon, for Bollingen Foundation, 1960), 52.

8. Johnson, *Letters* no. 559, October 27, 1777. Redford finds "slippery tonal ambiguities and theoretical inconsistencies" in this discussion of the intimacy a good letter can establish (214–15).

9. *The Works, In Verse and Prose of William Shenstone*, 3 vols., 6th ed. (London: 1791), 3: 234–35; quoted in Irving 261.

10. Malherbe 12. Cicero's letters are edited by D. R. Shackleton Bailey for Cambridge University Press and selected and translated for Penguin Classics. Bailey's *Cicero* (New York: Scribner's, 1971) puts them to splendid use.

11. Bolingbroke used that phrase for Seneca in a letter to Swift: "He is seldom instructive, but he is perpetually entertaining" (2: 414). Macaulay was less complimentary, comparing Seneca's letters to a meal of anchovy sauce; I owe this reference and some of the judgments in this paragraph to Donald Russell, "The Arts of Prose: The Early Empire," *The Oxford History of the Classical World*, ed. John Boardman, Jasper Griffin, and Oswyn Murray (Oxford: Oxford UP, 1986): 653–76.

12. The scant mention in Donald Lemen Clark, *Rhetoric in Greco-Roman Education* (New York: Columbia UP, 1957), 105–6, is indicative. See also Stanley K. Stowers, *Letter Writing in Greco-Roman Antiquity* (Philadelphia: Westminster P,

1986), which provides background for the New Testament Epistles; these had no discernible influence on the letters of the eighteenth century.

13. "Demetrius 'On Style,'" trans. W. Rhys Roberts, in *Aristotle, "The Poetics"; "Longinus," "On the Sublime"; Demetrius, "On Style"* (Cambridge: Harvard UP, 1960), 439 (italics added), 441–45. See also the introduction by W. Rhys Roberts 257–93; and Malherbe 4.

14. See pp. 281–82 of Roberts's introduction, cited in n. 13.

15. For Erasmus, see Binns; the *duo plaustra* are on p. 56. The response of the Italian humanists, especially Petrarch, to Cicero's letters was always complex and occasionally epistolary; see Jacob Burckhardt, *The Civilization of the Renaissance in Italy*, trans. S. G. C. Middlemore (New York: Harper & Row, 1929; New York: Harper Torchbook, 1958), 236–39, 256–58.

16. "Letter from Theon, an Egyptian boy, to his father Theon," in Adolf Deissmann, *Light from the Ancient East: The New Testament Illustrated by Recently Discovered Texts of the Graeco-Roman World*, trans. Lionel R. M. Strachan (New York: Hodder & Stoughton, 1910), 187–90.

17. I have used the fourth edition (London, 1763); for Chesterfield's granting of copyright, see 1 : 1. As the reader will see in James Tierney's essay, Chesterfield and Johnson both worked on Dodsley's behalf again, in promoting *Cleone*.

18. Winn 59–61 is especially good on the conventions of epistolary compliment.

19. Horace Walpole to John Pinkerton, June 26, 1785, in *Horace Walpole's Correspondence with Thomas Chatterton, Michael Lort, John Pinkerton, John Fenn and Mrs Fenn, William Bewley, Nathaniel Hillier*, ed. W. S. Lewis and A. Dayle Wallace, The Yale Edition of Horace Walpole's *Correspondence*, vol. 16 (New Haven: Yale UP, 1951), 273; also discussed in Irving 330–31.

20. Irvin Ehrenpreis, "Swift's Letters," *The Character of Swift's Satire: A Revised Focus*, ed. Claude Rawson (Newark: U of Delaware P, 1983), 227; first published in *Focus: Swift*, ed. Claude Rawson (London: Sphere Books, 1971), 197–215; quoted by Redford on p. vi. Fruman speculates on some ways in which correspondence might yield to "interpretation."

21. Samuel Johnson scrutinized the claims of the letter to project "character" in his "Life of Pope" (*Lives* 3: 206–8). Winn also subjects the concept to investigation (167–83).

22. The original term, *un présent tâtonnant*, is Rousset's.

23. Kaufman's book, *Discourses of Desire: Gender, Genre, and Epistolary Fictions*, explores the implications of every word in its title and the correspondences among them. But the focus on the amorous epistle draws Kaufman away from "natural" utterances like the ones explored in these essays and steers her toward the "poetic" texts of the epistolary novel. That distinction, frequently cited, belongs to Barbara Herrnstein Smith 19–20; see also 23–24 and 139–40.

24. See also Altman 112n and 204–5. *Les Liaisons dangereuses* is kinetic because the action proceeds through as well as in letters to protagonists and a polylogue because of the number of correspondents. Jost's taxonomy is both helpful and stimulating, but there are too many subgenres of actual letters even to attempt to illustrate them. Indeed, the letter is probably the genre with the most subgenres of any, because its genre, like its form, is dictated by character and occasion. And if its genre subdivides and modulates, its content is so various as utterly to defy cataloging. Any given letter may contain any or none of the following: anecdote, scandal, opinion, news, maxims, excuses, rebukes, apologies, propositions, requests, introspection, banter, congratulations, advice, moralizing, pedantry, preaching, and any or none of dozens of similar lists that might be extracted and put forward.

WORKS CITED

Altman, Janet Gurkin. *Epistolarity: Approaches to a Form*. Columbus: Ohio State UP, 1982.

Anderson, Howard, Philip B. Daghlian, and Irvin Ehrenpreis, eds. *The Familiar Letter in the Eighteenth Century*. Lawrence: UP of Kansas, 1966.

Austen, Jane. *Jane Austen's Letters to Her Sister Cassandra and Others*. Ed. R. W. Chapman. 2 vols. Oxford: Clarendon, 1932.

Binns, J. W. "The Letters of Erasmus." *Erasmus*. Ed. T. A. Dorey. London: Routledge & Kegan Paul, 1970. 55–79.

Boswell, James. *Boswell's Life of Johnson*. Ed. George Birkbeck Hill, rev. L. F. Powell. 6 vols. Oxford: Clarendon, 1934–50.

Chesterfield, fourth earl of (Philip Dormer Stanhope). *The Letters of Philip Dormer Stanhope, 4th Earl of Chesterfield*. Ed. Bonamy Dobrée. 6 vols. London: Eyre & Spottiswoode, 1932.

Cowper, William. *The Letters and Prose Writings of William Cowper*. Ed. James King and Charles Ryskamp. Vol. 1. Oxford: Clarendon, 1979.

A Dictionary of British and American Women Writers, 1660–1800. Ed. Janet Todd. London: Rowman & Littlefield, 1987.

Fruman, Norman. "Some Principles of Epistolary Interpretation." *Centrum* ns 1, no. 2 (Fall 1981): 93–106.

Genette, Gérard. *Figures III*. Paris: Seule, 1972.

Habermas, Jürgen. *The Structural Transformation of the Public Sphere*. 1962. Cambridge: MIT P, 1989.

Irving, William Henry. *The Providence of Wit in the English Letter Writers*. Durham, N.C.: Duke UP, 1955.

Johnson, Samuel. *The Letters of Samuel Johnson, with Mrs. Thrale's Genuine Letters to Him*. Ed. R. W. Chapman. 3 vols. Oxford: Clarendon, 1952.

————. *Lives of the English Poets*. Ed. George Birkbeck Hill. Oxford: Clarendon, 1905.

Jost, François. *Essais de littérature comparée*. Vol. 2, *Europaeana*. Urbana: U of Illinois P, 1969.

Kaufman, Linda S. *Discourses of Desire: Gender, Genre, and Epistolary Fictions*. Ithaca: Cornell UP, 1986.

MacArthur, Elizabeth J. *Extravagant Narratives: Closure and Dynamics in the Epistolary Form*. Princeton: Princeton UP, 1990.

Malherbe, Abraham J. *Ancient Epistolary Theorists*. Atlanta: Scholars Press, 1988.

Men/Women of Letters. Ed. Charles A. Porter. *Yale French Studies* 71 (1986).

Molitor, Helen. "Jonathan Swift and the Post Office: 1710–1713." *Eighteenth-Century Life* 13 (1989): 70–78.

The New Cambridge Bibliography of English Literature. Vol. 2, *1660–1800*. Ed. George Watson. Cambridge: Cambridge UP, 1971.

Ogilvie, R. M. *Roman Literature and Society*. Sussex: Harvester Books, 1980.

Pope, Alexander. *The Correspondence of Alexander Pope*. Ed. George Sherburn. 5 vols. Oxford: Clarendon, 1956.

The Preceptor: Containing a General Course of Education. 4th ed. London, 1763.

Redford, Bruce. *The Converse of the Pen: Acts of Intimacy in the Eighteenth-Century Familiar Letter*. Chicago: U of Chicago P, 1986.

Robinson, Howard. *The British Post Office: A History*. Princeton: Princeton UP, 1948.

Rousset, Jean. *Forme et signification: Essais sur les structures littéraires de Corneille à Claudel*. Paris: José Corti, 1963.

Smith, Barbara Herrnstein. *On the Margins of Discourse: The Relation of Literature to Language*. Chicago: U of Chicago P, 1978.

Spacks, Patricia Meyer. "Forgotten Genres." *Modern Language Studies* 18 (1988): 47–57.

Stewart, Keith. "Towards Defining an Aesthetic for the Familiar Letter in Eighteenth-Century England." *Prose Studies* 5 (1982): 179–92.

Swift, Jonathan. *The Correspondence of Jonathan Swift*. Ed. Harold Williams. 5 vols. Oxford: Clarendon, 1965.

Versini, Laurent. *Le Roman épistolaire*. Paris: PUF, 1979.

Winn, James Anderson. *A Window in the Bosom: The Letters of Alexander Pope*. Hamden, Conn.: Archon Books, 1977.

Accounts of an Eyewitness:
Defoe's Dispatches from the Vale of Trade
and the Edinburgh Parliament House

Paula R. Backscheider

Daniel Defoe to Robert Harley, September 10, 1705

SIR

My absence from the Bath, where I had Appointed my Brother to Meet me and where having waited Two dayes I Could not Satisfye my Self to spend my Time, Occasion'd me to Miss him Longer then I Intended and Consequently to Deferr my Giveing you an Account That by him I Recd as well the Supply as the Repeated Expressions of your Concern for my Safety, for both of which Sir I Owe More Acknowlegements than I Can Express this Way.

I spent about 8 dayes, the Intervall I Mention above, in Goeing back into Somersetshire and that Great Vale of Trade Extending from Warminster on the south bordr of Wilts to Cirencester in Gloucester shire, which lyeing so Out of the Road I Could no Otherwise take Either Goeing or Comeing without Omitting places of Equall Moment.

Here I shall give you an Account & I hope to satisfaction of strange and Unaccountable people as well as practises in the late Elections, with a survey something perticular of the Towns of Warminster, Westbury, Bradford,

Defoe to Harley, Sept. 10, 1705, from Defoe, *Letters* 103–4, no. 42; Defoe signs the letter "AG," for Alexander Goldsmith, one of his pseudonyms. Defoe to Harley, Nov. 5, 1706, from Defoe, *Letters* 142–43, no. 60.

Trubridge, Chipenham, Caln, Divizes, Malmsbury, Bedwin, Lutgersall, Marleboro', Cirencester, &ca.

Here I am to Note to you Sir that *Watt White* Member for Chipenham is Dead, and that all the Gentry of the high party who here act like Devills more than Men, *pardon the Expression,* are Embark't to get in if possible that scandall of the County Coll Chivers, and the Design is not so Much to have the Man in the house as to shelter him from the prosecution of my Ld Bishop of Salisbury who prosecutes him for most Impudent language, of all which I have the perticulars.

Sir there Can not be a greater peice of Service to the publick nor Can any Thing Tend more to Carrying future Elections in this County, which Now Run higher and worse than in most places in England, than to prevent this project, and One step above would do it Effectually Viz: putting Chivers Out of the Commission of peace to which he is Really a horrible scandall— for by being in that power he Influences the Town, Sitts Dilligently at Every petty sessions, and Aws the people. He was at this work when I was at Chipenham—This may be done Obliquely; No Man Need kno' who hurt them. His Character will most Clearly Justifye it and No man Can Object. If he is Out of the peace he Certainly looses the Election.

My Ld Mordaunt stands against Mr Chivers but his Intrest is but weak yet.

Bristoll, Gloucester, and Bath are Entirely Reform'd Cittyes and the Moderate Intrest prevails amain.

Divizes and the wholl County of Wilts are Corrupted and abused by the *Iron-Chest*, a Modern proverb now known in this Country as Universally as the Alphabet. The Meaning is the Reciever Genll of the County is Sir Fra: Childs Bro: [John] whose Influence so Rules by Lending Money that who ever is Needy is sure to be bought off.

The Remove of that One Article would make 20 Members more, of which I Reserve till I have the honour to see you.

I am Now Moveing North, shall be at Shrewsbury to morrow and at Manchester Thursday from whence Ile do my self the honour to write again, and where I may Reciev any Ordrs from you if you please to Direct to Robt Davis, to be left at the post house at Manchester Till Call'd for, for I shall Go to Leverpool & Come back thither.

I am I bless God Got Clear of all the Enemies I apprehended and am Every where Recd with Unusuall Respect.

It a little surpriz'd me At Gloucester when Mr Forbes the Dissenting

Minister bid me at parting Give his humble service to you for he knew I had the honour [to] be known to you. I Can no way Divine his Intelligence unless Mr Auditor might mention it to him.

I am, Sir, Your Most Obedient

A G

Kiderminster, Sept. 10. 1705

Daniel Defoe to Robert Harley, November 5, 1706

SIR

Since my Last the Face of affaires I hope are a little Mended and after a Very Long and Warm Debate on Fryday whether they should proceed on the Union or Go first on the security of the Church, it was past proceed.

On Saturday they sat till near 8. at night and the speeches on both sides were long and Warm.

D Hamilton Rav'd, Fletcher of Saltoun, and the Earle of Belhaven, Made long speeches, the Latter of which Will be printed—the Clamour without was so great That a Rabble was feared tho' the Guards are Numerous and were Drawn Out in Readyness.

Addresses are Delivred in from Severall places and More prepareing but tis observ'd the addresses Discover a Fraud which shows the party here at their shifts.

The addresses are found in the Cant of the Old Times Deploreing the Misery of scotland for want of a Further Reformation and the security of the Church and the Lords Covenanted people, but when the Names Come to be Examind'd they Are all sign'd by known Jacobites and Episcopall men.

There has been a farther Expectation of a Mob and some practises have been used to Infect the souldiers, but the E of Leven Call'd the Guards together to day and made a speech to them. They had been posesst with a Notion that they should be sent to the West Indees as soon as the Union was Over.

My Ld Leven I hope has Reestablisht them, and the proceeding since is more favourable.

Last night the Grand question was put whether the first Article—Or in short the Union it self should be approved or Not—and Carryed in the Affirmativ which being On King Williams Birthday is to me Very Remarkable and Encouraging.

I had to day the Honour to be sent for by the Lds Comittee for Examining the Equivalents and to assure them in the Calculateing the Draw back on the salt, the proportion of the Excise and some addenda About Trade.

They profess themselves Oblig'd to me more than I Merit and at their next Committee I am Desir'd to Dine with them. I am lookt on as an English man that Designs to settle here and I think am perfectly Unsuspected and hope on that foot I do some service—Onely I spend you a great Deal of Money at which I am Concern'd but see no Remedy if I will go thro' with the work.

I have Now Great hopes of it tho' to day the assembly men make a great stir; in short the Kirk are *au Wood* [all mad], pardon the scotticisme.

Your Most Obedt Servt
D F

Edinb. Nov. 5. 1706

Context of the Letters

For several months in 1704 and 1705 Daniel Defoe traveled through England collecting election opinion for Secretary of State Robert Harley; in the fall and winter of 1706 Defoe observed the political maneuvering that accompanied the passage of the Treaty of Union in Scotland and again reported to Harley. During these times Defoe wrote a set of highly characteristic letters. Although other letters he wrote include more intimate details, these reveal the qualities of mind that made him a valuable employee to the ministries of three monarchs and a groundbreaking journalist. They exhibit the attention to detail and presentation, the economy, and the accumulative syntax that are the hallmarks of his prose. Characteristically, that prose is exceptionally informed about taxes, trade, and elections, and its author frankly worries about appreciation, detection, and expenses. The letters reveal an ear for local phrases and an eye for local color, and they record utterances and events, using them to reveal principles, prejudices, and sentiments.

The first letter is from Defoe's second and most extensive fact-finding tour. Written near the halfway point of his journey, Defoe had already traveled from London through Reading and Salisbury down to Weymouth, then traced most of the coast from there around to Bristol, and moved along the Welsh border from Chippenham through Gloucester to Kidderminster on his way to Liverpool and Manchester.[1] He begins with a survey of his movement and the towns to be described, then analyzes in some detail the situation in one of these districts, Chippenham, and concludes with personal remarks, including how he can be reached by Harley. Defoe organizes the second letter, written about a month after his arrival in Edinburgh, around the Scottish Parliament and, particularly, the pressures being brought to bear on it. In the first and last paragraphs he alludes to the powerful Church of Scotland, and he writes at some length about the petitions from the electorate that were beginning to pour into Parliament. He artfully juxtaposes the names of the three most influential opponents to the union with a reference to the mob that gathered daily outside the chambers. He deftly develops the theme of a nation gone mad by playing the lords' long emotional speeches and "raving" against the "Clamour" of the opposite class, the "Rabble." This letter also includes the news that the first article of the Treaty of Union has passed, and both Defoe and Harley would have instantly apprehended the crucial nature of this event. In short, to pass this article was to effect an incorporating rather than a federated union of the two nations, something Defoe and the English ministry very much wanted. This letter too has extended references to two men who would become frequent contacts in Scotland, the earl of Leven and Alexander Campbell of Cessnock, and the letter ends on a more personal note as Defoe reports on his plans and progress.[2]

Defoe saw his job to be to write clear, accurate, informative letters and to give sound advice. He identified influential people, troublemakers, sources of discontent, and opportunities. As he said, he was to provide "plain, naked, and unbyasst accounts both of persons and things" (Backscheider, *Daniel Defoe* 254). Especially in 1704–5 when he had a sense of the possibilities for long-term consolidation and increase of strength for Harley's party, he gave advice for carrying the next election, as he does in the first letter. Here he cleverly explains how Henry Chivers's and John Child's influence may be reduced so that they can be defeated, as both were, in the next election. In the second letter, the advice is more veiled. Defoe appears to lament the money he is costing Harley (something he had done in very similar words on July 9 in reference to his travel through England [*Letters* 89]), but he is certainly encouraging Harley to continue, for he insists that there is "no Remedy if I will go thro' with the work." In addition to making these reports, Defoe saw himself responsible for inclining people toward moderation and the policies of Queen Anne's ministry and for "opening their eyes" to the "truth" and their "interest."[3] He carried out this work by writing and publishing periodical and pamphlet essays and through what must have appeared as informal conversations in a variety of settings.

Method of the Letters and the *Review*

The *Review*, the periodical that Defoe wrote single-handedly for nine years, often offers a second day-by-day record of his experience and opinions.[4] For instance, in the September 6, 1705, *Review* Defoe tells the story of the parson in Wiltshire, and in the 1705 letter he tells Harley that he has recently visited "Warminster on the south bordr of Wilts." Defoe's essays argue the same positions he presented to Harley and expounded on the road. Such pamphlets as the *Removing National Prejudices* series and *The Advantages of Scotland by an Incorporate Union with England* complemented the *Review*s and were often aimed at slightly different audiences.

One of Defoe's most able adversaries, Charles Leslie, wrote in 1714, "Defoe may change his name from *Review* to *Mercator* from *Mercator* to any other title, yet still his singular genius shall be distinguished by his inimitable way of writing" (Backscheider, *Daniel Defoe* 166, 178). Whether readers find his way of writing "inimitable" or not, Defoe's letters, periodicals, pamphlets, and novels do share a number of features that reveal the prose style characteristic of a mind in motion, one with a "singular genius." In one of the best articles on Defoe's style, George Starr concludes that Defoe is "less concerned with rendering [external things] objectively than with assigning them human significance" (293–94). This fact ties Defoe's style inseparably to his content. At any place in his writing, the reader can perceive Defoe observing, assigning meaning, and manipulatively creating what can best be called "transmissions." At one moment, we are present with Defoe: "He was at this work when I was at Chipenham," "I am Now Moveing North." Suddenly some value-laden words slip by—"strange and Unaccountable people," "Moderate Intrest"—while others begin to arrest the reader—"act like Devills more than Men," "that scandall of the County Coll Chivers." Unobtrusively repeating the word *scandal*, each time assigning it to Chivers, Defoe leads his reader toward a plan of action presented as public service rather than as party skulduggery. Thus, he inextricably joins interpretation to event and attempts to transfer his judgment to his receiver.

In the second letter, a theme clearly emerges that again asks that the reader assent to both description and interpretation: "the Face of affaires . . . are a little Mended," "the addresses Discover [meaning 'uncover' or 'reveal'] a Fraud," "the proceeding since is more favourable," "Very . . . Encouraging," "I have Now Great hopes." Suddenly the threatening environment and pessimism lift, and Defoe gradually lets the clouds break and concludes that all of the signs (including the auspicious date) promise that the treaty will be signed. In both letters Defoe reinforces a theme prevalent in the majority of his letters and periodical essays: his competence, dedication, and value. For instance, by writing that "there Can not be a greater peice of Service," he identifies himself with a cause and with Harley, the means of bringing it about. "Sent for by the Lds Comittee," he is summoned, solicited, in the position few spies could attain. As I have argued elsewhere, varied repetitions of *servant* and *service* work to evoke secular and biblical images that blend conceptions of the humble with the chosen, the self-sacrificing person with the valiant missionary. Defoe often self-consciously allied this role with St. Paul's description of his ministry: "I am made all things to all men, that I might by all means save some" (Backscheider, "Personality" 1–20). These two letters portray the man who could gather all "the perticulars," represent himself as "a little surpriz'd" at a Dissenting minister's conspiratorial message, recognize "the Cant of the Old Times" (Scottish cant, by the way), accommodate himself to a committee, and call attention to his *au courant* use of a "scotticisme." Both medium and message, Defoe mingles his designs for the good of his country and for the advancement of himself.

The two letters reveal a happy, fully engaged man. He believed in his work, thrived on a sense of importance and usefulness, and even enjoyed the risks involved. In an October 1704 *Review*, Defoe bragged that he was still "in the Country upon his Extraordinary and Lawful occasions," and in the first letter above he is obviously pleased that James Forbes has recognized that Defoe "had the honour [to] be known to" Harley.[5] To several people he wrote that he served "by Inclination and principle" (*Letters* 86; Backscheider, *Daniel Defoe* 183). Both missions carried risks, for violence was not uncommon. In Coventry, for instance, mobs fought in the street, and the mayor was clubbed and hit in the head with a stone.[6] Edinburgh seemed on the verge of anarchy, as ordinary citizens gathered around the Parliament House daily, as Highlanders poured into the city, as the "treaters" were scorned as "traitors" (and the Scottish pronunciation made this slide easy), and as a serious riot that required the troops of horse and foot to quell broke out on October 23, 1706. Defoe's letter of September 10, 1705, mentions that he is "Clear of all the Enemies I apprehended," and in one of his Scottish letters he remarks that he ran all the dangers of a soldier storming a counterscarp (*Letters* 242). Defoe's reaction was neither extreme nor unusual; the earl of Mar, an experienced soldier and a member of the Scottish Parliament, wrote, "I'm not very timerous and yet I tell you that every day here wee are in hazard of our lives." [7]

Defoe was in danger not just because he was where random violence broke out but also because he was notorious. Convicted in one of the most publicized seditious libel trials of the century, he had been the subject of newspaper advertisements, pamphlets, and satiric prints and had stood in the pillory three times. The purpose of the pillory was to make a person recognizable, to "stigmatize and dishonor," to "render infamous" (Backscheider, *Daniel Defoe* 116, 571 n. 2). Thus the man described in the advertisements as having a hooked nose, a sharp chin, and a large mole near his mouth would run the risk of being recognized on the street. Once known, people reacted to him with suspicion, wariness, and curiosity. One man wrote that Defoe's visit to Liverpool had been "the great Subject talked of and been a matter of Speculation." About the same time, the Scot John Clerk identified Defoe to his father as the man that was pilloried. Hugh Stafford, justice of the peace at Pynes, Devonshire, issued a warrant for Defoe's arrest "for spreading and publishing divers seditious and scandalous Libels and false news to the great disturbance of the Peace of this Kingdom." He, like many others, believed Defoe increased tensions. Thomas Johnson, another Liverpool resident, wrote, "I do not like such men let them be of what side they will—it's those creatures endeavours to influence us" (Backscheider, *Daniel Defoe* 186). Defoe wrote Harley of a frightening night when he had been recognized as English in Scotland and another when he had had to change his lodgings after being "Openly Threatened" (*Letters* 133–36, 184). His friend John Clerk believed that Defoe would have been "pulled to pieces" if his employment and mission had been widely known (Clerk 63–64).

In the great age of coffeehouses, Defoe was in his element in these convivial places that Jürgen Habermas has identified as centers for the free, relatively classless exchange of ideas so important to the development of "public opinion" as a major political force.[8] On his English trips, he would ride horseback fifteen to twenty miles a day and then spend time talking about trade, politics, and personalities. Defoe had long made it a habit to visit his favorite coffeehouses after 4:00 P.M. He received mail and messages at Jones's Coffee House in Finch Lane near the Exchange and at the Essex near the Temple (*Letters* 13, 102; Backscheider, *Daniel Defoe* 151, 198). He had his periodicals and pamphlets distributed to the coffeehouses and used the most hospitable to take subscriptions for his major works. In September 1704 at least eight coffeehouses, including the Essex, Jones's, and two others mentioned in Defoe's correspondence, were accepting the "half a crown down" for *Jure Divino*.[9] Like most men, he went there for the conversation, the generous stack of periodicals, and the convenience for arranged meetings (see *Letters* 107, 253). Each one had something of its own character, and now and then Defoe repeated a line that caught its special flavor. Of Snow's in the debtors' sanctuary in the Mint, perhaps also a location for a scene in *Moll Flanders*, he recorded "the ancient Language" of it: "If you won't take this you shall have nothing, I'll lie here and spend it."[10] Of the coffeehouse "generals" and "statesmen" he would demand more judiciousness and impartiality (*Review* 4: 521; 6: 159; 9: 9). As Paul Hunter has noted, the particular appeal of the coffeehouses was their timeliness and "the gazettes and other public papers" (174). Habermas is surely correct to credit them with making a major contribution to the increasing importance of "public opinion." César de Saussure, an eighteenth-century visitor to England, wrote, "Nothing is more entertaining than hearing men of this class discussing politics and topics of interest concerning royalty. You often see an Englishman taking a treaty of peace more to heart than he does his own affairs" (quoted in Hunter 174). Occasionally Defoe accused a group of habitués of real misconduct; in a 1701 pamphlet he wrote that he had heard the men at Jonathan's and Garraway's coffeehouses buy and sell elections.[11] Even the small towns had coffeehouses: correspondents mentioned them, and contemporaries sometimes wrote that they had seen or met Defoe in such local legends as Sue's in Edinburgh.[12]

In the coffeehouses, at pubs and meetinghouses, and at long convivial meals, Defoe discussed the state of the nation, gathered opinion, and propagated his views. Stafford complained that Defoe represented the young Tory M.P.'s as drinking at the Fountain until time for a vote and then voting as they were told by "Sir Edward, Sir Humphrey, or Sir John."[13] From the time of his release, Defoe had been suspected of being a creature of the Whig party. Even before Harley paid his fees and fine, sums collected in Whig coffeehouses had nearly reached the necessary amount, and an annoyed journalist wrote, "Every one is not a *Daniel de Foe* that has a Party to pay a Fine for him. . . . It's no ungainful thing to be a Whig" (*Heraclitus Ridens*). The alleged privileged association with the party and the obvious knowledge and insight displayed in the *Review* made him a desirable coffeehouse companion, and he often asked Harley for news "Other than the Prints" give. He would then swap his gossip for accounts of the elections and of local people's alliances and interests. When he was on the road, as he was when he wrote these two letters, Defoe went beyond the coffeehouse into private homes, committee rooms, markets, Dissenting meetinghouses, and post houses, where his coffeehouse manner enabled him to extract all sorts of information. The information he provided Harley about Chivers, remarkably detailed information for an outsider, was probably gleaned from a variety of places and kinds of people. Thus Defoe absorbed the information embedded in the free flow of coffeehouse discourse and intimate conversations and transmitted it, organized and shrewdly packaged, to Harley and the ministry and, packaged anew in the *Review*, to his readers, where it entered again the public forum of the coffeehouse.

Even the arrangements Defoe made to receive his mail presented him with problems as well as opportunities for meeting people and collecting information.[14] Having been received and sorted on the preceding "post days," mail left London shortly after midnight on Wednesdays, Thursdays, and Sundays; carriers transported a large bag holding an individual bag of mail for each designated stop on the six inland routes. Each postmaster took his bag, and the carrier continued. There were no official deliveries of mail; therefore, merchants and coffeehouse proprietors sent servants to pick up mail sorted by the postmaster or an "alphabet man." Some deliveries were made to shops and coffeehouses, because many of them served as official Letter Receivers; employees of the post office picked up letters left at these "substations" sometimes as often as hourly and would often deliver letters when they came. When he traveled, Defoe usually gave Harley the name of a merchant or printer, and, when in London, the name of a coffeehouse.[15] His letters make it clear that he used his brother-in-law Robert Davis as a private letter carrier more frequently than he used the mails.[16] The fact that Defoe asked Harley to direct his mail to the post house in Manchester shows that he was less acquainted with that city and its people than he was with other places in England. The post houses were inns licensed to furnish the horses used in relays by the carriers. They also furnished post horses for private travelers, and Defoe occasionally used them for that purpose. The Manchester post house was one of the smallest, and he soon began to have his mail sent to John Coningham in Manchester instead.[17] Concerned with security more than with using the receiving stations for gathering information, Defoe displays considerable anxiety about arrangements for the receipt of his mail, as his consternation over John Bell's trip from Newcastle to London shows (*Letters* 207).

In both England and Scotland, Defoe carefully cultivated useful contacts. When he traveled, he often stayed with substantial merchants or prosperous, established, Nonconformist clergymen. For instance, he stayed with the merchant Francis Bere, brother to Thomas, the Tiverton M.P., and with Nathaniel Priestley, a man wealthy enough to have purchased land and built his own Presbyterian chapel at Northgate End, Halifax. In Scotland, Defoe joined the Society for the Reformation of Manners, invested in business with men such as the former Deacon of Crafts for the weavers, and attended presbytery meetings with Hew Dalrymple, brother to the earl of Stair. These men supplied him with some information, reacted usefully to his writing, and distributed his pamphlets and selected numbers of the *Review*. The writings of a few of them suggest that Defoe could be very good company indeed. John Russell, the Edinburgh writer to the signet, jokes that he can be confident in Defoe's choice of wine for him, for "you expect a botle here when the h[igh Chur]ch shall make home too warm for you" (Backscheider, *Daniel Defoe* 198, 164). These letters capture much of the style, range, and purpose of Defoe's letters, but they are actually mere indications of their richness.

Like many men of his time, Defoe wrote many letters. Of those that survive, four types can be identified. Reports, many longer and more anecdotal and detailed than the ones printed here, make up the majority of Defoe's surviving letters. He also wrote a number of position papers, which he directed to Harley. Sometimes these were solicited, as was his discussion of the appointment of commissioner to the General Assembly (*Letters* 313–15), and came at Harley's often urgent request, "Let me have your thoughts." Others were done apparently at Defoe's own initiative, and some are shockingly cold and manipulative. For instance, in the summer of 1704 he had suggested that Harley establish a "Supreme Ministry," and of the Nonconformists whose interests he always insisted were his own and closest to his heart, he wrote, "I Might Possibly Grant The Temper of the Dissenters Not so Well Quallify'd for the Prosperity of Their Princes favour as Other Men . . ." (*Letters* 54). Another group of letters contains solicitations for money or for favors, most far more starkly directive than the oblique encouragement to continue spending that is found in the 1706 letter above. Harley was something of an irregular paymaster, and Sydney Godolphin, whom Defoe served from June 1707 until 1710, was apparently worse.[18] In fact, it was unusual for an author to receive regular payments as Defoe did at least through the years 1707–14 and 1716–24.[19] Even those who wrote consistently and by agreement for a ministry or party customarily presented their work and received a gift, often from the secret service money. Defoe wrote to be considered for employment and to be "remembered," in addition to pleading for money and reminding his patrons of overdue payments. All of these groups of letters reveal a manipulative, scheming man, and the reports are the only ones written with flair.

A final group of letters is made up of brief notes written to conduct small economic transactions or to maintain Defoe's network of hosts, informers, and paper distributors. Among the most interesting surviving Defoe letters are those written to him by some of these correspondents. These letters often give a glimpse of Defoe as opinion-gatherer and as convivial friend. The old images of Defoe as a humorless political journalist and as a writing machine drudging away in solitude hour after hour are quite wrong, and this set of letters fills out the picture of him that the reports imply. Even those who by long familiarity or political savvy recognized the ambiguities of Defoe's personality and the perils of relationships with him would not deny that he was good company. John Barber, who was criticized for printing Defoe's satirical poem *The Dyet of Poland*, said that "no Man could ever converse with [Defoe], without being wiser and better for that Conversation" (*Life and Character of John Barber* 9). Men like John Fransham, the Norwich linen draper, often encouraged Defoe to return to their homes. Fransham, John Russell, and others wrote with insight and humor about the London political milieu and Defoe's place in it.

Defoe's Letters as Manuscripts

The two letters above, both reports, illustrate admirably some of the challenges facing any scholar who works with letters.[20] The most obvious one is finding the letters. People do, of course, find large caches of letters carefully preserved in the families of writers or of their friends and acquaintances. Dozens of letters to and from Defoe may yet exist throughout the United Kingdom and even in the United States and Canada. For instance, it is common knowledge that Defoe and Cotton Mather corresponded, and yet neither Kenneth Silverman nor I have been able to locate the letters. We know that Defoe wrote his wife, Mary, two or three times a week when he was away from London, and from some of his letters to Harley, we know that she wrote him. Some of these letters may be among privately held papers in Scotland; others might have been in the papers Defoe left in the family home when he transferred it to Henry and Sophia Defoe Baker in April 1729 or when he moved in May 1730, the time of the loss of his final disastrous debt litigation.[21] A list of letters written kept by the earl of Hyndford shows that he regularly wrote Defoe, and evidence in surviving letters to and by Defoe indicates that Defoe replied. An entire set of letters written to Harley and routinely passed to Godolphin in 1706 has disappeared but probably survives. Dozens of letters like those by John Fransham and John Russell may exist, and surely more descriptions and opinions such as those by Thomas Johnson will be found and published.

At the end of the twentieth century, finding such letters for major literary figures is, of course, less likely than finding letters of people long neglected. A subject's circles of friendship and acquaintanceship must be carefully reconstructed, and then each name must be checked archive by archive. At the same time, the identification of those who would have cared about, for instance, Defoe's or the government's activities yields letters such as Johnson's and Norris's. Mayors, Whig and Tory leaders, Anglican clergymen, and chief citizens cared about election outcomes, about policies in formation and in practice, and about the conduct of outsiders that might disrupt the community, its economy, or its balance of power. These people often had a sense of history and of their own place in it; many of the leading families continue to live in the same locations. What may seem to have local interest only—for instance, the rise of a trading family—may actually reveal connections to the larger world and include descriptions of national public figures like Defoe. From such incidental comments a sense of Defoe's reputation and notoriety emerges and becomes both more complicated and more accurate. The number of resources available to scholars, such as the National Register of Archives, has increased greatly in recent years and promises the discovery of many letters.

In addition to files of names and collections of family papers, however, the meeting-by-meeting records of town councils, parish councils, vestries, city livery companies, and mayors' entry books yield important information and may even include letters or transcriptions of letters.[22] Poll books often record the occupation and place of residence of voters, and early tax records (such as those for the hearth tax) usually give the names of members of each household, including those of servants. Where these survive, individuals can be followed year by year and their relative prosperity charted. Like these sources, wills and the inventories that often accompany them may provide new names and locations where letters may be found.

Once the letters are found, the handwriting can be a problem. Those letters that survive in rough letter book copy alone are especially difficult. It is, of course, important to try to ascertain if they were in fact sent, which means locating answers or references to them in other documents. Copybook letters may be written in several different hands and by people who used different symbols and abbreviations. Particularly in manuscripts from the late seventeenth and early eighteenth centuries, the handwriting can increase the difficulty of the work substantially. Every individual's writing has eccentricities, but most people in that period were entirely familiar with both the secretary and italic hands and often mixed them with what was becoming the English round hand.[23] Some people still wrote in rather pure secretary hand, but combinations of secretary and other letters are often especially hard to decipher because of the unexpected and isolated older letter forms. Some letters differ markedly from modern letters (the "reverse *e*," for instance, and many capitals), and others are deceptively like other modern letters (*c*, *r*, and *p* resemble respectively our *r*, *w*, and ornate *x*). Combinations of letters, especially *ir*, *pr*, *es*, *th*, and *tion*, often vary from clerk to clerk. A common mixed hand links italic letters much like the round hand but uses secretary capitals. For years writers continued to find secretarial abbreviations and signs, many based upon Latin words, such as *qd* (*quod* for "that") and *vid* (*vidua* for "widow") economical and useful. Unfortunately, some common abbreviations could mean several things; *sol*, for instance, may be "shilling" or "paid," and *libr* can stand for "book" or be a pound-weight of some commodity. Scottish secretary is yet different and includes Scottish abbreviations such as *q* for "quhen," meaning "when." When Defoe wanted to disguise his handwriting, he wrote a more secretarial hand.[24]

Because people mixed their own ink from powder, a careless scrawl in weak, fading ink or blotchy, bleeding, thick strokes can be as hard to read as tiny writing. Similarly, letters written by elderly people can present special difficulties. Reading years of Robert Harley's letters and memoranda roughly in chronological order makes the fact that Guiscard stabbed and bruised him on the right side and that he was right-handed obvious, and the number of illegible words and phrases increases. In any event, what Samuel Johnson once said of writing definitions can be said of deciphering words and phrases: "What is obvious is not always known, and what is known is not always present . . . the writer shall often in vain trace his memory at the moment of need for that which yesterday he knew with intuitive readiness, and which will come uncalled into his thoughts tomorrow" (327).

Because most of Defoe's letters exist within a context of frequent face-to-face meetings and shared acquaintances, concerns, and even opinions, they lack the identifications and the kinds of explanation that would make the scholar's work easy. In these letters, Defoe supplies phrases that would instantly place people, places, or ideas for Harley, as "Member for Chipenham" does "Watt" White and as "Cant of the Old Times" does the content of the petitions to the Scottish Parliament. The phrase "Sir Fra: Childs Bro:" in the 1705 letter would have spoken volumes to Harley. Sir Francis Child was a staunch Tory and the first banker to give up the goldsmith's business; he had represented Devizes and London in Parliament and had been president of the board of Christ's Hospital in 1696 when Defoe's proposal to build twelve tenements had been turned down (Peterson 306–38; *DNB*). Ironically, Defoe's and Harley's shared and long-standing familiarity with local politics and influential individuals enormously complicates the work of modern scholars. The single word that allowed, for instance, Harley to distinguish between father and son, uncle and nephew, may now mean nothing or even go unnoticed.

Perhaps decisions about how much research into context and personalities is necessary are easiest for biographers, for they need to know as much as possible. Literary critics, however, may have no reason to go beyond what Defoe's *Letters*, the *Dictionary of National Biography*, or a good history of the period supplies. Some scholars and critics may need to know, for instance, what else Defoe said about Francis Child, and such information often contributes to interpretation of Defoe's objectivity, personal involvement, or tone (as the information about Child, Defoe, and Christ's Hospital does). Periodical and pamphlet literature of the time can be used to compare and contrast Defoe's reports and opinions with those of his contemporaries, and contemporaries representing a spread of opinion from radical Tory to radical Whig and with a range of similarities and oppositions to Defoe can usually be located. Papers such as the *London Gazette*, Samuel Buckley's *Daily Courant*, and Jacques de Fonvive's *Post-man* give fairly straightforward reports of events, and the state papers in the London Public Record Office often give important supplementary information. For men such as Henry Chivers and Campbell of Cessnock, however, the work is more difficult, for provincial papers—if there were any—and records are sometimes less complete and accessible. Even the social class and religious affiliation complicates; as late as the 1980s it was common for archivists to dismiss a gap in their records with "Oh, he was a Nonconformist."[25] Robert Davis, Defoe's brother-in-law, led an eventful and fairly well-documented life, and yet it took years for me to assemble information that finally came from such diverse places as Cornwall, Leith, Rockingham Forest, and London.

Defoe and Harley

Defoe's letters consistently belong in two contexts. They are, of course, the record of relationships, and surely his with Harley was one of the most important in his life. Not nearly so uncritical and slavish as some eighteenth-century critics have said, the relationship had undertones of deep understanding as well as elements of cynicism and pragmatism. Just as Defoe called on Harley when he needed money or legal help, so Harley would employ Defoe in quite specific projects at crucial times in Harley's career. Their pious natures and Dissenting backgrounds, which occasionally find expression in the letters, provided a set of allusions that they could count on being correctly and resonantly interpreted. Because he knew Harley well and wrote him frequently, Defoe could be elliptical. He could count on Harley to identify "Ld Mordaunt" and "Mr Forbes," and he knew Harley would recognize the three speech-making Scots' positions and degrees of influence. Using a symbol or a pseudonym (such as "A G" for "Alexander Goldsmith" in the first letter), Defoe kept a steady, narratively pleasing correspondence going. His understanding of Harley's objectives in these reprinted letters is confident, without the need for explanation or emphasis. Moving quickly and efficiently to identify the men and the means for Harley's advantage, Defoe often shows the same kind of diligence and attention to detail that Harley exercised in his best years as Speaker

of Commons and as Lord Treasurer. Both regularly mention and acknowledge expressions of concern, as Defoe does Harley's caution about his safety
in 1705 and as Defoe habitually does when Harley is promoted, ill, or in
politically tense situations.

The letters printed here testify to the complexity of the relationship.
Repeatedly vacillating among obsequious appeals, embarrassing flattery,
straightforward description, and presumptuous, confident advice, Defoe
addresses a politician whose silences could be punishment or procrastina-
tion. The tangled sentence that begins the 1705 letter suggests some of
the relationship's fraught nature. Defoe opens by explaining why he was
not where he had told Harley he would be—at Bath—and thereby admits
he could not receive messages or convey information to Harley expedi-
tiously. Simultaneously, he blames his "Brother," Davis, whom he often
characterizes as an unreliable messenger, and also depicts himself as diligent and active; rather than waste the time waiting there for Davis he has
made a productive eight-day trip. In the most contorted part of this sentence, he implicitly apologizes for not thanking Harley immediately for
"the Supply," Defoe's euphemism for money, and for "your Concern" and
rises to an effusive "More Acknowledgements than I Can Express." The
valued object of the great Harley's "Concern" is also the grateful, humble
servant. The movement in the sentence is from straightforward *thing* to be
explained ("My absence from the Bath"), through time organized by commitment and impatience (the pluperfect, an ablative absolute, and a simple
past) with the consequences stated ("to Miss" and "to Deferr"), through
to a tight joining of past and present ("I Recd," "I Owe"), finally rising to
"Can Express," a verb construction bearing the Old English *cunnan,* a form
in which the infinitive is not the inflected infinitive of modern English but
is the integrally attached infinitive carrying the connotation of "bearing
the gift." Thus Defoe begins with a simple statement that he complicates
in time, space, and tone, perhaps disingenuously admitting that he does
not "have the gift" of stating what he feels even as his sentence becomes a
hieroglyph of his complex actions, intentions, and feelings, a hieroglyph
we can read in quite uncommon ways.

Harley told Defoe what he thought he needed to know, felt no need
to tell him about his other agents even when they were working in the
same city, and neglected him when his services were unnecessary. Defoe,
in turn, occasionally lied to Harley about his authorship of pamphlets and
apparently hid the fact that he had known many Scots before his Edinburgh

assignment and probably planned to go to Scotland with them long before he and Harley struck their agreement. Despite scores of meetings and letters, there is no evidence that Harley shared his feelings about his loss of office or about the death of his favorite daughter; Defoe writes of family deaths, even that of the father to whom he would always refer with respect and powerful feeling, with strict restraint: "I Confess myself in Some Disordr to night, The Account of the Death of my Father Comeing just as I was writeing this" (*Letters* 180).

The Letters and the Expression of Personal Emotion

The other context for Defoe's letters is his journalistic career. In a time when it was common for newspapers and periodicals to quote the *London Gazette* or even foreign papers, Defoe was out, as these letters show, observing, interviewing, and questioning.[26] In the first year of the *Review*, he shows an acute sense of the weaknesses—and absurdities—of contemporary news reports. He notes the discrepancies and contradictions in reports and ridicules the way news was collected: "They write from *Tunbridge,* by way of *Edinburgh,* that the Duke of *Ormond* was safe arrived in *Dublin*" (Backscheider, *Daniel Defoe* 152–53). As he developed his distinctive style and his relationship with his imagined readers, he used material from his reports to Harley increasingly effectively and confidently. In 1705 he occasionally bragged in a self-important way and by doing so surely increased suspicion about his activities. In 1706 he used the *Review* to thicken the screen he had thrown up to confuse his enemies. Insisting that economic and political difficulties were motivating his consideration of relocation to Scotland, he wrote about investing in salt and in linen manufacturing (*Review* 4: 82). This time he bragged of clever investments rather than of undefined "Extraordinary" business. In the *Review* he carefully reported, mollified, and tactfully interpreted events. While he allowed frustration, amazement, and even fear to show in his letters, he resolutely "put the best Face on the proceedings" and insisted for his English readers upon a picture of a Scottish people with foolish but human and understandable reservations about the Union.[27]

The style of the letters quoted here is journalistic, as are most of the letters in this category and even in the categories of position papers and brief personal notes. They show alert observation, attention to the who, what, and where of events, willingness to make connections and assign cause and implications, and a gift for concise narrative. In a few lines he makes the image of Chivers who "Sitts Dilligently at Every petty sessions, and Aws the people" live. The credibility of such pictures is strongly enhanced by such additions as "He was at this work when I was at Chipenham." Defoe learned early the power of the eyewitness and often unobtrusively reinforces his most directive or manipulative points this way. In the Scottish letter, he introduces what will be a series of descriptions of the parliamentary committee appointed to check the Equivalents. His anecdote about Leven captures the atmosphere of wild rumor and might have come from Leven himself, a man Defoe had met in London the previous summer. The kinds of graphic metaphors found in his periodicals appear in the letters. Defoe says the proverb of the Iron Chest is as universally known "as the Alphabet," and the exaggeration, tone, and homeliness are entirely typical. Defoe often managed to convey a shared opinion, a shared derisive perception, and mundane common sense. The comparison to "Devills" in the 1705 letter suggests both evil and derangement, as in New Testament references to Christ driving the devils into swine. He could assume such a reading with Harley but would gloss it a bit for his *Review* readers.

The prefaces to the successive volumes of the *Review* can appropriately be read as letters. As the years pass, the intimacy of the prefaces grows, and the tones common to Defoe's letters to Harley increase. Some of them gloss the correspondence but still reveal the unity of Defoe's style. The preface to the 1706 volume, for instance, includes paragraphs in which Defoe preens himself on the importance and success of his work. In lamenting that the "Story" (a historical event) and the "Book" (the calendar year's printed volume) do not often correspond neatly, he explains that the previous volume "broke off in the middle of the great Undertaking, which the Author, at the utmost Hazard, went through, in pressing this Nation to Peace. . . . And thus it is now, when pursuing the same general Good of his Native Country, the Author has embark'd in the great Affair of the Union of *Britain*" (preface, vol. 3).

Even in the first volume (printed in 1705), Defoe allows the reader access to his thoughts and the evolution of the paper. In a rather stream-of-consciousness style, he explains how readers demanded diversion, how he supplied it, and how he now teaches by fables or stories, a form that fascinated him from his youth as the "Historical Collections" (1682) and the later memoirs and novels show. In each volume, he reflects upon the purposes he has for the paper, insists upon his moderation and commitment to giving his readers the facts regardless of the personal and political risks, and evaluates the nation's temper. These essays give yet more access to the mind formulating the personal letters of 1705 and 1706. The prefatory essay for volume 8 is a kind of stocktaking in which Defoe begins successive paragraphs with "First, *I look in,*" "Next, *I look up,*" "In the third place, *I look back.*" The inclusion of the middle term is typical of his thought. Here he says, "I submit with an entire Resignation to what ever happens to me," and "I may not yet see through [how things] will, at last, issue in good, even to me."

These personal remarks were made in an age when so many journalists were Nonconformists and deeply religious men, and yet they are highly singular and more in keeping with Defoe's letters than with the ordinary modes and addresses of periodical writers. In several letters he tells people that he has faith in God's purpose and the outcome but cannot yet imagine the resolution (*Letters* 17, 476). The whining and the frequent complaints of being underappreciated hardly balance the passages in which Defoe's energy, resilience, and quick intelligence appear, and yet some of the most human, revelatory statements are in these addresses to the readers of his *Review*: "In the School of Affliction I have learnt more Philosophy than at the Academy, . . . I have seen the rough side of the World as well as the smooth" (preface, vol. 8). The essay ends with his assessment of himself as cheerful, "enjoying a . . . clearness in Thought" and a "Resignation to the will of Heaven," all moods and tones common to personal, reflective passages in the letters. When he ends the *Review*, his essays combine the enthusiasm for new projects and the faith in new, interesting, significant work with a sense of a long relationship: He begins his last essay, "You must bear with my freedom a little, in reproving one epidemick Mischief," and ends with an endorsement of his new paper, the *Mercator*, and an understated "And so, Gentlemen fare you well." His letters usually convey such bounding toward new ideas and efforts along with ongoing harangues, advice, and allusions to an established relationship.

The paucity of letters and their insignificance in Defoe's novels sets him apart from writers of prose fiction in the Restoration and eighteenth century, for letters are crucially important to the early novel. Commentary on the major epistolary novels and the rich experimentation with the form are familiar to all students of the novel, as are analyses of the very important part individual letters play in such novels as Jane Austen's *Pride and Prejudice*. The anticipation, receiving, reading, and writing of letters seem consistently to be portrayed as moments of heightened tension and narrative significance in eighteenth-century fiction. Defoe's novels are, of course, more related to native English travel narratives, criminal literature, and spiritual autobiography than to those forms that engendered the prose fiction of the type that was published in the same year as *Robinson Crusoe* and competed successfully in sales with it: Eliza Haywood's *Love in Excess*. In the Continental memoirs, romances, and novellas that stand behind her book, writers had already developed the letter as a major, flexible, subtle narrative device.

The letters in Defoe's novels are often highly functional, but they have neither the emotional impact nor the interpretative richness of letters in other novelists' work. Perhaps this fact might be expected of a writer who wanted to make meaning transparent and interpretation unnecessary. From the many statements on style that he left emerges a dominant theme: "The best Rule in all Tongues [is] to make the Language plain, artless, and honest, suitable to the Story, and in a Stile easie and free . . . that the meanest Reader may meet with no Difficulty in Reading, and may have no Obstruction to his searching the History of things" (*Continuation* v). The heavy use of appositives, relative clauses, constructions beginning with "viz." or "that is to say," and what Furbank and Owens have called the "improvisatory sentence" are aimed at clarifying and at restricting the interpretations available to readers just as surely as Richardson's revisions were.

Unlike those of other eighteenth-century novelists, the letters in Defoe's novels are summarized, not quoted. Most perform the functions that Defoe's own surviving letters do: business associates receive requests, reply, and occasionally provide accounts. Colonel Jack's wife asks for help in obtaining a pardon for him, and characters give reports of events. A typical passage reads:

> The first thing I did upon this Occasion, was to send a Letter to my Maid . . . wherein I gave her an Account of my Disaster; how my Husband, as she call'd him (*for I never call'd him so*) was murther'd; and as I did not know how his Relations, or his Wife's Friends, might act upon that Occasion, I order'd her to convey away all the Plate, Linnen, and other things of Value, and to secure them in a Person's Hands that I directed her to, and then to sell, or dispose the Furniture of the House, if she could . . . Amy was so dext'rous, and did her Work so nimbly, that she gutted the House. (*Roxana* 55)

Here is largely a summary of "real" events. The man is dead; Amy has been told to secure everything of value, and she does. What interpretative possibilities there are (the parenthetical statement, for instance) hardly add anything new. This letter closes an interlude in Roxana's life, and others advance the plot, open lines of action, and provide impetus for character choices that will develop our judgment of the characters, as does Amy's letter telling Roxana that her first husband, the brewer, is dead (131–32). The letters are primarily devices for rapidly and efficiently summarizing action.

Of the 239 letters by Defoe that survive, 67 are roughly coeval with the two letters printed above, and another 92 are from the period between his return to Harley's service in 1710 and Queen Anne's death on August 1, 1714. Almost all of the letters are to Robert Harley; in 1706 all but two are, and in 1711 all but one are. It is to be expected that letters written to describe the unfolding of a historical event would share some of the narrative qualities of a periodical Defoe described as "history writing by inches" and of episodic novels that contemporaries called "general histories." Trained at the finest Dissenting academy in England to consider many points of view, to debate, and to persuade, Defoe could be expected to use anecdote, exhortation, analogy, carefully selected examples, and classical rhetorical strategies to present and reinforce his version of things and their implications in periodicals and pamphlets as well as in letters to powerful politicians.

The distinction between "public" and "private" also developed after Defoe's death, and even a work as personal as the "Historical Collections" (probably begun for himself alone when he was considering the ministry and then completed as a courtship gift to Mary) seems to suggest that for him the realms blended and that he would put what he conceived to be his duty or his work before personal feelings. Mary was his "faithful Steward" and was sometimes sent to do business or to negotiate for him. Does that mean that his letters to her were like those between lovers, husbands and wives, and intimate friends in the novels? Did he write no letters like James Boswell's to the Reverend William Temple or Jonathan Swift's to Stella? What does it mean that the letters in his novels do not extend the purposes and uses of his own surviving letters? Will we someday find a cache of letters in which the language of Defoe's heart flows more unreservedly than in the pages of the *Review* in which he does reveal his hopes, frustrations, petty triumphs, disappointments, discouragements, and even passing moods?

The small number of surviving letters and the fact about them that we must never forget—that they are almost exclusively addressed to a single person who was in status and position remote from Defoe and who was himself a secretive, difficult, complex personality—determine that they pose tantalizing questions more than they illuminate Defoe's life and personality. In any event, it is not surprising that a person who wrote as much as Defoe spoke intimately to his "ideal, imagined reader." Few letters go beyond statements like these: "Fate, that makes Footballs of Men, kicks some up stairs and some down . . . and no Man knows . . . whether his Course shall issue in a PEERAGE or a PILLORY; and time was, that no Man could have determin'd it between [Lord Haversham] and this mean Fellow" (*Reply* 8). And it would be hard in any of his letters to find a more convincing statement of Defoe's resilient courage and willingness to begin anew than that left in *Robinson Crusoe* and *Moll Flanders*.

NOTES

1. See the itinerary in Defoe, *Letters* 108–13 or on the Royal Geographical Society map reprinted in Backscheider, *Daniel Defoe* 185.

2. In the second letter, Defoe refers to the Committee for Examining the Equivalents. Cessnock was a member of that committee, and he was the most frequent host of dinner meetings.

3. These interests were not always synonymous with Robert Harley's; not only was Harley sometimes out of power, but occasionally Defoe's ideas differed from Harley's. See Backscheider, *Daniel Defoe* 153–56, 337–38, 341, 448–49.

4. It began as a weekly publication on Feb. 19, 1703/4, became twice weekly in Apr. 1704, and was expanded to three times per week in Mar. 1705.

5. Defoe, *Review* 1: 268; Defoe, *Letters* 72; Defoe, *Queries* 25.

6. See Defoe, *Letters* 95; Defoe, *Review* 2: 113–16 and 3: 393–96; Historical Manuscripts Commission 4: 188.

7. Mar to David Nairn, Nov. 19, 1706, Scottish Record Office Ms. GD 124/14/449/67.

8. Habermas notes that by 1670 the government was concerned about the freedom of discourse in them (59). Estimates are that there were over three thousand coffeehouses in London alone at this time. See also Eagleton 13–27.

9. Defoe, *Letters* 118; Defoe, *Review* 1: 251–52. Blackadder's in Edinburgh handled subscriptions to his *Review* in 1708 (Backscheider, *Daniel Defoe* 262).

10. Defoe, *Review* 5: 604. In his final *Review* Defoe mentioned the coffeehouses and how each drew a clientele obsessed with one subject of public debate (9: 214).

11. Defoe, *Freeholders Plea* 20ff. Yet it was Jonathan's that apparently raised

substantial sums for Defoe when he was in prison in 1703 (Backscheider, *Daniel Defoe* 148).

12. The establishment was actually named Fortune's, but it was called Sue's because it was the former mansion of Susannah, countess of Eglinton (Backscheider, *Daniel Defoe* 218). See also Defoe, *Letters* 107; Backscheider, *Daniel Defoe* 48.

13. Defoe, *Letters* 101–2, especially n. 3; the name of the tavern is from Hamilton 83.

14. In 1710 Defoe offered to make suggestions that Harley could use to improve the mail service and especially to raise more revenue from it (*Letters* 312).

15. Among the typical people and places Defoe suggested in 1704–7 were John Morley's in Bury, Francis Bere's in Tiverton, and John Bell's in Newcastle.

16. Defoe was surely influenced in this decision not only by the speed and care that Davis offered but also by the fact that post office employees had the legal right to open, read, and confiscate mail for forwarding to the secretaries of state. The Post Office Act of 1711 confirmed the "unassailable legal basis" of this practice; see Alan McKenzie's essay, below, and Ellis 62–63. At least once, Defoe's mail was picked up by the wrong Mr. Turner with embarrassing and complicating results (Backscheider, *Daniel Defoe* 186–87). Aside from this built-in problem, there were many complaints about slow mail; delivery time from London to Berwick, the last English post before the last two stages to Edinburgh, was more than five days. Yet the mail was quite reliable; Helen Molitor points out that not one of the more than 104 letters Swift and Stella sent each other was lost (75).

17. The Manchester postmaster received only £14 a year and paid only £11 a year for the mail; in comparison, the Birmingham postmaster received £140 a year, and even the postmaster at Hull paid £50 for his letters. Information on the postal service is from Robinson, *Britain's Post Office* 4–37; Robinson, *British Post Office* 91–95, 213; and Hemmeon 1–28.

18. In June 1707 Harley wrote Defoe that Godolphin had decided "it is not fit you should be longer at my Charge" (Defoe, *Letters* 229), and subsequent letters show that Defoe expected payment from Godolphin. Harley resigned in Feb. 1708. Defoe applied to Harley and went back in his service in July 1710 (*Letters* 270–74).

19. Records of payments to Defoe are in the Public Record Office, Kew, and have been published; see Downie 437; Alsop 225–26; Backscheider, *Daniel Defoe* 284–85, 385, 571 n. 6, 578 n. 38, 580 n. 4, et passim. The 1724 terminus is not altogether certain, but circumstantial evidence, including the transfer of Charles Delafaye, Defoe's primary contact after the fall of Townshend, to the Southern department and Defoe's decreasing involvement with London periodicals, argues for it; see Sainty 408.

20. Because these letters were part of the series of official reports that Robert Harley saved, they are among the most accessible; they are now the property of

the British Library. Some in this series are, however, already too fragile for readers to consult, and an entire group of Defoe's reports dating from his first weeks in Scotland were passed to Godolphin and the queen and have never been found.

21. Defoe left the manuscript of *The Compleat English Gentleman* and some letters in the house (Moore 230; Backscheider, *Daniel Defoe* 526–27; conversation with Mrs. Violet De Foe Vasey).

22. Until 1834 the parish was the local ecclesiastical and civil government. Although most parish records have been deposited in public record offices, some are in local diocesan record offices. Some vestry records are still in local churches, especially in Scotland. Linda Merians is admirably brief, clear, and helpful (15–19). I would like to acknowledge her help with this section of the essay as well as my use of it here.

23. Secretary hand, while familiar to Renaissance scholars, is often a surprise to Restoration and eighteenth-century critics on their first visit to archives. In fact, Martin Billingsley wrote, "There is hardly any true Straine of right Secretary" (B2r). Modern specialists in paleography often divide secretary hands into at least three distinct types.

24. See the original of the Sept. 10, 1705, letter, British Library Portland 70291.

25. Research into the lives and experiences of non-Anglicans can require some special knowledge. For instance, births and baptisms of these children were haphazardly recorded, particularly before a quite false idea spread that Dissenting children's births should be recorded at "Red Cross Street" in the time of Daniel Williams. Non-Anglicans' birth or baptism records are still hard to find. Some specialized and little-known record repositories exist; for example, information about Jewish families is available at the Beth Din in London (Merians 17–19). In spite of these facts, the lack of records, or, more commonly, the lack of knowledge of them, often seems to spring from class or religious feelings.

26. Black 64–79; Sutherland 123–45.

27. Defoe states this approach often; see *Letters* 187, and *Review* 3: 470.

WORKS CITED

Alsop, J. D. "Defoe and His Whig Paymasters." *Notes and Queries* 226 (1981): 225–26.

Backscheider, Paula R. *Daniel Defoe: His Life.* Baltimore: Johns Hopkins UP, 1989.

———. "Personality and Biblical Allusion in Defoe's Letters." *South Atlantic Review* 47 (1982): 1–20.

Billingsley, Martin. *A Coppie Book containing . . . Examples of all the Most Curious Hands.* 2d ed. London, 1637.

Black, Jeremy. "The British Press and Europe in the Early Eighteenth Century."

The Press in English Society from the Seventeenth to the Nineteenth Centuries. Ed. Michael Harris and Alan Lee. Rutherford, N.J.: Fairleigh Dickinson UP, 1986. 64–79.

——. *The English Press in the Eighteenth Century.* Philadelphia: U of Pennsylvania P, 1987.

Clerk, John. *Memoirs of the Life of Sir John Clerk.* Ed. John M. Gray. Publications of the Scottish History Society 13. Edinburgh, 1892.

Defoe, Daniel. *The Complete English Tradesman.* 2 vols. London, 1726.

——. *A Continuation of Letters Written by a Turkish Spy at Paris.* London, 1718.

——. *The Freeholders Plea.* London, 1701.

——. "Historical Collections." Manuscript, 1682. William Andrews Clark Memorial Library, UCLA.

——. *The Letters of Daniel Defoe.* Ed. George H. Healey. Oxford: Clarendon, 1955.

——. *Queries upon the Bill against Occasional Conformity.* London, [1704].

——. *A Reply to a Pamphlet Entituled, the L——d H——'s Vindication.* London, 1706.

——. *Review.* Ed. A. W. Secord. 9 vols. in 22 vols. New York: Columbia UP, 1938.

——. *Roxana: The Fortunate Mistress.* Ed. Jane Jack. London: Oxford UP, 1964.

Downie, J. Alan. "Secret Service Payments to Daniel Defoe." *Review of English Studies* ns 30 (1979): 437–41.

Eagleton, Terry. *The Function of Criticism.* London: Verso, 1984.

Ellis, Kenneth. *The Post Office in the Eighteenth Century.* London: Oxford UP, 1958.

Furbank, P. N., and W. R. Owens. "Defoe and the 'Improvisatory' Sentence." *English Studies* 67 (1986): 157–66.

Habermas, Jürgen. *The Structural Transformation of the Public Sphere.* 1962. Cambridge: MIT P, 1989.

Hamilton, Elizabeth. *The Backstairs Dragon.* New York: Taplinger, 1969.

Hemmeon, J. C. *The History of the British Post Office.* Cambridge: Harvard UP, 1912.

Heraclitus Ridens. Nov. 6, 1703. London.

Historical Manuscripts Commission. *The Manuscripts of His Grace the Duke of Portland.* 9 vols. London: HMSO, 1891–1923.

Hunter, J. Paul. *Before Novels: The Cultural Contexts of Eighteenth-Century English Fiction.* New York: Norton, 1990.

Jameson, Fredric. *The Political Unconscious: Narrative as a Socially Symbolic Act.* 1981. Ithaca: Cornell UP, 1986.

Johnson, Samuel. "Preface to the Dictionary." *Samuel Johnson.* Ed. Donald Greene. Oxford: Oxford UP, 1984. 307–28.

Kolodny, Annette. "A Map for Rereading." *The New Feminist Criticism.* Ed. Elaine Showalter. New York: Pantheon, 1985. 46–62.

The Life and Character of John Barber, Esq: Late Lord-mayor of London, Deceased. London, 1741.

Merians, Linda. "A Guide to Record Offices in England." *EC/ASECS Newsletter* (1987): 15–19.

Molitor, Helen. "Jonathan Swift and the Post Office, 1710–1713." *Eighteenth-Century Life* 13 (1989): 70–78.

Moore, J. R. *A Checklist of the Writings of Defoe.* 1960. Hamden, Conn.: Archon Books, 1971.

Peterson, Spiro. "Defoe and Westminster, 1696–1706." *Eighteenth-Century Studies* 12 (1978–79): 306–38.

Robinson, Howard. *Britain's Post Office.* London: Oxford UP, 1953.

———. *The British Post Office: A History.* Princeton: Princeton UP, 1948.

Sainty, J. C. "A Huguenot Civil Servant: The Career of Charles Delafaye, 1677–1762." *Huguenot Society Proceedings* 22 (1975): 398–413.

Starr, G. A. "Defoe's Prose Style: 1. The Language of Interpretation." *Modern Philology* 71 (1974): 277–94.

Sutherland, James. *The Restoration Newspaper and Its Development.* Cambridge: Cambridge UP, 1986.

Courtliness, Business, and Form in the Correspondence of Lord Chesterfield

Alan T. McKenzie

Lord Chesterfield to Henrietta Howard, May 18, 1728

The Hague, 18 May, N.S.

MADAM,

Among the many privileges I enjoy here, I exercise none with so much pleasure as I do that which you granted me of writing to you, in order to put you sometimes in mind of a very humble servant, too insignificant to be remembered by anything but his importunity.

Could I imagine that you had the goodness to interest yourself in the least in what concerns me here, I could yet give you but a very indifferent account of myself hitherto, the little time I have passed here having been wholly employed in ceremonies as disagreeable to receive as to relate; the only satisfaction that I have yet had has been to find, that the people here, being convinced that I am determined to please them as much as I am able, are equally resolved in return to please me as much as possible, and I cannot express the civilities I have met with from all sorts of people. Notwithstanding which, as far as I can judge, neither my acquaintances nor my pleasures here will make me forget, or even hinder me from regretting, those I left at London. My great comfort is, that I have all the reason in the world to believe that my stay here will be highly beneficial both to my body

Chesterfield to Howard, May 18, 1728, from Chesterfield 36–38, no. 21; Chesterfield to Newcastle, Mar. 5, 1745, from Chesterfield 563, no. 773; Chesterfield to his son, Sept. 5, 1749, from Chesterfield 1387–90, no. 1656.

and my soul; here being few temptations, and still fewer opportunities to sin, as you will find by the short but true account I will give you of myself.

My morning is entirely taken up in doing the King's business very ill, and my own still worse; this lasts till I sit down to dinner with fourteen or fifteen people, where the conversation is cheerful enough, being animated by the patronazza, and other loyal healths. The evening, which begins at five o'clock, is wholly sacred to pleasures; as, for instance, the Forault [Voorhout] till six; then either a very bad French play, or a reprize at quadrille with three ladies, the youngest upwards of fifty, at which, with a very ill run, one may lose, besides one's time, three florins; this lasts till ten o'clock, at which time I come home, reflecting with satisfaction on the innocent amusements of a well-spent day that leave no sting behind them, and go to bed at eleven, with the testimony of a good conscience. In this serenity of mind I pity you who are forced to endure the tumultuous pleasures of London. I considered you particularly last Tuesday, suffering the heat and disorders of the masquerade, supported by the Duchess of Richmond of one side, and Miss Fitzwilliam of the other, all three weary and wanting to be gone; upon which I own I pitied you so much that I wished myself there, only to help you out of the crowd.

After all this, to speak seriously, I am very far from disliking this place; I have business enough in one part of the day to make me relish the amusements of the other part, and even to make them seem pleasures; and if anything can comfort one for the absence of those one loves or esteems, it is meeting with the good will of those one is obliged to be with, which very fortunately, though undeservedly, is my case. There is, besides, one pleasure that I may have here, and that I own I am sanguine enough to expect, which will make me amends for the want of many others, which is, if you will have the goodness to let me know sometimes that you are well, and that you have not quite forgot that perfect esteem and respect with which I am,

Yours, etc.

P.S. May I take the liberty of begging you to make my compliments to those of my acquaintance who are ever so good as to mention me to you.

Lord Chesterfield to the Duke of Newcastle, March 5, 1745

The Hague, 5 March N.S. 1745

MY LORD,

After having read and writ for fourteen hours this day without intermission, I have very little time and as little power left to trouble your Grace. I have acknowledged your letter by a postscript to your brother; but having seen the Pensionary since, I can't help telling you that by this post he will do what you mentioned, and will repeat the dose occasionally. By your thinking it will be of use, I hope things mend. I never meant to exclude Lord Harrington from our private correspondence, and I mentioned at first *the four* to your brother, meaning him and the chancellor. He might have been examined about separate letters to him; the others I knew would not. I am your Grace's quite exhausted humble servant.

Lord Chesterfield to his son, September 5, 1749

London, 5 September O.S. 1749

DEAR BOY,

I have received yours from Laybach, of the 17th of August N.S. with the enclosed for Comte Lascaris, which I have given him, and with which he is extremely pleased, as I am with your account of Carniola. I am very glad that you attend to, and inform yourself of, the political objects of the countries you go through. Trade and manufactures are very considerable, not to say the most important ones; for, though armies and navies are the shining marks of the strength of countries, they would be very ill paid, and consequently fight very ill, if manufactures and commerce did not support them. You have certainly observed in Germany the inefficiency of great powers, with great tracts of country and swarms of men, which are absolutely useless, if not paid by other powers, who have the resources of manufactures and commerce. This we have lately experienced to be the case of the two Empresses of Germany and Russia. England, France, and Spain must pay their respective allies, or they may as well be without them.

I have not the least objection to your taking into the bargain the observation of natural curiosities: they are very welcome, provided they do not take up the room of better things. But the forms of government, the maxims of policy, the strength or weakness, the trade and commerce, of the several countries you see or hear of, are the important objects which I recommend to your most minute inquiries and most serious attention. I thought that the republic of Venice had by this time laid aside that silly and frivolous piece of policy, of endeavouring to conceal their form of government, which anybody may know, pretty nearly, by taking the pains to read four or five books, which explain all the great parts of it; and as for some of the little wheels of that machine, the knowledge of them would be as little useful to others as dangerous to themselves. Their best policy (I can tell them) is to keep quiet, and to offend no one great power, by joining with another. Their escape after the *Ligue of Cambray* should prove an useful lesson to them.

I am glad you frequent the assemblies at Venice. Have you seen Monsieur and Madame Capello? and how did they receive you? Let me know who are the ladies whose houses you frequent the most. Have you seen the Comtesse d'Orselska, Princess of Holstein? Is Comte Algarotti, who was the *tenant* there, at Venice?

You will, in many parts of Italy, meet with numbers of the Pretender's people (English, Scotch, and Irish fugitives), especially at Rome, and probably the Pretender himself. It is none of your business to declare war on these people; as little as it is your interest, or, I hope, your inclination, to connect yourself with them; and, therefore, I recommend to you a perfect neutrality. Avoid them as much as you can with decency and good manners; but, when you cannot, avoid any political conversations or debates with them: tell them that you do not concern yourself with political matters— that you are neither a maker nor a deposer of Kings—that, when you left England, you left a King in it, and have not since heard either of his death, or of any revolution that has happened, and that you take kings and kingdoms as you find them; but enter no farther into matters with them, which can be of no use, and might bring on heat and quarrels. When you speak of the old Pretender, you will call him only the Chevalier de St. George, but mention him as seldom as possible. Should he chance to speak to you at any assembly (as, I am told, he sometimes does to the English), be sure that you seem not to know him; and answer him civilly, but always either in French or in Italian; and give him, in the former, the appellation of *Monsieur,* and in the latter of *Signore.* Should you meet with the Cardinal of York, you will be under no difficulty, for he has, as Cardinal, an undoubted right to *Eminenza.* Upon the whole, see any of those people as little as possible; when you do see them, be civil to them, upon the footing of strangers; but never be drawn into any altercations with them about the imaginary right of their King as they call him.

It is to no sort of purpose to talk to those people of the natural rights of mankind, and the particular constitution of this country. Blinded by prejudices, soured by misfortunes, and tempted by their necessities, they are as incapable of reasoning rightly as they have hitherto been of acting wisely. The late Lord Pembroke never would know anything that he had not a mind to know; and, in this case, I advise you to follow his example. Never know either the father or the two sons, any otherwise than as foreigners; and so, not knowing their pretensions, you have no occasion to dispute them.

I can never help recommending to you the utmost attention and care to acquire *les manières, la tournure, et les grâces, d'un galant homme, et d'un homme de cour.* They should appear in every look, in every action—in your address, and even in your dress, if you would either please or rise in the world. That you may do both (and both are in your power) is most ardently wished you, by

Yours.

P. S.—I made Comte Lascaris show me your letter, which I liked very well; the style was easy and natural, and the French pretty correct. There were so few faults in the orthography, that a little more observation of the best French authors will make you a correct master of that necessary language.

I will not conceal from you that I have lately had extra-ordinary good accounts of you, from an unsuspected and judicious person, who promises me that, with a little more of the world, your manners and address will equal your knowledge. This is the more pleasing to me, as those were the two articles of which I was the most doubtful. These commendations will not, I am persuaded, make you vain and coxcombical, but only encourage you to go on in the right way.

Chesterfield's Courtliness

In testimony to the concern with courtliness, business, and form in Chesterfield's letters, I have exercised an editor's prerogative and included three of them, while holding the other contributors to this volume, strictly and with difficulty, to two. Doubtless these three terms always overlap; in the letters of Chesterfield they are quite inseparable. It is not just that his courtliness is often businesslike, or that the more business he had to transact, the courtlier he became, or even that both court and office have always been predominantly (some would say exclusively) given over to matters of form.

Chesterfield's concern with form extends beyond the overdeveloped conventions of the places and occasions from which the letters were written into the underdeveloped possibilities of the letter itself. Chesterfield himself manifestly had the form in which he was about to work in mind every time he picked up his pen: every letter he composed and sent conveys business and exhibits courtliness. Both concerns extend the form into which they are laid at the same time that they fold it back into itself. His letters frequently insist upon and exploit the fact that they are letters, reminding his readers, contemporary or subsequent, not only what they hold in hand but also why.

Chesterfield had mastered the arts of the court as a child, tutored by the splendid example of his maternal grandmother, the dowager Lady Halifax. He had learned the business of diplomacy on the job, or rather on several jobs, all of them important, and several of them extraordinarily difficult: member of the House of Commons, gentleman of the Bedchamber, captain of the Yeoman of the Guard, member of the House of Lords, privy councillor, ambassador at The Hague, lord steward, viceroy of Ireland, special ambassador to The Hague, and secretary of state.[1] He performed all of his business well, shrewdly, and with much more candor and integrity than most courtiers manage. And of necessity, he accomplished most of his business by letter. Assigned, or rather banished, first to The Hague and then to Dublin, he sometimes wrote fifteen letters a day, most of which exhibit all the courtliness the form can, or once could, bear.

When in 1748 he had tired of both office and court, Chesterfield turned, again by letter, to the task of enabling his sixteen-year-old illegitimate son to conduct the business of diplomacy by mastering the forms of the court. He sent this not very promising and not very eager correspondent letter after letter exploring and exhibiting this combination. He received, irregularly, replies reminding him of the difficulty of his task. Philip had, by several accounts, no gifts for business, no courtly graces, and little capacity for form, epistolary, social, or official. Even his spelling and his penmanship were disappointments.

His father, on the other hand, had a genius for form, a genius he had cultivated, tested, and displayed for years, and one that he was not yet ready to lay aside. His positions and his assignments had prevented him from separating courtliness and business in his life or his letters, and he was determined to instruct his son in their effective combination.

The Letter to Henrietta Howard

The first letter is an early one, written within two weeks of Chesterfield's arrival at The Hague as ambassador charged with persuading the Dutch to consent to the Treaty of Seville. It is the sixth surviving letter in a lifelong correspondence with Henrietta Howard, a favorite of the new king, a friend of Swift and Pope, and soon-to-be countess of Suffolk.[2] The letter compensates for its lack of matter by becoming courtly in a very businesslike manner. Like several of the earlier letters, this one exploits the differences between the stodgy place it was written and the elegant place it would be read. It flatters and amuses the well-connected (and well-liked) recipient, while keeping in her mind the absent ambassador and his efforts on behalf of the king, the man who had sent the writer to the place where the letter was written and condemned him to the tasks from which it was a respite.

The repeated and playful emphasis on form rectifies and embellishes the lack of content. It reminds the reader, initial and subsequent, how clever and thoughtful the writer could be. There is no content because there is nothing to do in The Hague but business (the king's business), and Chesterfield is too polite, and too shrewd, to send a business letter to a lady in waiting.[3] On the other hand, much of that business had to be conducted by correspondence, and a clever letter to a well-connected friend at court would hardly reflect badly on the capacities of the writer.

This letter presents Chesterfield as diligent, courteous, and clever, in that order, and suggests that he is putting all three qualities equally at the disposal of his correspondent and his king. The partitioning of business and pleasure (a habitual one in Chesterfield's writings) reflects the simple fact that the letter is written in a place of business and read in a place of pleasure. None of the reflections from the fancy mirrors of this period, however, are simple or unadorned; Chesterfield's cleverness puts a high polish on all the sentiments and events he transmits. The distrust of ceremony, determination to please, and willingness to socialize (and to gamble) evident in this early letter continued throughout his career, strengthening it considerably.

The letter goes on to embellish the business and denigrate the pleasures of The Hague while suppressing the business and exaggerating the
pleasures of London: "In this serenity of mind I pity you who are forced
to endure the tumultuous pleasures of London." Even in the midst of all
these flourishes, Chesterfield's pen gives evidence of the workings (I wish
there were a more elegant term) of the mind behind it: he distinguishes
ceremonies from civilities and makes clear his preference—a lifelong preference—for the latter; he assesses the quality of both conversation and
the language in which it is conducted; he balances the satisfactions of the
parts of the day devoted to business with the mild disappointments of the
parts wasted on insipid pleasures and finds ways to combine the two that
seem thoughtful, candid, and ingratiating. Finally, he manages a fillip of
innuendo, in the reference to temptations, sin, and the age of his card part-
ners, and a touch of romance, the last and least businesslike refuge of the
courtier, in the prospect of rescuing three damsels in distress.

The letter opens by calling attention to itself as an elegant but unworthy
go-between, and it closes by inviting a reply. In between, Chesterfield
takes considerable comfort in doing his business well, and he did do it
well. The goodwill he developed and detected in The Hague was so good
that he would be asked to return at another crucial diplomatic juncture
in 1744. But he claims to find true pleasure only in personal correspondence, not just in writing this letter, but in anticipating the reading of it,
in envisioning the sharing of it with others, and in expecting a reply to it.
This invocation and extension of the form of the document contemplates
its extended effects, but it also dictates those effects. In doing so, it heightens the expectancy of the writer and raises the obligations of the reader,
first to respond and then to reply. The eliciting of a reply, whether by en-
ticing, cajoling, or badgering, is a regular feature of the correspondence of
Chesterfield and many others.

It certainly worked in this case, as this correspondence lasted nearly forty
years. Chesterfield's first letter to Henrietta Howard, written in 1716 (no.
10), purports to be to her lapdog, while the last one, written in November
1766 (no. 2465), insists that it is from his footman.[4] These two exceedingly
courtly appurtenances, the lapdog and the footman, enable Chesterfield to
bend the form and brighten the page. All of his letters to this correspondent, including this one of May 1728, are intimate, polite, and clever; none
of them have much in the way of real business to transact.

The Letter to the Duke of Newcastle

The next letter, written seventeen years later, is much more businesslike, but no less courtly. This one was written when Chesterfield was sent back to The Hague as part of the "Broad Bottom" ministry. His extraordinarily difficult task was to charm the Dutch into exerting themselves against the French, contrary to their inclinations, their interests, and their unworkable constitution.[5] "The choice was an obvious one. Chesterfield had the rank to which so much importance was attached in the eighteenth century, his diplomatic skill and tact were unquestioned, his previous embassy had given him an intimate knowledge of political and social conditions in Holland, and he had maintained friendly relations with the leading Dutch politicians."[6]

That his chief correspondent was the bustling, erratic, and fussy duke of Newcastle did not simplify Chesterfield's epistolary task.[7] Moreover, Newcastle showed as much of his correspondence as suited him to the king, a touchy reader much distracted by his Hanoverian possessions and not at all well disposed to his special envoy in The Hague. In all of the letters from this period Chesterfield was very much upon his epistolary mettle, alert—in a statesmanlike rather than a literary sense—to multiple readers, multiple meanings, and a constant need for clarity, firm civility, ingenuity, and tact.

That this letter of March 5, 1745 N.S., survives in holograph reminds us that much of Chesterfield's business correspondence was conducted by a secretary and that much of it was in code. Chesterfield sometimes calls attention to the hand that has written each letter and frequently alludes to those who will hold it in addition to the addressee. Some of these will be intended, but secondary, readers, meant to be manipulated by the document they are allowed to see by the recipient. Others will be unauthorized readers, on whom, as we shall see, the effects are no less calculated. Chesterfield wrote most of his business letters in layers, calculating their effects on secondary readers and including careful instructions as to whom, how, and when they were to be shown. All of them, including this one, supply evidence of a constant awareness of the probability of secondary and the likelihood of unauthorized readings.

Apparently not the rival of Lovelace and Valmont in some things, Chesterfield competes with both of them in disclosing his documents in layers. He often employs the efficient device he calls the "ostensible letter"

(749, no. 923). His correspondence bristles with comments like: "I showed your letter as far as it related to that point to the Duke of Newcastle" (812, no. 980); "I hope I may depend upon those letters that I trouble your Lordship with, in my own hand, being kept secret" (91, no. 149); and "I must desire that your Lordship's answer to me upon this particular may be in a separate letter, and such a one that I may show the Pensionary the whole letter" (96, no. 165).

The layers in the letter of March 5, 1745, occur in the care Chesterfield took not to write to Harrington for fear he "might have been examined about separate letters to him" by the king. Elsewhere he manipulates ostensible letters with more elaborate skill. He concludes a letter to Lyttelton as follows: "Pray lay me at His Royal Highness's Feet, but without showing this letter, which is in too free a style." But then he continues, evidently on a separate sheet—this is one of a number of cases where one really needs access to the manuscripts: "I add this to my other letter to tell you that, notwithstanding the postscript, you may show it the Prince or not, as you think proper; if you would have him see it, make a seeming difficulty at first, and make him force you at last."[8]

A year later Chesterfield refused, characteristically but impolitically, Lord Malton's request to appoint a bishop. He did so in an exquisitely layered letter to Newcastle: "But as you are entirely out of this affair, provided that you can convince that little puppy that you were in earnest in it, and lay it all upon me, I send you an enclosed letter writ on purpose that you may show him. I'll answer for it neither he nor his dependants will quarrel about it" (721–22, no. 906).

A second layer, the "ostensible" letter (no. 907), refers to yet another, earlier letter to Malton that should have rendered this exchange unnecessary. This third layer seems to be missing, but we can estimate its manner and effectiveness from the other two. All Newcastle could do in the face of so well documented a strategy was to refuse to write to Chesterfield for a month (Lodge, *Studies* xxxiii).

These intricate manipulations of form depend upon shrewd assessments of character, made during years of doing business with all the recipients. Circumstances dictated form, content, and tone, but the writer controlled the conditions and techniques of disclosure. The king's curiosity combined with Harrington's jealousy and distrust to complicate the letter writer's task. The resulting letter challenges the reader, whether that reader is immediate, secondary, illicit, or merely scholarly.

Often during this period, especially when the king was concerned, Chesterfield exploited the form by sending unsealed letters to intermediate recipients, who were to read them, then seal them and send them on to the ultimate addressee. This "flying seal," as he called it, saved his secretary time and ink, while establishing varying levels of confidence into which he could take his several correspondents: "I leave my dispatch to that Minister under flying seal, for your Royal Highness's perusal, and you will be pleased when you have read it, to order it to be sealed and sent forward by this messenger to Vienna, with all possible diligence." [9] Chesterfield was still availing himself of this device, a device both businesslike and courtly, for extending the form as late as 1758 (2280, no. 2038).

The elliptical phrase "he will do what you mentioned, and will repeat the dose occasionally," according to Lodge, means that the pensionary will write to his agent, Hop (*Studies* 12n). It is a compliment to, and defense against, another layer of readers that Chesterfield had constantly in mind, one over which he had somewhat less control. Nobody knew better than a retired ambassador and secretary of state that diplomatic mail got read by many unauthorized readers. The Walpole administration had been so notorious for opening the mails that the House of Commons conducted an official investigation in 1735. [10] Chesterfield was unfailingly courtly in addressing this layer of extremely businesslike readers: "I make my compliments likewise to those who will open and peruse this letter before you [Lady Suffolk] do" (271, no. 586). When letters of different dates arrive simultaneously, he wonders whether it is out of negligence or curiosity (no. 425).

He sometimes reminds those writing to him that the form is porous: "But remember, too, that I shall then be no longer master of the post; therefore let such of your letters as come by it contain nothing but what will bear an opening previous to mine. But when you can have a safe opportunity of conveying a letter to me, write more fully" (1089, no. 1526, to Dayrolles). When he had a chance to send a letter by courier, as he did one to Lord Huntingdon, he was more candid: "For in those that go by the common post I must be less explicit than I have been in this" (1711, no. 1767).

Chesterfield was himself a master of this form of intrusion. Evidently in the eighteenth century some gentlemen did read one another's mail. He had arranged to have the letters of suspected Jacobites opened, and he frequently forwarded surreptitious copies of the letters of others along with comments of his own (e.g., no. 198). A postscript to a letter to George Tilson, literally Townshend's right-hand man, in that as undersecretary of state he prepared the documents by which the business of the state was conducted, indicates that Chesterfield found the Dutch post offices especially porous: "The Postmaster of Leyden informs me that he has already sent you several copies of Count Degenfeldt's correspondence; the Pensionary will do his utmost to get at those letters, but there are two difficulties: one is that the post offices belong to burgomasters who often will not do it; and the other is, that they have nobody here expert at opening and closing letters, so that the affair would immediately be discovered by their bungling" (149, no. 309). When his son was granted access to the secret correspondence of Colonel Yorke, the diplomatic father expressed rare and unmitigated approval (1766, no. 1786).

The indication of the date as "5 March N.S. 1745" was essential for a letter being sent from The Hague to London, where, according to the Julian calendar, it was only February 23. Chesterfield contended with this inconvenience repeatedly, and not just in his business letters. Letters to and from his traveling son were especially difficult to keep track of, in time as well as space, and his numerous Continental correspondents, among them Algarotti, Fontenelle, Montesquieu, and Voltaire, struggled with this inconvenience.[11]

Chesterfield took it upon himself to correct this discrepancy between the Julian and Gregorian calendars, slipping the chronological intricacies past the House of Lords in a cloud of eloquence and disdain: "It was not, in my opinion, very honourable for England to remain in a gross and avowed error, especially in such company [Russia and Sweden]; the inconvenience of it was likewise felt by all those who had foreign correspondences, whether political or mercantile. I determined, therefore, to attempt the reformation."[12] Those writers represented in the present volume who were still corresponding after 1752, their editors, and all their readers, immediate and subsequent, are very much in Chesterfield's debt for taking the trouble to adjust this small but essential feature of the form.

In the course of his long epistolary career as a diplomat, Chesterfield manipulated every other component of the letter too. The top and bottom of the form, the salutation and the close, lent themselves especially well to his exquisite sense of civility. The "My Lord" on the letter in question seems straightforward, but Lodge points out that the "semi-official letters always begin 'My Lord', whereas the really confidential letters are to 'My

dear Lord'" (*Private Correspondence* xxvii). His promotion of his son from
"Dear Boy" to "My Dear Friend" in 1749 (1474, no. 1681) is the most
noticeable of several other calculated salutations. To a captain on the verge
of promotion he hesitates between major and captain and settles for "Sir"
(no. 1668), and he withholds the salutation to the Reverend Dr. Chenevix
in hopes that he will be "my Lord of Chlonfert" (i.e., a bishop, promoted
by Chesterfield's influence) by the time the letter arrives (no. 786).

The closing variation of "I am your Grace's quite exhausted humble servant," though nice, is not drastic or elusive. It does make a point worth
making about the effort that went into the letter at hand. Dobrée points
out the increased formality of closings of letters to Sandwich after he began
jockeying for Chesterfield's position as secretary of state (Chesterfield 981n,
no. 1332).

No formal or mechanical aspect of a diplomatic letter was beneath
Chesterfield's notice. Once he found out that the king was reading his son's
official letters, he urged Philip "to get the blackest ink you can: and to
make your Secretary enlarge his hand[writing]" (no. 2019). He complained
repeatedly about his son's handwriting and insisted on "neatness in folding
up, sealing, and directing your packets" (1801, no. 1801). That same letter,
however, enlarges on the content of business letters as well, insisting, as
Chesterfield always did in discussing manners, that they must indicate a
rich interior, not disguise a poor or an evil one: "The first thing necessary
in writing letters of business is extreme clearness and perspicuity; every
paragraph should be so clear and unambiguous, that the dullest fellow
in the world may not be able to mistake it, nor obliged to read it twice
in order to understand it. This necessary clearness implies a correctness,
without excluding an elegancy of style" (1799, no. 1801). This letter insists
on attention to pronouns and "the usual terms of politeness and good-
breeding" and "*certain graces* . . . scattered with a sparing and a skilful hand"
as especially important in business letters (1800–1801). It recommends
the business letters of Cardinal d'Osset and Monsieur D'Avaux and, with
reservations, Sir William Temple. Like the letters we have before us, this
one proves that Chesterfield knew what he was doing, and what he was
planning to do, whenever he wrote a letter.

So brief a letter as the one to Newcastle of March 5, 1745, cannot do
justice to the content of his business letters. This letter is more about letters than about business, or perhaps about letters as business. Others have
nearly as much civility and much more in the way of details and principles.

Attentive to the workings of several courts and conscious of the volatile cargo of information his letters had to carry, Chesterfield exploited the form every time he picked up his pen—which he did three or four times a day, often more. Working out of what he regarded as the whispering gallery of Europe, he had many whispers to sort, amplify, and redirect. Some of them were his own, many of them were gleaned from his numerous social and political contacts, and some of them had been purloined from the letters of others. He could always tell the difference between whispers that were worth conveying and those that were not, and he could frequently impart substance to the most evanescent utterance or behavior. These abilities, diplomatic and stylistic, made his letters unusually valuable to his employers and his contemporaries, as well as to subsequent historians.[13]

If the subtle control of tone and convention and the clarity, variety, and accuracy of content are not enough to qualify the letters Chesterfield dispatched from The Hague as works of art, perhaps it is time to discard that term. It is certainly past time to reclaim the letters.

The Letter to His Son

We come now to the four hundred didactic letters to his illegitimate son for which Chesterfield is notorious. The letter of September 5, 1749, is a fair sample of the depth and intricacy of Chesterfield's understandings of the workings of the state, the court, and the human mind and an indication of some other unsuspected excellences in his correspondence. The correspondence course in which he had enrolled his son was a demanding one, based on Chesterfield's own considerable experience in the ways of the world. He had no intention of subsidizing his son's travels merely for the sake of entertainment; letter after letter sets forth the places he is to visit, the things he is to notice, and the lessons he is to learn. In this letter he puts his unillusioned understanding of the connections between manufactures and commerce on the one hand and internal and external political power on the other at the disposal of his son and subsequent readers. His exasperating years negotiating treaties as ambassador in The Hague underlie the discussion of subsidies and mercenaries, while his year of reading history in retirement strengthens the part of the lesson dealing with Venice. The court is foremost in the father's mind here, and the forms in which business is transacted there figure in every line. Nonetheless, the comments about manufactures and mercenaries prove that the statesmanship of this courtier was both perceptive and current. Chesterfield did not maintain or exhibit the courtier's usual disdain for the business of the world around him.

The brief paragraph on the "assemblies at Venice" and the concluding flourish of French may confirm the expectations of those who know Chesterfield merely by reputation. It does inquire into Philip's behavior and drop a number of socially correct and politically powerful names. Those who know only this aspect of the correspondence, however, will not know what to make of the next two paragraphs—historically, socially, and politically among the most remarkable paragraphs from any correspondence of the period. In them Chesterfield instructs his son, for whom he planned a diplomatic career, how to behave in social and political circumstances fraught with opportunities for embarrassment and compromise.

The presence of the Pretender and his predatory court in Italy provided young Philip with several tests of his intelligence, his manners, and his good sense.[14] The letters of Sir Horace Mann to Walpole confirm that the diplomatic currents in Rome were subtle and treacherous: "The very subjects of princes in alliance with us, of which such numbers reside at Rome, are by the maxims of that Court taught publicly to profess what they might not [dare] to own in their own countries, and must do it to advance their fortunes at Rome, till it becomes habitual to them, and so the poison spreads everywhere. The very ambassadors of those princes in alliance with the King, when they reside at Rome are forced to adore another in that quality" (Walpole 18: 428). The retired statesman worried that his son's instincts and intelligence could not resist the courtly intrigues of the Jacobites, whose business he had been keeping an informed eye on for years.

Chesterfield developed this wary eye for the Jacobites as early as 1714, when he and they were in Paris, and one of his tasks in The Hague, both self-appointed and official, had been to report on the movements and machinations of the Jacobites there. He employed his Dutch sources for this purpose long after he had departed.[15] When Charles Edward invaded England in 1745, Chesterfield was lord lieutenant of Ireland (by all accounts the most successful and the most popular viceroy ever), and he handled the threat, the danger, and the numerous Irish Catholic supporters of the bonny prince firmly, fairly, and bravely (120–36). As Horace Mann reported to Walpole in 1748, "the Pretender's people exult extremely on Lord Chesterfield's retiring" (Walpole 19: 475); Chesterfield knew whereof he spoke when he wrote this letter of caution. If, after 1745, the Jacobites were no longer a military threat, their court in exile still constituted an enormous diplomatic complication, one that could easily halt the diplomatic career of a young man already handicapped by illegitimacy and a father now out of power.

This strong sense of the actual danger combines with Chesterfield's acute insight into the workings of a court to provide a lesson, and not just for his son, in the intricacies of power and *politesse* in the eighteenth century. The emphasis on manner is, as so often in this correspondence, enlarged by principles and supported by good sense: "It is none of your business to declare war on these people." Availing himself of the language of diplomacy throughout this paragraph ("I recommend to you a perfect neutrality"), he offers his son a little wit to mingle with his undoubted loyalty and his suspect discretion ("when you left England, you left a King in it, and have not since heard either of his death, or of any revolution that has happened").

He then turns, precisely and in detail, to the modes of reference and address his son must adopt. While courtiers are notorious for their overnice linguistic conventions, this passage reminds us of the crucial importance of both language and titles in this unique diplomatic context. The former ambassador is not urging his son to seek refuge in safe titles and prescribed languages; he is assessing the established ones and invoking them shrewdly and with precision. The didacticism is reinforced by good information ("as, I am told, he sometimes does to the English") and a good script—a script that makes the letter that contains it witty, honest, and serviceable. That good sense and civility mingle with the more pragmatic qualities of this passage even Chesterfield's detractors will have to acknowledge: "Answer him civilly, but always either in French or in Italian; and give him, in the former, the appellation of *Monsieur,* and in the latter of *Signore.* Should you meet with the Cardinal of York, you will be under no difficulty, for he has, as Cardinal, an undoubted right to *Eminenza.*"[16] The hand that wrote that passage was witty, principled, and well informed—politically, socially, and linguistically well informed. Even the reminder, at the end of the paragraph, of the Catholicism that was the primary objection to the Stuarts' return is effectively incorporated and well managed.

Though serious, very serious, this letter exhibits no trace of excessive weight. That weight might well have been paternal, diplomatic, political, or stylistic, but Chesterfield's courtliness controls every aspect of his prose. It is doubtless unfortunate that he did not trust his son's wit or discretion (even though there is no evidence that his distrust was misplaced).[17] Subsequent readers may savor the polite and informed instructions and at the same time regret the personal assumptions behind them. The passage itself testifies to how much wit, discretion, and discernment the author of this letter had at his own disposal.

The next paragraph in the letter reminds us, in its acerbic tone, generalized comment, and detached distrust, that Chesterfield had written more than letters. His speeches in the House of Lords were both feared and admired, and his political essays for *Fog's Journal* and the *World* can still be read with profit by those with a taste for the severe and balanced judgments that Augustan humanists passed on the activities of others. "Blinded by prejudices, soured by misfortunes, and tempted by their necessities, they are as incapable of reasoning rightly as they have hitherto been of acting wisely." That passage draws its abstractions from the part of the lexicon employed with similar effect by Burke and Gibbon. The nouns evaluate the human condition, while the past participles indict human nature. The syntactic structure of a triplet of past participles followed by a neat antithesis imparts rotundity and steadiness to the weighty abstractions, enabling as fragile a vehicle as the letter to convey a substantial cargo of meaning. The invocation of the example of "the late Lord Pembroke," a characteristic and perhaps effective maneuver of social didacticism, proves that we have not left the court.

Preceded by two paragraphs as full as these are of wisdom and good sense, the closing flourish of courtliness and French can no longer be read as contemptible instructions for the constructing of a mere facade. If Philip was to have a career at court, he would need to increase his own skill and attention with his father's experience, help, and instruction. And Philip is not the only reader who can derive instruction about courtly maneuvers from this letter.

For reasons of discretion and convenience, Philip's education was to be conducted abroad. At that distance, his father tried, frequently and repeatedly, to impart his own considerable fund of wisdom, gained by his years of experience of courts at home and abroad. He did so in letters that exploit all the courtly forms they undertake to explain, including the most nearly businesslike of them, the epistolary form on which they are laid.

NOTES

1. The best biography is Bonamy Dobrée, "The Life of Philip Dormer Stanhope, Fourth Earl of Chesterfield," in Chesterfield 1–225; see also Connely.

2. Pope praised her as "a Reasonable Woman, / Handsome and witty, yet a Friend"; Alexander Pope, *Minor Poems*, ed. Norman Ault, completed by John Butt, The Twickenham Edition of the Poems of Alexander Pope, vol. 6 (New Haven: Yale UP, 1964), 250–51. Swift praised her sagacity and dexterity, while doubting she could retain her virtues at court; Jonathan Swift *Miscellaneous and Autobiographical Pieces, Fragments and Marginalia*, ed. Herbert Davis, vol. 5 of *The Prose Works of Jonathan Swift* (Oxford: Basil Blackwell, 1962), 213–15. For her own letters, see *Letters to and from Henrietta, Countess of Suffolk, and her second husband, the Hon. George Berkeley, from 1712 to 1767*, ed. John Wilson Croker, 2 vols. (London, 1824).

3. Chesterfield did not write to any women as if they were, in his notorious adaptation of Dryden, "children of a larger growth" (1209, no. 1585). His letters to Madame de Monconseil, though courtly to the point of rococo, are neither paternal nor childish; see, for example, the letter of Sept. 8, 1747 (no. 1373).

4. Horace Walpole was enlisted to help with the reply, as if from "Elizabeth Wagstaff." See Chesterfield 2775n, no. 2463, and *Horace Walpole's Correspondence with Hannah More, Lady Browne, Lady Mary Coke, Lady Hervey, Mary Hamilton (Mrs. John Dickenson), Lady George Lennox, Anne Pitt, Lady Suffolk*, ed. W. S. Lewis, Robert A. Smith, and Charles H. Bennett, The Yale Edition of Horace Walpole's Correspondence, vol. 31 (New Haven: Yale UP, 1961), 431–32.

5. For a succinct account of the historical and political circumstances and the diplomatic disadvantages with which Chesterfield had to contend, see Dobrée, "Historical Note II," in Chesterfield 542–48; also Lodge, *Studies* 77–85.

6. Lodge, *Private Correspondence* xv. Lodge sets forth the complications of George II's epistolary expectations and pronounces Chesterfield's success remarkable (xv–xvii).

7. See Reed Browning, *The Duke of Newcastle* (New Haven: Yale UP, 1975). Chesterfield understood this character perfectly and described him at length; see his *Characters*, Augustan Reprint Series nos. 259–60 (Los Angeles: William Andrews Clark Memorial Library, 1990), 48–49.

8. Chesterfield 313, no. 610. These are by no means mere epistolary games. Lyttelton may have been easy to deal with, if notoriously inattentive, but the Prince of Wales was impossible to deal with, the circumstances were touchy, and the stakes were high. This letter was written during the height of the contest with Walpole after the death of Queen Caroline, so that each document had to be precisely drawn up and carefully handled. A later letter (no. 1281) offers Dayrolles elaborate instructions on how it is to be shown to the prince of Orange, predicts the prince's comments, and dictates Sandwich's replies. The reply from Dayrolles shows that the whole transaction transpired precisely as Chesterfield had predicted (953–54n).

9. Chesterfield 957, no. 1290. Cf. 191, no. 406; 558, no. 767.

10. Robinson 119–25. This was not, however, a new abuse. Cromwell's secretary of state employed an expert letter opener who went about his business every

post night in a private room "adjoyning to the forreign office," and Charles II
delighted in, and employed, a device for opening sealed letters, copying them,
and then resealing them, quickly and undetectably. The Dutch in particular complained about this practice. Robinson 45, 54–55; see also Ellis 60–77.

    11. The letter to his son, to be considered next, is dated "5 September O.S.
1749" because it was sent from London; it is in reply to "yours from Laybach, of
the 17th of August N.S."

    12. Chesterfield 1698, no. 1764. The rest of this account, in a letter to his
son, deserves to be read in full. See also no. 1768. Chesterfield worked harder to
master, if not to convey, the intricacies of chronology than this letter suggests. He
consulted the president of the Royal Society, the astronomer royal and the recently
retired chancellor of France. See Connely 311.

    13. They are infinitely more valuable, in every sense of the word, than the
merely gossipy letters of Sir Charles Hanbury Williams (see Chesterfield 795 and
1006n). Chesterfield did, however, send on all the gossip he could come by pertain-
ing to the king of Prussia (no. 299), knowing that this gossip would be welcomed
by his own king, for whose intelligence he did not have much respect.

    14. The deep contradictions, continuing threat, and seductive appeal of Jaco-
bitism to young men on the Grand Tour are developed in Monod, esp. 278–79,
284–85, 343–50; see also Lewis 113–14, 149–50.

    15. See Dobrée, in Chesterfield 20; see Chesterfield's letters no. 1091 (p. 862)
and no. 1098 (pp. 864–65); also Connely 32.

    16. The cardinal of York was Henry, the Young Pretender's second son and
later, to a few stalwart, romantic, but not very canny Scots, "Henry IX." It still
gives one a start (especially if one is a McKenzie) to come upon the burial place of
the last Stuart in one of the side chapels of St. Peter's in Rome.

    17. He may not even have trusted his languages. One of the nicknames he used
for Philip as a boy, partly to inspire him and partly to shame him, was Polyglot. He
never gave up exhorting him to learn German, French, and Italian or inspecting
the epistolary results (e.g., no. 1774). Boswell knew Philip "at Dresden, when he
was Envoy to that court; and though he could not boast of the *graces*, he was, in
truth, a sensible, civil, well-behaved man"; Boswell 1: 266n.

WORKS CITED

Boswell, James. *Boswell's Life of Johnson*. Ed. George Birkbeck Hill, rev. L. F.
    Powell. 6 vols. Oxford: Clarendon, 1934–50.
Chesterfield, fourth earl of (Philip Dormer Stanhope). *The Letters of Philip Dormer
    Stanhope, 4th Earl of Chesterfield*. Ed. Bonamy Dobrée. 6 vols. London: Eyre &
    Spottiswoode, 1932.

Connely, Willard. *The True Chesterfield: Manners—Women—Education*. London: Cassell, 1939.

Ellis, Kenneth. *The Post Office in the Eighteenth Century*. London: Oxford UP, 1958.

Lewis, Lesley. *Connoisseurs and Secret Agents in Eighteenth-Century Rome*. London: Chatto & Windus, 1961.

Lodge, Sir Richard, ed. *Private Correspondence of Chesterfield and Newcastle: 1744–46*. London: Royal Historical Society, 1930.

———. *Studies in Eighteenth-Century Diplomacy, 1740–48*. London: Murray, 1930.

Monod, Paul Kléber. *Jacobitism and the English People, 1688–1788*. Cambridge: Cambridge UP, 1989.

Robinson, Howard. *The British Post Office: A History*. Princeton: Princeton UP, 1948.

Walpole, Horace. *Horace Walpole's Correspondence with Sir Horace Mann*. Ed. W. S. Lewis, Warren Hunting Smith, and George L. Lam. The Yale Edition of Horace Walpole's *Correspondence*, vols. 18–19. New Haven: Yale UP, 1954.

Banter and Testimony,
Supplication and Praise, in the
Letters of Christopher Smart

Betty Rizzo

Christopher Smart to Arthur Murphy, late July 1753

. . . Num tu, mî Arture, hominum longè longéque ignavissime, adèo
diligentèr otiaris, ut ad amicum mittas ne verbum quidem. Jamdudum
expecto—sed perperam—Quid agis? in quâ mulierculâ operam navas? &
cuius honesti viri agilis thyma circumvolitas? Cave ne silentium tuum me
nimis faciat disertum. Mirum est, cum tibi insit tanta dicendi copia, ut
in Patriam populumque totis fluas voluminibus, te virum sicco praeteriri
calamo, qui te libens legit, libentior audit, & summoperè amat atque
admiratur.

Felicissimè situs sum ad marginem Oceani, qui meus est, inter comites
non inurbanos virginesque quàm pulcherrimas.—Non temere (ut opinor)
Scriptores antiqui Venerem praedicabant è mare oriundam, &c. &c.

(Are you not, my Arthur, both far away and faraway the laziest man and

Smart to Murphy, July 1753, from Smart, *Annotated Letters*, no. 12. The holograph of
this letter was apparently discarded by Arthur Murphy's biographer after he had quoted the
portion reprinted here in *The Life of Arthur Murphy, Esq.* (London: J. Faulder, 1811), 59n.
Though Dr. Jesse Foot was credited with writing the biography, it was actually compiled by
William Combe.

Smart to Panton, Jan. 10, 1766, from Smart, *Annotated Letters*, no. 17, reprinted by
permission. I am grateful to G. B. G. Thomas, senior assistant archivist at the National
Library of Wales, for providing a copy of this letter and permission to use it.

68

so industriously idle that you send no word to your friend? For a long time now I've been waiting—but in vain—What are you doing? With what fair lady are you hard at work? And around what honest man's thyme do you lightly buzz? Beware lest your silence provoke me to say too much. It is a wonder that you, in whom is such a plenitude of words that you gush forth to your country and your people in whole volumes, pass over with a dry pen the man who willingly reads you, more willingly hears you, and exceedingly loves and admires you.

I am most happily situated on the seashore, which is my element, among not uncultivated companions and the most beautiful girls.[1]—Not by accident {I think} do the ancients describe Venus arising from the sea. &c. &c.)

Christopher Smart to Paul Panton, January 10, 1766

Storey's Gate Coffee House St James's
2 pm [2]   Park Janry 10th 1766.
I shou'd have dispatched your books according to your commands, but lost your letter & the directions therein contained. _____ It will be a very kind thing to collect the 2d payments for me & send them & you shall have the books as soon as I am repossessed of the directions——For you must know I was lately arrested by my printer for Eighty Six pounds & must have gone to jail for that very book, from which I was in hopes of ingenuous bread, if it had not been for a kind friend, who cou'd not bear to see my tears _____ I am again to impose another tax upon my friends for a new Volume of Miscellaneous Poems, which nothing but absolute want shou'd have compelled me to __ Pray let me hear from you soon.————Your most obliged
    & affectionate

Christopher Smart

Smart's "Madness" and the Survival of His Letters

The full correspondence of any habitual letter writer would fall naturally into a variety of subcategories and then of sub-subcategories. There would be found, for instance, the family letter, the love letter, the business letter; in the subcategory of the love letter there might be letters of supplication, seduction, and mutual gratulation, letters planning assignations, letters of rebuke and reproach, letters of excuse, letters of repudiation. In the case of Christopher Smart's correspondence, the question of the subcategory becomes particularly important because of the small number of his letters that survive and the nature of those letters. The majority are letters of business; but as can be readily seen from the second letter provided above, a letter of business may be a letter of request so urgent that it becomes supplication and may also, when written to an old friend, be warm and may include personal detail.

Apart, however, from this obvious kind of categorization, a generic division dependent upon the relationship of the author to the recipient, Smart's scanty correspondence suggests another less obvious but equally valid method of division into only two subcategories, a division according to stylistic mode dependent upon the author's intention of producing either a bellettristic document or a communication that is simply, *faute de mieux,* a substitute for conversation. This kind of modal division would occur most often in the correspondence of literary people. It would not be invariably present, for some literary people—Elizabeth Montagu is an example—almost always wrote bellettristic letters, and there might conceivably be an author who invariably did so. The surviving letters of Smart do very usefully demonstrate this division, however. And they suggest the use, by Smart at least, of an index that would inform the recipient of a letter at once whether it was a formal or an informal communication, a literary set piece or a casual communication. This index, the common mark of punctuation the dash, I will discuss in the concluding section of this essay.

Correspondents in the eighteenth century seem often to have preserved their correspondence more carefully than they do now. It might have been expected that letters from Smart, a famous poet in his own lifetime (1722–71), would have been saved as the letters of Gray were saved. The fact that so few of Smart's letters did survive—twenty-five have been found to date, and five others have been noted in booksellers' catalogs and may yet resurface—may be an effect of the view people then took of mental derangement.[3] It was generally regarded with horror and without that scientific curiosity otherwise so characteristic of the educated.[4]

Smart had become famed as a poet and had attracted patronage even as a precocious boy and certainly at Cambridge; in the first phase of his adult career (from about 1749 to 1756) he had become well known in London. His various incarcerations for madness in 1756–63 therefore escaped no one's notice, and his postincarceration career, from 1763 to 1771, was not only the period in which he wrote his greatest poetry, fulfilling his early promise, but, ironically, was also the period in which he suffered contempt and neglect for the first time in his long life as a poet. It was almost certainly at this time that his family and friends discarded or destroyed the letters he had written earlier as well as later. The interpretation of the madhouse manuscript as potentially a vatic document was not yet, in that period, conceivable. Because Smart had been mad, even the virtually flawless *Song to David* was to be dismissed among the other documents displaying "the melancholy proofs of the recent estrangement of his mind" by Smart's nephew, namesake, and editor, the Reverend Christopher Hunter (xliii); it was dismissed as well by Smart's daughter the novelist Elizabeth LeNoir as having been only fancifully thought meritorious when it was imagined to be lost (71–72). Smart's exquisite control in the *Song*, its fierce faith, its perfect form and balance, its elaborate plan, and its tail-rhyme stanza scheme were not calculated to attract the favorable notice of the Romantics, and an 1819 reissue of the *Song* attracted a little critical but apparently no general attention.[5] The enormous virtuosity of the *Song* was to be proclaimed only in 1887 by Robert Browning (77–95). In the killing climate in which Smart persistently wrote his last and best work, and particularly in the 116 years following his death, some of his latter-day work as well as many of his letters may have perished. The manuscript of *Jubilate Agno* apparently survived accidentally, not as an innovative poetic work, but as a madhouse document that might, two friends of Cowper thought, shed some light on Cowper's derangement (Stead 15).

Among the letters of Smart that were discarded must have been those saved during his early days of promise and then of notoriety as a mad genius in London as well as those supplications received from the madhouse and from the last sad years. His mother and sisters must have proudly saved early letters from Smart written when he was a boy at Durham Grammar School, letters recounting his triumphs as a Latin scholar and poet and his promising acceptance by the Vanes at nearby Raby Castle, letters from Cambridge, as well as later letters from London. All these are gone with the letters about his conversion, his struggles in the madhouse. Indeed, not one letter to any of the women Smart loved has survived; not one letter to a woman survives. Apart from two early letters sent to friends—one to

Burney and the other that to Murphy given above—and two others sent to
Burney, those letters that do survive were letters of business that survived
in business files: four from the publisher Robert Dodsley, one from the
publisher Thomas Carnan, one from the theater manager George Colman,
six from the files of Paul Panton, a Welsh antiquarian and landowner with
coal mining interests. Dr. Charles Burney, an exception, had saved all his
correspondence, intending to illustrate the life of his time. Smart's letters
to him must have been many, as their friendship was lifelong, but Burney's
daughter and editor, Frances Burney, had no compunction about discarding
all but two. As she intended to publish these, it is not surprising that one
was a set piece and the other was a short informal communication containing one of those jewellike sentences that she knew how to savour: upon
receiving a sum of money from Burney, Smart had written, "I bless God
for your good nature which please to take for a receipt" (*Annotated Letters*,
nos. 10, 26). The third letter to Burney, removed from Dr. Burney's collection in his lifetime, fortuitously from our point of view, survived in private
collections and has lately been rediscovered (*Annotated Letters*, no. 31).

We are reduced, therefore, to dealing largely with the business letters of
Smart, those that survived routinely in files with all other correspondence.
Still, the variety of these letters is notable. Almost all supplicate in one
manner or another for money or assistance from the recipient, but in one
letter Smart is abject, driven to his knees; in another he remains the proud
poet, able to repay, if not in kind, then in the verses or prayers that he
always considered to be an equal if not superior commodity. In some letters
he is thoroughly businesslike and impersonal; in others pathetic personal
details creep in, one suspects to enhance the appeal. In some there is nothing to suggest the letter was written by a poet at the height of his powers;
in others occurs an example of that succinct and happy turn of phrase that
Frances Burney appreciated, that caused the letter to be remembered and
quoted: once she noted a letter lost or discarded that said Smart had assisted
a fellow prisoner "according to his willing poverty" (Burney, *Early Journals
and Letters* 166). Even after his loss from his papers of the 1770 letter from
the King's Bench Prison (Smart, *Annotated Letters*, no. 31), Charles Burney
was able to recall its structure: "Sir, After being *six* times arrested; *nine*
times in a spunging house: and *three* times in the Fleet-Prison, I am at last
happily arrived at the King's Bench." [6]

The Letter to Murphy

The first of the two letters given above, however, though it is in some part an application letter, was saved not as a business letter, but from appreciation of its literary quality, and perhaps also out of pride that the recipient, not a university man but definitely an ally of the classically educated wits in the wars against the dunces, had attracted a letter written in such correct and elegant Latin.[7]

Smart's had been a premature birth, and he had been predisposed to drunkenness, his nephew noted, by his having been fed cordials as a baby (Hunter xxx). One can scarcely assert that as an adult he was of delicate health, for his frenetic life in the ten years before his breakdown in 1756, added to his heavy drinking habits, suggests a phenomenal resilience. But Smart did show a tendency throughout that period to physical breakdowns, sometimes serious ones, that were characterized by bouts of fever and occasionally of delirium (*Annotated Letters* 56–58). One of these illnesses, a serious one, occurred in the spring of 1753, at about the time of the birth on May 3 of the Smarts' elder daughter, Marianne. Perhaps this illness had been brought on by the stress of working for the bookseller John Newbery, whose stepdaughter, Anna Maria Carnan, Smart had married in 1752. Newbery was patently determined to look after the interests of his stepdaughter and her children by procuring from Smart services commensurate with the disbursements he made to support the young, proliferating family.

Smart's 1753 illness had been noted by his close friend Arthur Murphy in the *Gray's-Inn Journal* of May 26, where Murphy announced that though lately indisposed, Smart has recently been seen and "has again held Dalliance with the Muse," a point proven by his production of lines now printed by Murphy, "To the Rev. Mr. Powell on the Non-performance of a Promise he made the Author of a Hare" (Smart, *Poetical Works* 4: 269–70, 449). These lines contained one of Smart's most famous *jeux,* the couplet "Thou valiant son of great Cadwallader, / Hast thou a hare, or hast thou swallow'd her?"[8] (The lines may also have revealed to the astute the importance of the hare to the Smart dinner table.) And it can also be inferred from Murphy's remarks that Smart wanted his perfect recovery certified so that his creative powers would be known to be unimpaired—some suggestion, at least, that symptoms of derangement may already have manifested themselves.

In the summer Smart, probably with his wife and infant daughter, visited the Hunters, his sister's family, at Ramsgate, the coastal resort east of Canterbury where his brother-in-law John Hunter, fortuitously a physician, was in practice. The purpose of the visit was undoubtedly to ensure Smart's continued recovery, and one purpose of the letter to Murphy was to demonstrate, to him and to their circle, the perfect restoration of his faculties. Murphy had found political patronage in the Opposition, and the Opposition had that summer focused on the unobjectionable bill for the naturalization of Jews that had been passed in the spring and was attempting to embarrass the government through questionable means that were probably most egregiously, certainly most successfully, demonstrated by Murphy in his famous or infamous *Gray's-Inn Journal* essay of July 14, 1753. The piece, purporting to present news of a hundred years hence, reported the circumcision of twenty-five children at the Brownlow Street Lying-In Hospital, the whipping of a nonjuring clergyman for speaking in disrespectful terms of the coming of the Messiah, the transformation of the city livery companies into tribes, and the ejection of Christians from the Sanhedrin (by which Murphy probably meant the higher courts but may also have meant Parliament).

According to Murphy's biographer, who by printing the surviving portion of Smart's letter preserved it, Smart had written to Murphy to congratulate him upon having contrived an excellent piece of party propaganda. As Smart was always on the search for patronage himself, he may also have been indirectly applying to Murphy's employer, to whom he hoped Murphy would show his elegant congratulatory remarks. The surviving part of the letter has all the characteristics of a literary set piece, very much like a letter that Smart had sent to Charles Burney in 1748, while Burney enjoyed the patronage of the wealthy Fulke Greville (*Annotated Letters*, no. 10). And like the letter to Burney, Smart's letter to Murphy was preserved, probably, because of its formal excellence.

The letter demonstrates one consistent characteristic of Smart's writings in both poetry and prose, a characteristic he very much valued: concision. Latin is, of course, a concise language, and in English Smart often utilized Latinate constructions that sometimes compressed his prose to the point where it is not easily comprehensible. The Latin of this letter is concise as well as beautifully balanced: *hominum longè longéque ignavissime*.

Smart's very small stature may have had something to do with his determined dedication to concision. His argument in "The Author apologizes to a Lady, for his being a little man" applies to his verse as well:

The less the body to the view,
The soul (like springs in closer durance pent)
Is all exertion, ever new,
Unceasing, unextinguish'd, and unspent;
Still pouring forth executive desire,
As bright, as brisk, and lasting, as the vestal fire.
(*Poetical Works* 4: 170–71, 434)

None of his surviving letters extend beyond a single page, an anomaly in a period of voluminous correspondence; probably the letter to Murphy was confined to one page as well.

Smart is also unabashedly allusive in his writings, often supplying additional significance to his work by referring through allusion to an important model. The letter to Murphy is in its entirety an allusion to Horace's *Epistles* 1.3, which incidentally is, like its imitation, also both an informal letter and a finished literary piece. Horace's letter opens, like Smart's, with a series of questions in which Horace inquires of Julius Florus, campaigning with Tiberius, where he is and what he is doing. "Quae circumvolitas agilis thyma?" (Over what beds of thyme are you busy?). Compare Smart's "& cuius honesti viri agilis thyma circumvolitas?" This line is the most obvious allusion to the Horatian epistle, but it identifies the model and would have done so for any classically educated reader. A letter based upon an epistle of Horace must live up to its original or incur ridicule upon its author; Smart has put considerable effort into the letter and has produced a work that was, wrote Murphy's biographer, "as might be expected, in very classical Latin."

There is another indication in this letter that Smart has fully recovered himself: he may in part have written in Latin lest someone look over his shoulder to see that he was revealing not only the literary but also the rakish interests the two friends shared.

Because between 1750 and 1755 Smart was the author of five Seatonian Prize poems on the attributes of the Supreme Being, it is often assumed that he was always of a religious turn and that in the madhouse he altered only the models for his religious verse, switching from Miltonic to scriptural models. In fact, until his shattering conversion in early 1756, Smart had played the role of rake in his life and in much of his verse. The Restoration rake did survive throughout the eighteenth century, both in life (Lord Sandwich, Old Queensbury) and in letters (Richardson's Lovelace, Burney's Sir Clement Willoughby), and arguably still does survive. Many eighteenth-century men did adopt the role, and no role could have been more radically unchristian. The rake had two natural and abiding enemies: the parent figure determined to keep riches and power from the next generation, and the woman determined to manipulate the men who lusted after her to suit her own purposes and to withhold her favors unless she could marry or satisfy her own lust. Rakish values reflect a universe not so much unrealistic as devoid of Christian principle, a universe in which everyone is determined to have his or her own will at the expense of almost everyone else. This was the world that Smart encountered as a child at Raby Castle—home of his patrons, the totally unregenerate and dissolute Vanes. Dean Spencer Cowper noted in his own correspondence the drinking bouts of Harry Vane, first earl of Darlington, the rumors of his incestuous connection with one of his daughters, his unprincipled misuse of money, and the dissolute behavior of his children (Cowper 113, 153–54, 183). At Raby Castle in his teens Smart confirmed his character as a rake. Undoubtedly it was from Vane that he learned how to use the drunken debauch to liberate wit and song. His early songs and poems are characteristically misogynistic, memorializing women as promiscuous, or as prey, or at best as provocative, responsible for male lust; he writes an excellent seduction poem. "The Precaution" of 1746, his most successful Vauxhall song, cataloged women's capacities for deception and had for a refrain "The Blind eat many a Fly" (*Poetical Works* 4: 107–8, 422). His "Ode to Evening" is comically derailed at the end when Nell, the lovely country girl, admits the philosophic Sophron for the night, the ode stanzas change to the ballad form, and the ode abruptly ends (*Poetical Works* 4: 144–45, 429). Nell has simply ruined the mood, diction, form, philosophy, and poem. The plot of Smart's lost comedy turns upon the manner in which a young lover outwits his mistress's father in order to obtain both the mistress and her fortune: the father is gulled into performing the part of a magistrate onstage and instructed to sign the paper put before him as part of the stage action (Hunter xiii–xiv).

Probably, in those early years, most of Smart's intimates played the rake as well. Charles Burney is almost always presented by his contemporaries as a sympathetic figure, but even granted that his father had serious failings, one is jolted by the response Smart made in 1748 to the news that the senior Burney had died: "I condole with you heartily for the loss of your Father, who (I hope) has left behind the cole [money], which is the most effectual means of consolation" (*Annotated Letters*, no. 10). If Smart could express such an opinion in a most carefully composed letter, he must have been using the mode of conversation customary and acceptable among his friends.

In the same way Smart is able to inquire of Murphy what man's wife he is seducing (or, given the metaphor of the bee and thyme, inseminating). There is the playful blackmail, too, with which Smart threatens to divulge secrets about Murphy: "Beware lest your silence provoke me to say too much." Though his married sister and his wife are present, the pleasure Smart finds in beautiful "virgines" tells us his eyes and thoughts stray secretly from the family group, and he invites Murphy to share his own vision of lovely bathing Venuses.

If the rake had little sympathy toward the rights or feelings of his father or his mistress, he was at least fully committed to wit. Wit, according to its eighteenth-century definition as the demonstration of a similarity between two objects apparently unlike, "the assemblage of ideas . . . wherein can be found any resemblance or congruity" (Locke, quoted by Johnson, *Dictionary*), was a kind of temporary union between two entities that appear to be irreconcilable, brought together solely by the ingenuity and will of the wit into the unlikely union of seeming incompatibles, a forced concourse that left to itself promptly dissolves again. Appropriately, this is the emblem of the brief sexual union without commitment. Nor is wit often kind; more often it is cruel. It is therefore the natural instrument of the rake, and it very much appealed to the unregenerate Smart. He begins this letter with a balanced construction, both pun and ploche, in which *longè* is used first literally, then figuratively: far away and faraway. He continues with an oxymoron: Murphy is diligently lazy, industriously idle. Then Murphy in metaphor becomes Horace's bee, fertilizing some honest (that is, dull) man's thyme. And finally in metaphor his manly pen becomes a fountain gushing forth enormous quantities of words sufficient to lave an entire nation. Here the analysis threatens Smart with having introduced a suggestion of homosexual intent, when he complains that the pen does not gush forth to him. A homosexual interpretation, which suggests another aspect of the rake's economy, his reluctance to limit potential amorous satisfaction by confining himself to sexual congress with only 50 percent of humankind, is perhaps tenable, but happily is beyond the scope of this paper to develop. What does emerge, figuratively, from the letter, is an expanding image of Murphy the prolific fertilizer and inseminator, first as a bee and then as an authorial pen gushing forth "in whole volumes" to his entire country, to which gargantuan gushing Smart obligingly juxtaposes "the most beautiful girls. . . . Venus arising from the sea." This carefully wrought letter is constructed in images, like a poem.

Smart's general rakishness was well known, and the disbelief of one acquaintance in the poet's sincerity when he wrote the religious Seatonian Prize poems (1750–55) has been recorded. Until his 1756 conversion, the Seatonian poems appear to be the only religious poetry Smart wrote; after 1756 his work was predominantly religious. The pre-1756 Smart was shy when sober and a consummate entertainer and exhibitionist when drunk. Francis Gentleman, the actor-writer who knew both Smart and Samuel Derrick well, wrote an epigram charging that neither wrote "from the heart." Derrick, he said, was sober, but celebrated wine; Smart, "for the sake of a legacy," "tho' devoted to wine, sings the glories of God" (Derrick 154). Smart himself airily referred to the prize premium, which derived from the bequest of the Kislingbury estate of Thomas Seaton, as "my Kislingbury estate." Almost certainly had it not been for the forty-pound premium and the challenge of the contest Smart would not have written the Seatonian Prize poems. And there is that other point that casts some doubt on the sincerity of Smart's earlier religious sentiments: although like other poor literary men he might have been expected to take orders and then slide, eventually, into a college living, he failed to do so.

Therefore, in 1756 Smart threw off almost all his old habits and attitudes with the old man; the new one (temporarily at least) abstained from the grape "even at the Lord's table" (*Poetical Works* 1: B5), gave up the theater, which he had once so loved, and, separated from his wife, practiced sexual continence. This abrupt change must have been disorienting; perhaps Smart's celebrated attempt to pray without ceasing was necessitated by his need to exile the old man by preventing the old man's thoughts from creeping in. In any case, Smart was, before his crucial illness in early 1756, a conventional rake, and after it he was an exceptional Christian.

The Letter to Panton

The second letter, written in 1766 to Smart's rich and supportive old friend Paul Panton, is very much a product of the new man. After his release from the madhouse in 1763, Smart was temporarily well settled. He lodged with excellent people in a house on Birdcage Walk just across the street from St. James's Park; he had begun to publish again regularly; he was leading a temperate life. But soon the old habits of improvidence caught up with him. He continued to spend more than he owned. This meant that when he collected the first half of the subscription money for his books—paid down in advance to cover the printing and paper fees—he had to use it for his living expenses and then could not pay the printer. The great endeavor of those last years was the printing and distribution of his poetic version of the Psalms. Toward this endeavor he directed the best energies he could summon, for these Psalms were also at the heart of his great delusion: that he had been born to reform the English church, which would be inspired to its reformation by adopting his versions of the Psalms into the liturgy.

Smart conducted his business not from his lodgings but from the Storey's Gate Coffee House opposite St. James's Park. From a table in this coffee-house he wrote an untold number of letters soliciting subscriptions and acknowledging payments. In the latter part of 1765, when Smart's *Psalms* had already been printed for him by Dryden Leach, he had been incapable of paying the printing charges, which probably amounted to the eighty-six pounds Leach claimed. Leach, a beneficent man, had doubtless realized that unless he arrested Smart as a debtor, no one would ever redeem the books. He had Smart arrested and taken to a spunging house, a holding place from which the debtor might make one last attempt to find the money owed. Here, as was usual in Smart's affairs, a friend came forward and paid the debt. Judging from Smart's next dedication, that to Sir John Blake Delaval identifying him as a patron of literature in *The Works of Horace, Translated into Verse*, published in July 1767, it was probably Delaval who came forward, a committed rake and a man of fashion equally improvident and about as proportionately impoverished in his own high rank as Smart was in his lowly one.[9]

Panton had been a good and steady friend to Smart, with whom he had become friends either at Cambridge or in London, where he had been entered at Lincoln's Inn. Now living almost entirely in Wales at his estate in Holywell, Flintshire, where he was developing extensive mines, Panton served Smart by subscribing to and enlisting other subscribers for a yearly charitable subscription of two guineas per subscriber organized by William Mason and Charles Burney and designed to provide Smart with a steady means of subsistence. He had also obtained many Welsh subscriptions to Smart's *Psalms*.

When Smart wrote, Panton, in Wales, had probably been awaiting the delivery of the books for some time; Smart's letter apprises him of the arrest, of his redemption, and of the redemption of his books. He is now ready to send the books, but he is apparently so impoverished that he requests Panton to take up the second payments and remit the money even before the books are delivered. It is possible that he had no money with which to send the books until the rest of the subscription money arrived.

Few of Smart's acquaintance and few even of his friends now praised his work or believed in his promise. His belief in his mission, his obligation to expiate for his past life by sowing God's seed, was so great that in the face of every discouragement he continued to work. He had the greatest belief in the *Psalms*, but for the most part those who subscribed—the list was long and filled with eminent names—probably did so as a charity. If Smart deceived himself on this score, he did accept with equanimity the charitable subscription undertaken in his behalf by Mason and Burney. In addition, though loath to publish a second large collection of poems, one that would gather up all the verse he had written since the publication of *Poems on Several Occasions* in 1752, because he was embarrassed by so frequent levies made upon his acquaintance, nevertheless he prepared to do so. (The proposed new volume never went to the press.)

The letter to Panton therefore outlines the kind of troubles that became the burden of Smart's latter-day correspondence. The recipients of his letters, one can imagine, laid them down with a sigh and murmured, "Poor Smart." The letter to Panton, however, also demonstrates a certain assurance, almost a touch of brass. In it Smart requests one service after another: Panton was to collect the second payments (from, the subscription list demonstrates, a formidable list of the Welsh), send the money to Smart, receive and distribute the books, and then be prepared for a new subscription for which again he would have to canvass all his acquaintance.

Smart's assurance derives from the sense of his special importance that he had always had and never lost. In his early years it was as a chrismed poet that he exacted tribute; he repaid material favors with verses and never doubted that the value of his own tribute at least weighed equally with that of his friends. After his conversion he paid with prayer, never doubting that his special position in relation to God as a chosen prophet gave him special influence.

In one sentence he very deliberately allows Panton a glimpse of his sad position: "I was lately arrested by my printer for Eighty Six pounds & must have gone to jail for that very book, from which I was in hopes of ingenuous bread, if it had not been for a kind friend, who cou'd not bear to see my tears." The letter with which he had summoned a friend qualified to give a note for eighty-six pounds would make a valuable addition to Smart's correspondence! Smart liked his recapitulation of his latest catastrophe, and it was demonstrably effective, for Granville Sharp reported a letter from the poet, now lost, dating from the end of December, and quoted his statement that he "must have finished an unfortunate life in jail had it not been for the good nature of a Friend, who could not bear to see his tears." The effect upon Sharp was to ask his brother, the archdeacon of Northumberland, whether some employment could not be found for poor Smart (Smart, *Annotated Letters*, no. 16). Smart was a man who always sought new patronage and new protection and never doubted that he ought to have it, first as a poet, then as a prophet.

The words *ingenuous bread* provide an example of Smart's characteristic use of words according to their literal meaning in Latin; from *ingenuus,* "noble," "honorable," Smart adapts the word to signify "honorable bread" or "honorably gained bread." This is a habit he shared with Johnson, who cites a meaning of this word as "freeborn; not of servile extraction."

Though this informal letter characteristically employs no figures or tropes, as the production of a poet it does have a composition that might be conveyed in painting or perhaps even better in sculpture by the centered image of the disconsolate poet sitting and weeping over his lost books, surrounded by various attentive friends.

Perhaps a point that needs to be made here is one developed in my introduction to the letters of Smart (*Annotated Letters* xix–xxi): the point that his letters of request were only one-half of the correspondence as he himself envisioned it. His vision was of a cycle that, in the first or secular half of his career as a poet, connected the poet and the poet's subject for praise in a perfect state of reciprocal generosity. In the second half of his career as poet and prophet, he envisioned a grander cycle running from the God-inspired benefaction to the God-inspired poet who by means of prayer and praise conveyed benefaction back upon the benefactor. The correspondence of Christopher Smart ought ideally to include most of his poems, for no poet wrote his poems in a more epistolary fashion. Many of his poems were actual notes or letters; many of the rest, including the *Song to David*, were directly addressed to the subject. In juxtaposition to all those letters asking for benefits, then, should be read those epistolary poems conferring due honor and praise.

The Dash and Its Grammar

A comparison of these two letters of Christopher Smart, one a carefully composed set piece, the other a quick and more casual composition, suggests that it may be useful to identify and to examine a seemingly minor component of many eighteenth-century letters, the dash used as a mark of punctuation.

Considering the dash in letters of the eighteenth century is not as simple a matter as at first it might appear. The dash was at that time in no way an acceptable mark to grammarians, and probably accordingly, it has been a widespread editorial practice cavalierly to remove this mark from the correspondence of those who utilized it. When it is rendered, it is invariably rendered, despite the length or placement that the writer has given it, as a midline mark of 1, 2, or 3 ems. In order to consider accurately the use of the dash, one must therefore work with holograph materials.[10]

This offending mark has often been identified as nothing but a semi-literate resort of the woman writer who knows no more proper form of punctuation, and in some cases—that of Frances Burney, for instance—it has been extensively edited out of the published journals and letters.[11] Indeed, the dash has been a favorite of many a woman writer, including (only as examples) Frances Burney, Mary Wollstonecraft, Jane Austen, Mary Shelley, Emily Dickinson, and Virginia Woolf. But whether edited out or left in their published work, male authors use the dash as well. The manuscript letters of Sir William Hamilton in the British Library, for instance, contain dashes that have often been silently removed when the letters have appeared in his biographies. Smart, too, in many of his letters makes a liberal use of the dash.

Smart did so well aware that the dash was in ill repute. Bishop Robert Lowth (whom Smart much admired) in his *Short Introduction to English Grammar* (1762) ignored the dash entirely, naming as the conventional four points the comma, the semicolon, the colon, and the full stop. These points, or stops, the only ones acceptable at the time, were, by Lowth and by other grammarians, often viewed as a sort of musical notation: there was to be a pause for a count of one for the comma, two for the semicolon, three for the colon, four for the period. There were no precise rules for the use of these stops, Lowth explained, because their use depended upon the length of the pauses judged advisable by the writer, to whose taste all final decisions must conform. Additional marks of punctuation that could be utilized were the parentheses, the question mark, and the "mark of admiration" or exclamation point. The parentheses required a pause greater than the comma to be accompanied by a depression of the voice. The pause required for the marks of interrogation and admiration was less determinate and was to be varied as required by the sense, but both were to be indicated by an elevation of the voice (Lowth 154–72).[12]

One conclusion to be reached from Lowth's instruction is that much of what was written was in the eighteenth century still considered very much, even primarily, as material to be read aloud. It was set down with instructions quite like musical notations to guide the reader in delivering it. Most grammarians made the same assumption. William Ward, master of a boy's school in Yorkshire, in his 1765 grammar confessed that it was impossible to give certain directions about the proper tone of voice, except in the case of the full stop, but "if anyone has a clear conception of the meaning of what is written, he will easily perceive where the points are to be placed; and if he has observed good speakers or readers, he will easily perceive what tones are to be used previous to each point" (9). A "reader" was in his terms the same thing as a "speaker."

Here may well be one reason women employed the dash—they had little to do with public speaking, reading sermons, or delivering speeches. Moreover, most of them would have been appalled at the prospect of their private letters being read aloud. So one purpose of the dash may well have been deliberately not to provide the conventional points because the letter was not to be read aloud. The dash might in fact proclaim the private status of the letter. A bellettristic letter, on the other hand—like most of Elizabeth Montagu's—seems designed to be read aloud, as a literary work. And so to some extent the dash might in part have functioned as a mark that helped to distinguish the letter as literary set piece from the letter as casual communication.[13] If to employ it was virtually to announce that one's purpose was not literary, that would help to explain why the mark was blacklisted by the grammarians—never mentioned. John Newbery's Circle of the Sciences volumes on grammar and rhetoric list the greatest number of punctuation marks I have noted: in addition to the seven already mentioned are included the apostrophe, hyphen, brackets, new paragraph sign, quotation mark, section mark, the mark for ellipsis within a word (a dash), the index mark (a hand), the asterisk, obelisk, and caret. There is no dash, other than that used as a mark of ellipsis within a word. None of the dozen eighteenth-century grammars that I have examined legitimate the dash.

Johnson does include the mark in his *Dictionary*, defining it as "a mark in writing; a line— , to note a pause, or omission." He therefore in some sense authorizes the dash used to denote a pause, in his commonsense fashion reflecting not pedagogical dogma but common usage. But his illustration of the use is from Swift: "In modern wit all printed trash is / Set off with num'rous breaks and dashes"—an example not calculated to inspire much respect for that common usage, an example that in fact again suggests that the dash was regarded as an informal mark not properly used in "literature."

The dash, as it was commonly used by Smart and others, also appears to represent, as Johnson noted, a pause, and, in the light of the contemporarily received idea of punctuation as musical notation, clearly a pause more weighty than any of the four orthodox points. The dash most often represents a transition to a new subject. If the period at the end of a sentence deserves a count of four, then the dash, marking what in a more literary work would be the end of a paragraph, might require a count of five or even six. When Smart employs the dash as a transition between subjects, often he also fails to develop the subjects into paragraphs, typically leaving them as lone topic sentences.

Conversation sometimes proceeds in the same fashion, by an exchange of undeveloped topic sentences, and the informal, unliterary letter seems once again to approximate and to substitute for conversation, while the literary set piece has the additional function of serving as art. Thus the use of the dash may have intimated at once to the recipient that the letter with its rapid transitions imitated conversation and did not purport to be polite literature. It provided a visual signal in somewhat the same way that the amount of paper left blank on the first page of the letter before the salutation was an indication of the amount of respect in which the writer held the recipient. Whether or not the recipients accorded the dash a longer count than the period when they uttered the letters to themselves is not clear.

Letter writers, I postulate, knew they had the Ciceronian choice of the plain, the middle, or even the high style. The plain style is often characterized, in the eighteenth century, by the use of the dash; it is meant to be for the most part purely informative. The middle style uses tropes and is meant to please. And it is unusual but not impossible for letter writers to aspire to the high style, the sublime, on occasion, as the letters of Elizabeth Montagu can illustrate. That the distinction could be recognized is seen in a comment made by Frances Burney in 1796 on some letters of William Mason that she had formerly seen and that she thought better than his general letters. "But he has two styles in prose, as well as poetry; & I have seen compositions rather than Epistles, which he wrote to Mrs. Delany, so full of Satire, point, & Epigrammatic severity & derision . . . that I feel not the least scruple for my opinion [that Mason was the author of Mathias's *The Pursuits of Literature*]" (Burney, *Journals and Letters* 3: 247).

Turning to the two letters of Smart with which we began, we can see again by the employment of the dashes that the first is a formal effort, the second an informal one. In the first Smart has employed a pair of dashes where he might have employed a pair of parentheses, to set off a parenthetical remark. A pair of dashes used in this fashion represents an orderly procedure. In the second paragraph he has used one dash that does not really represent a change of subject at all, but rather in this instance seems to claim close attention to the observation that follows—a usage that is not rare. A colon might have done as well. But in the second letter the dashes proliferate in a rich riot of a kind that modern typesetting is not equipped, it seems, to represent. Dashes employed nowadays must be 1 to 3 ems. Smart's dashes, however, defy such standardization. Some of them are laid in low, like underlining, while others rise to the midletter position. They vary in length. There may be messages in these variations. True to the conclusion that dashes are often employed to signal changes of subject, the dashes here do set off four successive changes and enable Smart to skip from the lost address to the request for the second payments to the arrest by his printer to his plans for a new volume of poems to the signature. The low-lying dashes may indicate the abrupter, more radical changes but seem also to follow the gloomier of Smart's remarks. One midline dash, preceding information about the arrest, is of the kind used in the second paragraph of the letter to Murphy: it might have been a colon and is meant to throw emphasis on what follows. The length of the dash is probably some additional indication of the pause Smart intends, for this is one mark that can be varied in length. The fact that the classically educated Smart utilizes the mark so scorned by the grammarians suggests that he, like others, desired to disclaim for his more hastily composed notes—notes literally dashed off—the status due his more serious work.

I would argue, therefore, that the dashes in eighteenth-century letters

should not be edited away, should not be so standardized in the printing that their difference cannot be assessed, and should be considered in
the light of the scorn accorded them by grammarians and of the musical
notation theory of punctuation.

It is reasonable to assume that even when one deals with a genre as simple
in appearance as correspondence, various subcategories of that genre will
make themselves evident. The division by subject into letters of business,
courtship, gossip, and so on is more obvious, however, than the division
by style into formal set pieces and casual communications. But the letter
writers of the eighteenth century were probably aware of both kinds of
distinction.

NOTES

1. Smart's meaning here is unclear but may simply be that he feels an affinity
for water.

2. Smart's figures are difficult to read; the numeral here may also be 7 or 8.

3. This reckoning is necessarily arbitrary. Some of Smart's letters survive in
holograph; some, like the 1753 letter to Murphy, survive because they were published; and of those published, some are incomplete, as, for instance, letters from
which excerpts have been published in booksellers' catalogs. From the five noted in
booksellers' catalogs, no excerpt has been provided. After the Rizzo and Mahony
edition of Smart's letters was completed, James Tierney noted a reference to a
previously unknown letter from Smart to Dodsley dated 1749 in a John Gray Bell
sale catalog of September 1856. See Tierney 533; Smart, *Annotated Letters* xvi–xvii
n. 2. This latest discovery makes up the sum of four letters to Dodsley and one to
Panton that have been noted but that are presently missing.

4. The newspapers and magazines published dozens of remedies for rabies,
for instance, but I have seen no popular discussion of the treatment for mental
derangement.

5. It was reviewed at least three times (Mahony and Rizzo, items 1329–31)
and praised for sublimity, but with a caveat concerning the poet's incoherence or
irregularity of mind. Until its rediscovery by Browning in 1887, it had very little
influence.

6. The letter actually began: "After being a fortnight at a spunging house, one
week at the Marshalsea in the want of all things, I am this day safely arrived at
the King's Bench." Smart went on to note he had been seven years in madhouses
and eight times arrested in six years. This letter, missed from his papers by Charles
Burney in 1808, reappeared on exhibition (from a private collection) at the Morgan
Library in 1980 and is now the property of the Morgan.

7. Mahony and Rizzo, items 34, 38, 55, 71–72, 134, 1168–69. I owe a debt of gratitude to Marshall Hurwitz of the classics department of the City College of New York, who reviewed my translation of Murphy's letter, noted the allusion to Horace's *Epistle* 1.3, to be discussed below, and characterized Smart's Latin as elegant, correct, and yet stylistically having a light, vernacular, and jocular tone all Smart's own.

8. Williamson prefers the text, with title as above, from Smart's *Midwife* of June 1753 (Smart, *Poetical Works* 4: 120–21); Murphy published the lines with minor differences and the title "An Epistle to the Reverend Mr. Evan Pritchard of ———— in Glamorganshire."

9. Delaval, the eldest son, had sold the family estate to his next brother in exchange for an annual income of four thousand pounds. A newspaper obituary, when he died in Aug. 1771, less than three months after Smart's death, noted that he had "always paid particular compliment to DISTRESSED AUTHORS nor was there ever an approach made to him for this purpose that he did not cheerfully come into with generosity that reflected the greatest honour to his heart"; Francis Askham, *The Gay Delavals* (London: Jonathan Cape, 1955), 142.

10. This is true, and of course the first letter discussed here, that to Arthur Murphy, exists only in a printed text. In the following discussion that must always be taken into account. But the fact is that Smart uses the dash in only about half of his existing letters and uses it rarely in his most carefully wrought ones, of which this is the most carefully wrought of all. Letters 10 and 30, probably the two next most carefully written, show a similar pattern. Letter 10 uses three dashes, two of them actually at the end of proper paragraphs, one at the end of the signature. Letter 30 uses no dashes at all.

11. Compare the journals and letters of Frances Burney as edited in the nineteenth and early twentieth centuries by Barrett, Dobson, and Ellis with the recent, accurately edited editions of Hemlow and Troide.

12. For a fuller view of conflicting punctuation theories in the eighteenth century, see Park Honan, "Eighteenth- and Nineteenth-Century English Punctuation Theory," *English Studies* 41 (1960): 92–102, and his chapter "Points," in *Author's Lives* (New York: St. Martin's, 1990).

13. The effect of gender differences on the use of the dash probably ought to be explored further in the light of the continued refusal of grammarians to recognize it well into the nineteenth century at least and the contumely male writers have heaped upon female writers for using it, as if its use were merely the result of female ignorance of the rules. I began such an exploration in several conference papers that I am preparing for publication. It seems to me that Richardson uses the dash to express what cannot or should not be expressed, often in imitation of what he perceives to be the style of women writers; Sterne uses it to express disjointed ratiocination, a disturbance of orderly reflection that may be associated

with feminine logic. Whether, in fact, women used the dash more frequently than
men remains an open question.

WORKS CITED

Browning, Robert. "With Christopher Smart." *Parleyings with Certain People of
Importance in Their Day*. London: Smith, Elder, 1887. 77–95.

Burney, Frances. *Diary and Letters of Madame d'Arblay*. Ed. Charlotte Barrett.
7 vols. London: Henry Colburn, 1854.

———. *Diary and Letters of Madame d'Arblay (1778–1840)*. Ed. Austin Dobson.
6 vols. London: Macmillan, 1904–5.

———. *The Early Diary of Frances Burney, 1768–1778*. Ed. Annie Raine Ellis.
2 vols. London: George Bell & Sons, 1907.

———. *The Early Journals and Letters of Fanny Burney*. Vol. 1, 1768–1773. Ed.
Lars E. Troide. Oxford: Clarendon, 1988.

———. *The Journals and Letters of Fanny Burney (Madame d'Arblay)*, *1791–1840*.
Ed. Joyce Hemlow et al. 12 vols. Oxford: Clarendon, 1972–84.

Cowper, Spencer. *Letters*. Ed. Edward Hughes. Publications of the Surtees Society
no. 165. Durham: Surtees Society, 1956.

Derrick, Samuel. *A Collection of Original Poems*. London, 1755.

Grammar and Rhetorick, Being the First and Third Volumes of the Circle of the Sciences.
London, 1776.

Hunter, Christopher. "The Life of Christopher Smart." *The Poems of the Late Christopher Smart, M.A.* [Ed. Francis Newbery]. 2 vols. Reading, 1791. 1: v–xliii.

Johnson, Samuel. *A Dictionary of the English Language*. 2 vols. 1755. New York:
AMS, 1967.

LeNoir, Elizabeth Anne Smart. *Miscellaneous Poems*. 2 vols. Reading, 1826.

Lowth, Robert. *A Short Introduction to English Grammar*. London, 1762.

Mahony, Robert, and Betty Rizzo. *Christopher Smart, An Annotated Bibliography,
1743–1983*. New York: Garland, 1984.

Smart, Christopher. *The Annotated Letters of Christopher Smart*. Ed. Betty Rizzo and
Robert Mahony. Carbondale: Southern Illinois UP, 1991.

———. *Poems on Several Occasions*. London, 1752.

———. *The Poetical Works of Christopher Smart*. Vol. 1, *Jubilate Agno*. Ed. Karina
Williamson. Oxford: Clarendon, 1980.

———. *The Poetical Works of Christopher Smart*. Vol. 4. Ed. Karina Williamson.
Oxford: Clarendon, 1987.

———. *A Song to David. By Christopher Smart, A.M.* London, 1763.

———. *A Song to David. By the late Christopher Smart, M.A., Fellow of Pembroke Hall, Cambridge; and Prose Translator of Horace*. [Ed. the Reverend Richard
Harvey.] London, 1819.

————. *A Translation of the Psalms of David*. London, 1765.
Stead, William Force. Introduction. *Rejoice in the Lamb, A Song from Bedlam*. New York: Henry Holt, [1939]. 13–49.
Tierney, James, ed. *The Correspondence of Robert Dodsley, 1733–1764*. Cambridge: Cambridge UP, 1988.
Ward, William. *An Essay on Grammar*. London, 1765.

Real Business, Elegant Civility, and Rhetorical Structure in Two Letters by Charles Burney

Alvaro Ribeiro, S.J.

Charles Burney to Samuel Johnson, February 16, 1755

Lynn Regis, Norfolk.

SIR

Though I have never had the happiness of a personal knowledge of you, I cannot think myself wholly a stranger to a man with whose sentiments I have so long been acquainted: for it seems to me as if the writer who was sincere had effected the plan of that Philosopher who wished that men had windows at their breasts, through which the affections of their hearts might be viewed.

It is with great self-denial that I refrain from giving way to panegyric in speaking of the pleasure & instruction I have rec^d from your admirable writings; but knowing that transcendent merit shrinks more at praise, than either vice or dulness at censure, I shall compress my encomiums into a short compass, & only tell you, that I revere your principles & integrity in not prostituting your genius, learning, & knowledge of the human heart, in ornamenting vice or folly wth those beautiful flowers of Language, due only

Burney to Johnson, Feb. 16, 1755, from Burney, *Letters* 16–18; ALS copy, William Luther Lewis Collection, Mary Couts Burnett Library, Texas Christian University. Burney to Mrs. Thrale, Jan. 11, 1778, from Burney, *Letters* 241–43; ALS, MS Vault File, Beinecke Library, Yale University.

to wisdom & virtue. I must add that your periodical Productions seem to me models of true genius, useful learning, & elegant diction, employed in the service of the purest precepts of religion, & the most inviting morality.

I shall wave any further gratification of my wish to tell you, Sir, how much I have been delighted by your productions; & proceed to the *business* of this letter; wch is no other than to beg the favour of you to inform me, by the way that will give you the least trouble, *when,* & in *what manner,* your admirably-planned, & long-wished-for Dictionary, will be published? If it should be by *Subscription,* or you sh^d have any books at your own disposal, I shall beg of you to favour me with 6 Copies for myself & friends, for which I will send you a draught for the money, as soon as I shall know the requisite sum.

I ought to beg pardon of the public, as well as yourself, Sir, for detaining you thus long from your useful labours; but it is the fate of men of eminence to be persecuted by insignificant friends, as well as enemies; & the simple cur who barks through fondness & affection is no less troublesome, than if stimulated by anger & aversion.

I hope however that your Philosophy will incline you to forgive the intemperance of my zeal & impatience in making these enquiries, as well my ambition to subscribe myself with very great regard, Sir,

Your sincere admirer,
and most humble servant.
Chas Burney.

Feby 16. 1755.

Charles Burney to Hester Lynch Thrale, January 11, 1778

St Martin's Street.
Jany 11th 1778.

DEAR MADAM.

What a *way you have* to make obligations of the greatest weight sit lightly on the Stomach of those who receive them at your Hands!—And then our good, great, & dear Doctor, so readily to second your Kindness, & my wish to be obliged to you both!—You are delightful Folks, & have so rivetted the affection of all under this Roof, who were before your willing Captives, that your names are never mentioned without such Gleams of Pleasure appearing in every Countenance; such smirking & smiling, that a by-stander, unacquainted with the Cause, w^d think us all bewitched: as, indeed, I believe we are.

My Conscience w^d not let me rest till Thursday without thanking you for all you *have* done, & Dr J. for all he so kindly *intends* to do, for our little Boy. You love Children too well not to know how nearly Benefits conferred on them come to a Parent's Heart. Heaven grant that the Ricciardetto may become worthy of such Patronage!

I am wholly in Leading-Strings as to the disposal of this Dicky-Bird. He shall certainly go no more to Hendon, if he can be received at Winchester after the Holydays. As I am entirely ignorant of the Institution, I know not at what Age, upon what Notice, or what Conditions Children are admitted. Something makes me fear there may not be an immediate vacancy, & in that Case, what is to be done? I think Dr J. said he w^d be rec^d as a Boarder, by Dr Warton—But, why do I talk of things beyond my Ken? The business is in such excellent Hands that it cannot go amiss, and I comfort myself, & quiet all Doubts with that Consideration.

But now, to transfer my Thoughts in a more particular Manner to Streatham: Do you know, my good Mad^m, that I returned from that dear Habitation more dissatisfied with myself than usual, at the thoughts of the little Service I had been able to do Miss T. during my last Visit? It is neither pleasant to a Pupil to hear, nor a Preceptor to tell Faults, in *Public*—Pray, if you can, let us fight our A, B, C-Battles in private, next Time. Miss B–ns are very goodnatured Girls, & as little in the way as Possible; but yet it is not easy for Miss T. or myself to forget that they are in the Room. When *real Business* is over, I shall rejoice to talk, laugh, sing, or play with them, till the Instant I am obliged to depart—But let our downright *Drumming* be first finished.

You must by this Time have seen, my dear Madam, that the Language of Music, like every other that has been cultivated, has its Letters, Syllables, Words, Phrases, & Periods; with Grammatical Difficulties equivalent to those of Declensions, Conjugations, Syntax, &c. The *Theory* of these is an Employment for the *Head,* only; but The *Practice* upon Instruments, Embarrasses the *Hand* as much as the Pronunciation of a new Speech does the Tongue. If my Utility in smoothing the road for my Fair Pupil to Musical knowledge & Abilities did but correspond wth my Zeal, she would then be exempted from that Progressive Drudgery to wch even Orpheus & Amphion must have been obliged to submit—But I forget that I am writing, & my Pen prattles away your Time about *Tweedledum* & *Tweedledee* with as much sober sadness as if you were a Musical Rapturist, an Enthusiastic *Dilettante*—Perdona! amica mia Colendissima! & remember that as yours was the first Letter of mere business wth wch you have honoured me, so this is the first from me to you without attempts at *Badinage;* but if any Terrestrial Concerns merit seriousness, & awaken sensibility, it must be such as relate to our Children; such Kindness as yours & our revered Friend Dr Johnson's; & such Gratitude as that of, dear Madam,

your obliged and
most obedient servant.
Chas Burney.

Cicero's Epistles . . . are letters of real business, written to the greatest men of the age, composed with purity and elegance, but without the least affectation; and, what adds greatly to their merit, written without any intention of being published to the world.

—Hugh Blair, *Lectures on Rhetoric and Belles Lettres*

Hugh Blair's statement might, with minor emendation, justly be applied to these two letters by Dr. Charles Burney (1726–1814), the celebrated eighteenth-century historian of music and man of letters. The letters I have chosen for critical appraisal are indeed "letters of real business" and are written to one of the "greatest men of the age" and to one of the greatest women, Mrs. Hester Thrale, the cultivated focus of the literary coterie that assembled around her at Streatham Park. They were not intended for publication to the world.[1] Whether Burney's letters here presented are "composed with purity and elegance, but without the least affectation," is a verdict that depends on that intractable and controversial article of belief called the reader's taste. I happen to believe that they are so composed— and here lies the crux of the matter. These letters are *composed*. Notwithstanding the surface ease with which his letters seem to have been written, I hope to show how Burney carefully structured these business letters along ancient rhetorical lines and thereby succeeded in what William H. Irving calls "the art of seeming artless in letter writing" (22).

That Burney composed his letters along rhetorical lines should not be surprising, for it was a commonplace of contemporary epistolary writing theory to remark on the close association of letter writing with conversation. Irving informs us that the early English books on style include letter-writing theories under eloquence: "Letters should be written, as a speech should be made, on the basis of rhetorical rules . . . and the test of success was the sound they made when read aloud. . . . Hence the continued emphasis on the idea of conversation. A friend is talking to a friend" (6–7).

Bruce Redford accurately and significantly entitles his recent study of the genre *The Converse of the Pen* and announces the principal subject of his study as "the familiar letter as intimate conversation" (1). His fundamental premise is that "the eighteenth-century familiar letter, like the eighteenth-century conversation, is a performance—an 'act' in the theatrical sense as well as a 'speech-act' in the linguistic" (2). Given the well-known connection between letter writing and conversation, it is not surprising to find in both these Burney letters strong evidence of the speaking voice. What is surprising, however, is that no eighteenth-century letter has to my knowledge so far been scrutinized for its rhetorical structure: precisely on what grounds does the letter-conversation link stand? I propose to address this lacuna in our critical understanding of the eighteenth-century letter as a verbal construct, as communication from one person to another; to apply to two Burney letters the techniques academic critics usually apply to more formal genres; and to suggest a way to read letters that would justify Hugh Blair's observation: "Epistolary Writing becomes a distinct species of Composition, subject to the cognizance of Criticism, only or chiefly, when it is of the easy and familiar kind; when it is conversation carried on upon paper, between two friends at a distance. Such an intercourse, when well conducted, may be rendered very agreeable to Readers of taste" (2: 297–98).

The two Burney letters presented here are carefully wrought, formally structured, and replete with the rhetorical devices of echo and allusion. What follows is an experiment in rigorous literary critical method applied to eighteenth-century familiar letters—an avenue of approach unattempted yet in prose or rhyme.

The Letter to Johnson

In his introduction, Bruce Redford argues that the critical neglect suffered by the familiar letter as a "marginal" form is attributable in large part to "the vexed issue of generic placement." He asks, "How can we do more than talk impressionistically about the letter until we can fix a category for it and then formulate appropriate aesthetic criteria?" (8). This is indeed the case. Whether we like it or not, the familiar letter, by its very nature, stands in between the Aristotelian categories of history and poetry. Any critical theory that would do justice to the genre cannot disregard either pole of this bivalency. An approach to the form along purely literary-historical lines runs the risk of treating the letter as a "mine of information," concentrating on the evidential facts that might be gleaned for other purposes. The opposite approach, considering exclusively the "poetic" aspects of the familiar letter, runs the risk of coming adrift from its moorings, only to be shipwrecked on the rocks of impressionistic chatter. What is needed is not an "either-or" criterion of critical assessment, but a much more difficult "both-and" critical endeavor.

Since letters plant one foot irreducibly in the stream of time, considerations of historical background and circumstance form a constitutive part of their meaning. Burney's letter of February 16, 1755, to Samuel Johnson yields up its full riches and interest only if we take the trouble to acquaint ourselves with its context. In 1751 ill health forced Charles Burney, at the age of twenty-five, to interrupt a blossoming musical career in London. He retreated to a country organist's post at King's Lynn in Norfolk, where he and his wife joined a bookish little circle of friends. Before his move to Lynn, Burney had read with excitement Johnson's *Plan for a Dictionary of the English Language* (1747), had seen and admired Johnson's *Irene* (1749) at Drury Lane, and, at the prompting of his friend Christopher Smart, had faithfully read each installment of the *Rambler* from its first appearance in March 1750.[2] Finding Johnson's essays virtually unknown in Norfolk, Burney recommended them to his friends, so that, as he says, "Before I left Norfolk in the year 1760, the Ramblers were in high favour among persons of learning and good taste" (Boswell 1: 208 n. 3).

Burney, buried in the darkness of deepest Norfolk, ambitiously looked for opportunities to resume his London career. To this end he traveled up to the capital each winter during the fashionable season to spend "3 weeks or a month in London every winter, to keep up his acquaintance, and prevent professional rust" (*Memoirs* 132). This tendency to "keep up his acquaintance," one of the most enduring and endearing of Burney's personal traits, lies behind his lifelong habit of penning familiar letters. He also used the letter to open and foster friendships, as this well-crafted epistle to Johnson shows. When the *Dictionary* was on the point of publication in 1755, the "insignificant" country organist assiduously collected a list of purchasers from among his Norfolk acquaintance and, greatly daring, plucked up the courage to write his first letter to Johnson, the forty-five-year-old London author and lexicographer.

The letter is ostensibly a business letter. It is, on its surface, a polite inquiry about the publication date and manner of publication of Johnson's *Dictionary*. Burney declares as much in his third paragraph where he proceeds "to the *business* of this letter." If we read this letter as it has hitherto been read, with only the literary historian's eye open, the first two and last two paragraphs might well appear to be virtually irrelevant bowing and scraping: here is the social-climbing Burney wheedling his way into Johnson's good graces. Roger Lonsdale has read this letter in this way. He writes: "Burney concluded his letter with more elaborate compliment and more profession of his own humility on this occasion" (*Burney* 46).

Without denying the truth of Lonsdale's faintly censorious assessment of what Burney was up to in this letter—Burney was undeniably a social climber—I want to open the other, poetical or rhetorical, critical eye and focus again on the letter with both eyes open.

Look at the five-paragraph structure of this letter. Notice how Burney carefully places the central "*business* of this letter" at the central hinge of his composition. Then work outward from this center to perceive how the second and fourth paragraphs go together, as do the first and fifth. This balanced structure of inverted parallelism around a central point has a name in rhetoric: *chiasmus*.

Biblical exegetes and scholars of biblical poetry such as the Psalms are fond of discovering the ubiquitous use of chiasmus in Scripture, and critics of English eighteenth-century poetry point to its use in the heroic couplet.[3] That such a rhetorical device should be found in an eighteenth-century familiar letter written in English is surprising only because we, as literary critics and scholars, out of long habit, have been looking at these letters askew with only a single eye, the literary historian's one, open. The chiastic structure of Burney's letter to Johnson of February 16, 1755, might be shown in schematic form:

a   "that Philosopher," Momus
    b   Johnson's "admirable writings"
      c   "the *business* of this letter"
    b'   Johnson's "useful labours"
a'   "your Philosophy," Johnson

The "business" center of the composition (*c*) both in content and in form is bracketed on either side by considerations of praise and censure of Johnson's writings which constitute the subject of the second (*b*) and fourth (*b'*) paragraphs. Johnson's "admirable writings" in the second paragraph is echoed by reference to his "useful labours" in the fourth. Such verbal echoes abound in these two paragraphs, which are thus inextricably linked through their diction. The critic might point to how "praise" and "censure" in (*b*) are balanced by "friends" and "enemies" in (*b'*). Johnson's knowledge of the "human heart" (*b*) finds its counterpart in the "simple cur" (*b'*), whose bark (*b'*) resounds in contradistinction to the paean of "panegyric" in the second paragraph, whose "vice or folly" and "wisdom & virtue" are echoed in the fourth paragraph by inverted parallelism in "fondness & affection" and "anger & aversion." Burney in these two paragraphs is signaling to Johnson that he is aware that Johnson's "admirable writings" and "useful labours" are not universally applauded by the critical press and fashionable opinion in the London of his day. If read only from the point of view of the literary historian, these paragraphs might indeed appear to smack of gross flattery. If read only from the point of view of the rhetorician, they might well be dismissed as verbal cadenzas on the theme of deference. The critic who only highlights the presence of rhetorical "flowers of Language" is always open to the disconcerting riposte, "So what?" This is where the "both-and" method of critical scrutiny of familiar letters is essential. Burney's rhetorical echoes serve the purpose of *communicating* to Johnson that this stranger who writes to him from remote Norfolk is in touch with the literary and fashionable trends of the day. As such, the second and fourth paragraphs of Burney's letter serve as a self-revelation, an "act of intimacy," in Redford's phrase, in which Burney draws close to Johnson.

This act of intimate self-revelation is precisely the subject of the first (*a*) and fifth (*a'*) paragraphs of Burney's letter. Whereas his second and fourth paragraphs resort to echo as their principal rhetorical "flower," here at the beginning and end of his letter Burney turns in addition to allusion. Burney alludes to "that Philosopher who wished that men had windows at their breasts," referring to Momus, the faultfinder of classical legend. In Lucian's *Hermotimus* 20, Momus judges a contest between Athena, Poseidon, and Hephaestus in which these deities each invent an object. Carping Momus finds fault with all three products: Athena's invention, a house, lacks wheels; Poseidon's bull has its horns inconveniently situated above its eyes so that it cannot see what it butts; and Hephaestus's invention, a man, is found to want a window in the bosom through which thoughts, sentiments, and affections might be viewed. Burney refers to Momus as "that Philosopher." Why "Philosopher"? Momus was no philosopher. All becomes clear, however, in the last paragraph, where Momus's traditional arrogance and unforgiving, unadmiring intemperance is balanced by Burney's invocation to Johnson's own "Philosophy," which, he hopes, will "forgive the intemperance" of Burney's zeal to subscribe himself "with very great regard, Sir, Your sincere admirer, and most humble servant."

Thus far do the to-and-fro echoes go between the first and fifth paragraphs. But the allusion itself creates a rich complex of interrelated meanings that contribute to the communication from Burney to Johnson. Burney himself most probably became aware of the Momus legend through reading the published correspondence of Alexander Pope. In 1735 Pope had published a letter to Charles Jervas that begins: "The old project of a Window in the bosom, to render the Soul of Man visible, is what every honest friend has manifold reason to wish for" (Pope 2: 23). James A. Winn calls this figure Pope's "most interesting metaphor about self-revelation" (200). By using the Momus legend filtered through the optic of Pope's letter, Burney appears to be doing several things at once. In the use of this allusion, Burney pays Johnson the compliment of assuming that Johnson will recognize the allusion. He also communicates to Johnson the message that they share a common "world" of letters—what Redford has called "a feeling of cultural consensus, which allows them to spin a delicately allusive web. Such a web substitutes for the physical presence that fosters intimacy between actor and audience" (6).[4] Most interesting, however, is the way in which the allusion works as a device by which Burney, to use Pope's phrase, renders his own soul visible to Johnson.

Through his writings Johnson had, for Burney, "effected the plan of that Philosopher who wished that men had windows at their breasts." Through this allusion and this letter Burney now returns the favor. The mutual intimacy thus established is not simply the baring of one soul but a mutual drawing close in self-revelation on the part of both parties. It is, in fact, a communion, an offer of the self and a response by an answering offer of self. Winn observes that Pope had learned from Voiture not only that "a letter should compliment its recipient" but also that "a letter might be used to display learning" (60–61). While Burney's letter does compliment Johnson in its use of literary allusion, I would argue that the reference to Momus (via Pope) does not here function primarily as a compliment to Johnson but rather as a display of learning through which Burney endeavors to establish his own literary credentials in order to win the older man's notice. Burney communicates to Johnson—the "sincere" writer (*a*)—the message that the letter Johnson holds in his hand is penned by no "mere" musician, no obscure country organist warbling his native wood-notes wild, but by Johnson's "sincere" admirer (*a'*). Burney's ambition to open an intimacy with Johnson through this familiar letter explains the careful rhetorical structure of its composition. The point was not lost on Johnson, who replied on April 8, 1755:

> If you imagine that by delaying my answer I intended to shew any neglect of the notice with which you have favoured me, you will neither think justly of yourself nor of me. Your civilities were offered with too much elegance not to engage attention; and I have too much pleasure in pleasing men like you, not to feel very sensibly the distinction which you have bestowed upon me.
>
> Few consequences of my endeavours to please or to benefit mankind have delighted me more than your friendship thus voluntarily offered, which now I have it I hope to keep, because I hope to continue to deserve it. (1: 68)

The Letter to Mrs. Thrale

We have noted how the familiar letter should compliment its recipient and how it might be used to display learning. Winn goes on to remark that Voiture's more lasting influence on Pope's letter writing was the "incorporation of the fanciful and romantic into his letters" (61–62). He also observes that when Pope began writing letters "the idea of a special style for writing to ladies was a cultural norm . . . Voiture's letters betray an assumption, usually tacit, that *all* ladies, whatever their age or marital status, are to be approached as if they were objects for romance" (63). All these precedents and assumptions are discernible in Burney's letter of January 11, 1778, to Hester Thrale.

In marked contrast to the circumstances in which Burney found himself when he wrote his first letter to Johnson, here, over twenty years later, Dr. Burney, now London's most fashionable music master, is an intimate member of the Streatham coterie. He had established his reputation as a man of letters by publishing the accounts of his Continental musical tours and had in January 1776 published the first volume of his highly successful *History of Music*, with its dedication to Queen Charlotte ghostwritten for him by Samuel Johnson, by now his friend.[5]

In December 1776 Burney had journeyed to Streatham for the first time
to begin giving music lessons to twelve-year-old Queeney Thrale, eldest
daughter of Henry and Hester Thrale. Mrs. Thrale recorded the event
under the date December 13, 1776, in her private journal entitled "The
Children's Book": "Yesterday . . . [Queeney] begun studying Musick under
Dr Burney, who is justly supposed at present the first Man in Europe, &
whose Instructions I have long been endeavoring to obtain for her. Says
Miss Owen this Burney's Name is MacBurney by rights His Family is Irish
& they were all MacBurneys till of late—*Hibernias* perhaps then quoth
Queeney" (Hyde 172).

Young Queeney's playful pun and her mother's evident delight in it
were apt tokens of things to come in the sparkling correspondence that
ensued between Mrs. Thrale and Dr. Burney, for professional contact
soon led to close family friendship between the Thrales and the Burneys.
Mrs. Thrale's particular favorite early in the relationship between the families was Burney's youngest son, nine-year-old Richard Thomas, who was,
by all accounts, a beautiful child. Burney's letter of January 11, 1778, to
Mrs. Thrale stands early in the run of their correspondence. It has to do with
their children and is, as Burney says, his reply to "the first Letter of mere
business" with which she has "honoured" him. Mrs. Thrale's letter is not,
alas, preserved, but we can infer from Burney's reply presented here that
it dealt with Mrs. Thrale's efforts to enlist Johnson's help in getting young
Dick Burney into Winchester, whose headmaster at this time was Johnson's
friend, the scholar and critic Dr. Joseph Warton.[6] Mrs. Thrale's letter about
Dick furnished Burney with the perfect excuse to communicate to her in
a familiar letter what was really on his mind: the disruption of his latest
music lesson with Queeney. The situation is full of the makings of comic
drama: How is Burney to tell Mrs. Thrale the unpalatable news that her
other guests at Streatham are a confounded nuisance? How is Mrs. Thrale's
embarrassment at receiving Burney's rebuke to be ameliorated?

Once again, as in the letter to Johnson, Burney couches the "real Business" of his music lessons—and of his letter—in a chiastic structure in
which his central point is propped up on either side with carefully plumped
cushions of courtesy. This time, however, Burney's chiastic structure is
disguised beneath the disposition of the paragraphs and emerges only if
we examine its rhetorical echoes and allusions as well as the parabola of
Burney's line of thought. I suggest the following formal division of the
letter:

a   "Dear Madam . . . believe we are." (par. 1)

   b   "My Conscience . . . Consideration." (par. 2, 3)

      c   "But now . . . first finished." (par. 4)

   b′   "You must . . . *Dilettante*" (par. 5a)

a′   "Perdona! . . . Burney." (par. 5b)

From the point of view of its contents, this disposition of the composition can be schematized thus:

a   Letter re Dick, Thrales/Johnson/Burneys, gratitude for "Kindness"

   b   Thrale's and Johnson's utility in Dick's education. Dismissal

      c   "real Business"

   b′   Burney's utility in Queeney's education. Dismissal

a′   Letter re Dick, Thrales/Johnson/Burneys, gratitude for "Kindness"

The "real Business" that is centrally placed in the letter might be read two ways, preferably simultaneously: looking outward into the "real" world, the "real Business" of Burney's last visit to Streatham; and, looking inward into the "world" created by an exchange of familiar letters, the "real Business" of Burney's letter itself. I would argue that here we have a good example of that Janus-like quality that Redford rightly identifies as the peculiar richness of the familiar letter genre: "The familiar letter . . . turns on the complex interplay between the natural and the fictive—between reflection and creation, history 'outside' and artifice 'within.' The peculiar richness of the genre results from this very ambiguity of status. Like the Japanese poetic diary, we might say, the letter is 'at once related to fact and freed by art'; like the diary, it moves between two poles, the historical and the artistic" (13).[7]

In this instance the historical pole is the disruption caused by the "Miss B–ns" who were present in the same room at Streatham while Burney and Queeney were fighting their "A, B, C-Battles." A little digging reveals that the "goodnatured Girls" were daughters of a director of the Bank of England and that one of them, Frances ("Fanny") Browne, had, according to Burney's most famous daughter, Frances ("Fanny") Burney, a "wild, careless, giddy manner, . . . loud hearty laugh, and general negligence of appearance" (Frances Burney 1: 234). Burney's protest to Mrs. Thrale, the "real Business" of his letter, is boxed into the center of his chiastic structure. It might not be too fanciful for the critic to suggest that this rhetorical boxing-in reflects and reinforces Burney's uneasy sense of entrapment by the historical incident as well as by his need to communicate his dissatisfaction to his hostess. The comic irony of Burney's situation is

heightened by the surrounding "Kindness" of everybody and everything
else associated with Streatham. He feels himself almost killed with kindness. Far from being mere decorative courtesies, therefore, the internal
parallels that frame Burney's central point take "Kindness" for their main
theme: form follows function.

In the first pair of surrounding parallels Burney elaborates on what
Mrs. Thrale has already done and what Johnson, ever sluggish, "*intends
to do*" for the literary education of Dick Burney (*b*).[8] The corresponding section (*b'*) speaks of Burney's own "Utility in smoothing the road"
for Queeney Thrale's musical education. Burney undergirds the correspondence between these two sections of his letter with allusion.

In (*b*) Burney makes reference to "Ricciardetto," a many-layered literary pun on his son's name. Only a month before the date of this letter,
in December 1777 Mrs. Thrale had recorded a snatch of conversation at
Streatham: "I told Dr *Burney* I would have his little Son *Dick* to spend some
holy days here with my Children when he was gone; What is the Joke of
that says Mr Johnson? why a Classical Joke replied I if any:—for you know
Ricciardetto succeeded to *Berni*" (Thrale 1: 219). This is as impenetrable to
the modern reader as it was to Johnson until we learn that *Ricciardetto* (1738)
is a poem by Niccolò Forteguerri written in the burlesque *bernesco* genre,
so called after its creator, Francesco Berni, the sixteenth-century Italian
humorous poet. The jest belongs to the same category as Queeney Thrale's
"Hibernias," and in using it Burney not only compliments Mrs. Thrale on
her literary learning and wit but also shares with her in the joke that most
private part of himself, his name. This section (*b*), which discusses the literary education of Dick Burney, equipped with its own apt literary allusion,
ends with a light-handed dismissal: "But, why do I talk of things beyond
my Ken?"

The corresponding section (*b'*) about the musical education of Queeney
Thrale also comes equipped with its appropriate musical allusion to Orpheus, whose dulcet tones on the lyre enchanted even trees and rocks
in addition to humans and beasts, and to Amphion, whose magical lyre
charmed the stones to assemble of their own accord into the fortifications
of Thebes. Without overemphasizing the musical aspects of his allusion,
Burney appeals to Mrs. Thrale's considerable knowledge of mythology. In
the graceful dismissal (the counterpart to "But, why do I talk of things
beyond my Ken?"), however, Burney surpasses himself: "But I forget that
I am writing, & my Pen prattles away your Time about *Tweedledum* &

Tweedledee," which, as a literary-musical allusion, shuts tight the clasp that binds together the two sections of Burney's letter and, in addition, unites Burney's and Mrs. Thrale's mutual efforts on behalf of their children. The allusion refers to John Byrom's *Epigram on the Feuds between Handel and Bononcini* (1727):

> Some say, compared to Bononcini,
> That Mynheer Handel's but a ninny;
> Others aver that he to Handel
> Is scarcely fit to hold a candle:
> Strange all this difference should be
> 'Twixt Tweedle-dum and Tweedle-dee![9]

The sheer inconsequence of the Handel-Bononcini partisan feuding evoked by Burney's allusion to Byrom's epigram serves as a corrective lens through which Burney views his "A, B, C-Battles" with Queeney. Burney also communicates through the allusion to Mrs. Thrale his hope that should any difference arise between them over the incident in the music room at Streatham, it should be no greater than that " 'Twixt Tweedle-dum and Tweedle-dee!"

The five-part chiastic structure of Burney's letter is completed at the beginning (*a*) and at the end (*a'*) of the composition with matching references to Mrs. Thrale's now-lost letter; the "smirking & smiling" (*a*) of the Burney household finds its modulated echo in "Badinage" (*a'*); and the friendship between the families is crowned by their mutual regard for "our good, great, & dear" (*a*) Samuel Johnson, who is "our revered Friend" (*a'*). The keynote "Kindness" rings out in the exposition of the theme and returns again in the recapitulation. Burney's "obligations" and "wish to be obliged to you both" (*a*) are adroitly worked into his coda (*a'*), where the very conventions of the complimentary syntactical close of the eighteenth-century familiar letter are pressed into service: "dear Madam, your obliged and most obedient servant. / Chas Burney."

THE RHETORICAL SKILL evidenced in the two Burney letters selected for scrutiny in this essay is by no means confined to these exemplars alone. Convinced that letters should be a supplement to friendly conversation, Burney throughout his life practiced the "art of seeming artless in letter writing" and instilled the habit in his large and talented family. The extant Burney family archive of over ten thousand letters, now becoming available in modern editions, is beginning to draw the critical attention it deserves.[10] To study these documents according to historical as well as aesthetic criteria will make comprehensible contemporary assessments of the Burney family correspondence such as this of Mrs. Thrale's:

> The Family of the Burneys are a very surprizing Set of People; their Esteem & fondness for the D^r seems to inspire them all with a Desire not to disgrace him; & so every individual of it must write and read & be literary; He is the only Man I ever knew, who being not rich, was beloved by his Wife & Children: tis very seldom that a person's own Family will give him Credit for Talents which bring in no Money to make them fine or considerable. Burney's Talents do indeed bring in something, but still I sh^d expect a rich Linen-draper to be better beloved in his own house—and nobody is so much beloved. (Thrale 1: 399)

This verdict raises many questions for the modern literary historian and critic; it also furnishes the germ of an answer. The sheer copiousness and variety of the Burney family correspondence testifies to a sense of epistolary vocation. I submit that in their stream of letters to one another and to their friends, the Burneys, not originally "fine or considerable," took the raw material of their daily encounters and fashioned them into a coherent "world" of their own devising, populated by the personalities of their wide and varied acquaintance, and supplied with incidents drawn from their real-life experience. No other explanation seems to account for their incessant letter writing, nor for their versatility in the form from the briefest note indicating simply that one was "alive," through what they liked to call "a few pleasing words," to the enormous journal letters of Frances and Susanna Elizabeth Burney. The Burney family correspondence, including the letters of Dr. Burney himself, would meet the three tentative criteria Redford suggests for identifying outstanding practitioners of the familiar letter genre: autonomy, fertility, and versatility (9–11). Redford writes: "At its most successful, . . . epistolary discourse . . . fashions a distinctive world at once internally consistent, vital, and self-supporting. The letters of a master thereby escape from their origins as reservoirs of fact: coherence replaces correspondence as the primary standard of judgment" (9).

It is this insistent, creative reaching out from the time- and place-bound self to the other in the converse of the pen that suggests to me a possible theoretical framework for understanding the genre. We have noted in Burney's letter to Johnson a gratuitous self-revelation in grateful response to Johnson's own self-revelation in his "admirable writings." In the letter to Mrs. Thrale, Burney draws close to his correspondent by writing about their mutual concerns for their children. These acts of intimacy seem to me to go beyond mere communication between friends apart. They establish a communion between the writer and the recipient. The letter thus becomes more than a physical object held in the hand of its recipient; it becomes in a symbolic sense the presence with the recipient of the writer's self. It might therefore be salutary for literary scholars and critics to reach across the boundaries that divide the disciplines in our fragmented academy in order to borrow some helpful notions about grace and presence from contemporary theology.

Karl Rahner, the German theologian whose contribution to theology in the twentieth century might be put on a par with Aquinas's in the thirteenth, centers his theology on the question of grace: What is grace? How is it possible for the divine and the human to communicate? For Rahner, grace is not a distinguishable "thing" that God pours into the human soul thereby justifying and divinizing it. Rather, grace is the gratuitous and free self-communication of God to the creature in which the giver and the gift are one. The giver is the gift: "It is decisive for an understanding of God's self-communication to man to grasp that the giver in his own being is the gift, that in and through his own being the giver gives himself to creatures as their own fulfillment. . . . What we can say by way of explaining grace and the immediate vision of God, then, does not give a categorical explanation of some definite thing which exists alongside of other things, but rather it gives expression to the nameless God as someone given to us" (120, 125).

We return from these heady heights of speculative theology to our little world of letters perhaps enlightened. I venture to suggest that at their best the eighteenth-century writers of familiar letters, in their self-revelatory acts of intimacy, created in the converse of the pen more than the illusion of physical presence. In a way analogous to Rahner's theology of grace, these writers sent their correspondents not so much a "thing which exists alongside of other things," but rather a "someone"—the writer's self—sent (as the title of this volume suggests) as a gift.

That Burney's self appeared in his letters was a feature of his correspondence commented on by his brother-in-law, Arthur Young, the traveler and agricultural reformer. In the following passage from his *Autobiography*, Young significantly makes no notable distinction between the "picture of the man" that emerges either from Burney's letters or from his conversation:

> In a letter from Dr. Burney . . . he rallied me with much wit on my culture of the earth instead of the Muses. This friend of mine had a happy talent of rendering his letters lively and agreeable, indeed they were a picture of the man, for I never met with any person who had more decided talents for conversation, eminently seasoned with wit and humour, and these talents were so at command that he could exert them at will. He was remarkable for some sprightly story or witty *bon mot* just when he quitted a company, which seemed as much as to say, "There now, I have given you a dose which you may work upon in my absence." (100–101)

The two fine letters studied in this chapter give us a small but true "picture of the man" that Burney was. Yet his characteristic and agreeable liveliness, wit, and humor described by Arthur Young must not blind us to the real business, the deeper purpose that sustained Burney's lifelong devotion to composing exquisite letters. That purpose might with justice be called a campaign for intimacy with the people to whom he wrote with such elegant civility. Armed with formidable talents to wield rhetoric skillfully, Burney waged his campaign by sending himself as a gift in his letters. In this way he successfully crossed most of the geographic, social, and psychological distances that lay between him and his correspondents.

NOTES

1. Burney to Johnson, Feb. 16, 1755, was published in Madame d'Arblay, *Memoirs of Doctor Burney*, 3 vols. (London: Edward Moxon, 1832), 1: 119–20; and in *The Harmonicon* 11 (1833): 53. Burney to Mrs. Thrale, Jan. 11, 1778, was published in Alexander M. Broadley, *Doctor Johnson and Mrs. Thrale* (London: John Lane, 1910), 127–29.

2. See Lonsdale, *Burney* 45–47, and Lonsdale, "Johnson and Dr. Burney."

3. See, for example, Robert Alter, *The Art of Biblical Poetry* (New York: Basic Books, 1985), 127, 167; *The Literary Guide to the Bible*, ed. Robert Alter and Frank Kermode (London: Collins, 1987), 52, 148, 190–94, 613–14; and David Fairer, *The Poetry of Alexander Pope* (Harmondsworth, Eng.: Penguin, 1989), 28.

4. See also Redford, chap. 3, "The Allusiveness of Thomas Gray."

5. *The Present State of Music in France and Italy* (London: T. Becket, 1771); *The Present State of Music in Germany, The Netherlands, and United Provinces*, 2 vols. (Lon-

don: T. Becket, J. Robson, and G. Robinson, 1773); *A General History of Music, from the Earliest Ages to the Present Period. To which is prefixed, a Dissertation on the Music of the Ancients* (London: T. Becket, J. Robson, and G. Robinson, 1776). See also Lonsdale, *Burney* 168–69, 182.

6. For further details, see Lonsdale, *Burney* 242.

7. Redford is quoting *Japanese Poetic Diaries*, trans. Earl Miner (Berkeley: U of California P, 1969), 10.

8. Johnson eventually got around to writing on Dick's behalf to Warton, who replied in a letter dated Jan. 27, 1778 (MS Winchester College). Mrs. Thrale records in her *Anecdotes of the late Samuel Johnson, LL.D.* (1786) that Johnson needed much prodding to produce this letter of recommendation: "After he had faithfully promised to do this prodigious feat before we met again—Do not forget dear Dick, Sir, said I, as he went out of the coach: he turned back, stood still two minutes on the carriage-step—'When I have written my letter for Dick, I may hang myself, mayn't I?'—and turned away in a very ill humour indeed"; *Johnsonian Miscellanies*, ed. G. B. Hill, 2 vols. (Oxford: Clarendon, 1897), 1: 280.

9. *The New Oxford Book of Eighteenth Century Verse*, ed. Roger Lonsdale (Oxford: Oxford UP, 1984), 207.

10. *The Journals and Letters of Fanny Burney (Madame d'Arblay), 1791–1840*, ed. Joyce Hemlow et al., 12 vols. (Oxford: Clarendon, 1972–84); *The Early Journals and Letters of Fanny Burney*, ed. Lars E. Troide et al. (Oxford: Clarendon, 1988–), in progress in projected 12 vols.; *The Letters of Dr Charles Burney*, ed. Alvaro Ribeiro, S.J., et al. (Oxford: Clarendon, 1991–), in progress in projected 4 vols. Recent book-length studies include Judy Simons, *Fanny Burney* (Basingstoke: Macmillan, 1987); D. D. Devlin, *The Novels and Journals of Fanny Burney* (Basingstoke: Macmillan, 1987); Margaret Anne Doody, *Frances Burney: The Life in the Works* (New Brunswick, N.J.: Rutgers UP, 1988); and Julia Epstein, *The Iron Pen: Frances Burney and the Politics of Women's Writing* (Madison: U of Wisconsin P, 1989).

WORKS CITED

Blair, Hugh. *Lectures on Rhetoric and Belles Lettres*. 1783. Ed. Harold F. Harding. 2 vols. Carbondale: Southern Illinois UP, 1965.

Boswell, James. *Boswell's Life of Johnson*. Ed. George Birkbeck Hill, rev. L. F. Powell. 6 vols. Oxford: Clarendon, 1934–50.

Burney, Charles. *The Letters of Dr Charles Burney*. Vol. 1, *1751–1784*. Ed. Alvaro Ribeiro, S.J. Oxford: Clarendon, 1991.

———. *Memoirs of Dr. Charles Burney, 1726–1769*. Ed. Slava Klima, Garry Bowers, and Kerry S. Grant. Lincoln: U of Nebraska P, 1988.

Burney, Frances. *Diary and Letters of Madame d'Arblay (1778–1840)*. Ed. Austin Dobson. 6 vols. London: Macmillan, 1904–5.

Hyde, Mary. *The Thrales of Streatham Park*. Cambridge: Harvard UP, 1977.

Irving, William Henry. *The Providence of Wit in the English Letter Writers*. Durham, N.C.: Duke UP, 1955.

Johnson, Samuel. *The Letters of Samuel Johnson, with Mrs. Thrale's Genuine Letters to Him*. Ed. R. W. Chapman. 3 vols. Oxford: Clarendon, 1952.

Lonsdale, Roger. *Dr. Charles Burney: A Literary Biography*. Oxford: Clarendon, 1965.

——. "Johnson and Dr. Burney." *Johnson, Boswell and Their Circle*. Ed. Mary Lascelles et al. Oxford: Clarendon, 1965. 21–40.

Pope, Alexander. *The Correspondence of Alexander Pope*. Ed. George Sherburn. 5 vols. Oxford: Clarendon, 1956.

Rahner, Karl. *Foundations of Christian Faith: An Introduction to the Idea of Christianity*. Trans. William V. Dych. New York: Crossroad, 1978.

Redford, Bruce. *The Converse of the Pen: Acts of Intimacy in the Eighteenth-Century Familiar Letter*. Chicago: U of Chicago P, 1986.

Thrale, Hester Lynch. *Thraliana: The Diary of Mrs. Hester Lynch Thrale (Later Mrs. Piozzi), 1776–1809*. Ed. Katharine C. Balderston. 2d ed. 2 vols. Oxford: Clarendon, 1951.

Winn, James Anderson. *A Window in the Bosom: The Letters of Alexander Pope*. Hamden, Conn.: Archon Books, 1977.

Young, Arthur. *The Autobiography of Arthur Young with Selections from His Correspondence*. Ed. M. Betham-Edwards. London: Smith, Elder, 1898.

Responses to Tyrants:
Robert Dodsley to William Warburton
and to David Garrick

James E. Tierney

Robert Dodsley to William Warburton, January 6, 1756

Pall mall Jan^{ry} 6th

SIR

I was favour'd with two letters from you, one on Monday, the other on Tuesday last, which I should have answer'd sooner but that I was then going out of town.[1] In the first of your letters I am charg'd (tho' without proof and I hope without foundation) with a want of regard to the Memory of Mr Pope, in suffering little scribblers to defame him thro' my press: and this is given as the reason why you did not chuse to treat with me for a share in his works.[2] In the second this charge is d[ropt?] and I am tax'd with a want of Sensibility, in applying to you for favours, after having, seven years ago, printed a book in which the Author (who put his name to his work) had treated You with ill manners.[3] I am also charg'd with not resenting properly, a forg'd Letter sent to You in my name: which last, as I was entirely ignorant of it, and You then did me the Justice to acquit me, have now even forgot on what occasion it was written.[4] As to the first charge, my

Dodsley to Warburton, Jan. 6, 1756, from Dodsley, *Correspondence* 215–17; the holograph is in the Hyde Collection, Somerville, N.J. Dodsley to Garrick, Dec. 5, 1758, from Dodsley, *Correspondence* 383–84; the holograph is in the Victoria and Albert Museum MS F. 48 F. 7, ff. 3–4. To some degree, the texts of these letters have been normalized for the reader's convenience.

want of respect to the Memory of Mr Pope; as it is my pride that he was my friend, so it is my consolation under the misfortune of your censure, that I cannot charge my self with the least forgetfulness of what I owe him. But You will pardon my remarking by the way, suppose I had been somewhat remiss in this respect had not you employ'd as the Printer of his works, the person who publish'd the most virulent Libel that has yet appear'd against him? I mean a Preface to ye Patriot King.[5] As to my having printed a book in which you was disrespectfully treated—I would beg leave to ask, what You would have said to Mr Knapton had he refused to print some of your Pieces? Did you object to him, that he had, before You employ'd him, printed Dr Sykes's book, professedly written agst You?[6] It does not appear that you did. I do not mention these Instances as charging either Mr Knapton or Mr Millar with the least crime, but only to shew, that what You have thought proper to make an objection against *me,* was not thought so in regard to *them.* Another charge upon me is, my want of Sensibility in applying to You for favours. I must own I was not conscious that I had ever given you any just cause of Offence: neither can I look upon my offer to You of purchasing at reasonable price, a share of that Property, part of which you had already dispos'd of to others, as an application for any singular favour. + But I give my self the air you say, of one who had some merit with you—I do not believe, on a perusal of my letter, that You will find me guilty of any such Presumption:[7] but I did so presume, how strangely was I mistaken! for by your uncharitable sneer on the morals of a Bookseller, and from the very hard conclusion of your last Letter, it appears that You cannot allow me even the merit of common Honesty; but treat me as one with whom You would by no means chuse to have any dealings.[8] This last stroke I must own would have given me some pain, were I not in hopes that the opinions of all who best know me, and of the public in general, are somewhat different from that which I am so unfortunate as to find is yours of

Sir

Your very humble Servant

Dodsley

p. s. + However, grant it was a favour, I never ask'd but once, & never rec^d a denial till now; & therefore your reproaches of Importunity, of not being content with a simple denial, but forcing You to tell me all your mind, I think might have been spar[ed.][9]

Robert Dodsley to David Garrick, December 5, 1758

Decr 5th

SIR

I thank you for your Compliments on the success of Cleone, and could have wish'd You had thought proper to have put it in my power to have thank'd you for contributing towards it: but I think it is not now in your own to redress the injury you have done me. You know full well that *profit* was but my second motive for bringing this piece on the Stage,[10] and you have taken effectual care to nip its *Reputation* in the bud, by preventing ye Town, as far as lay in your power, from attending to it. As to my proposing any means in which you can now be of service to me, I hope you do not think that, after what has past, I can possibly bring my self to ask a favour of you. In short, if your behaviour to me has been right, I see no cause you have to be concern'd about it; if wrong, why was it so? I am certain I gave you no provocation for it. I therefore leave it on your self to pursue what measure you may think most consistent with your own reputation; as to mine, you have certainly in this instance done all you could to lessen it. However, I beg you will believe it is with some regret I feel I cannot at present subscribe my self, with that cordiality I have always wish'd to be,

Sir

Your friend and Servant

R Dodsley

[Garrick's Endorsement:] Dodsley's Answer

Dodsley's Advocacy of the Common Man

Before his rise to fame as popular London playwright and eminent bookseller, Robert Dodsley struggled to reconcile his perception of his own genius with the degradations he suffered in his lowly station as a footman. Frustrated, he complained in his *Miseries of Poverty* (1731): "The miseries of a thinking man are intolerably aggravated by . . . the contempt with which the world looks upon him in a mean and despicable habit . . . and the many insults, inconveniences, and restraints which he undergoes . . . are themes which afford him a great many melancholy reflections" (138). Once he began to make his mark, however, Dodsley saw that, all along, what he had resented most was the artificial structure of English society that allowed worthless elements of a privileged class to exercise despotic sway over true merit when found in humble dress. And it is indeed a tribute to his integrity that success never blinded him to his origins and to the similar plight of humble "thinking" men and, more significant, that throughout his rise to the status of London's premier bookseller, Dodsley championed—both in his own writings and in the works he published—the cause of the common man. The wrongful oppression of true natural worth by a privileged aristocratic class (whether civil or clerical) became a regular theme of his democratic shop at the sign of Tully's Head. In his very first play, *The Toy-shop* (1735), Dodsley leveled his charge at the vanity of wealth and clerical pretension. His satirical shopkeeper instructs a customer: "You shall find Infidelity mask'd in a Gown and Cassock . . . Oppression is veil'd under the Name of Justice. . . . In short, Worthlessness and Villainy are oft disguis'd and dignified in Gold and Jewels, whilst Honesty and Merit lie hid under Raggs and Misery" (Solomon, *Toy-shop* 30–31).

The commonalty of all men is at the heart of his even more popular afterpiece *The King and Miller of Mansfield* (1737). Foundering by himself in the dark of Sherwood Forest after a day of hunting, King Henry II realizes: "Of what Advantage is it now to be a King? Night shows me no Respect: I cannot see better, nor walk so well as another Man. . . . in losing the Monarch, I have found the Man" (Solomon, *King* 11–12). Enlightened to common humanity, the king then proceeds to right the cruel deception one of his own courtiers had worked on his new, humble but noble country acquaintances, punishing the lord and rewarding the simple miller with a knighthood and a pension.

But Dodsley's advocacy of the common man was not limited to gentle satire and sentimental moralizing; his campaign as patriot for English liberties took on more aggressive proportions in the public forum, sometimes even emerging as a bitter or cynical attack on traditional "assumed" authority. A dangerous venture was his publication of Paul Whitehead's *Manners* (1737), a Juvenalian indictment of dishonorable intentions among particular members of both court and government. The publication landed the bookseller a week in prison, after a prosecution by the House of Lords. Twelve years later, under the guise of an ancient setting, Dodsley's own pantomime, *Rex et Pontifex*, caustically arraigned the collaborative tyranny of Church and monarch:

Kings the rights of priests defending,
More securely hold their own;
Priests to kings assistance lending,
Merit succour from the throne.
                                    (*Trifles* 154)

It is not surprising that Dodsley, as Harry S. Solomon notes, would later be publishing Hume's *Remarks upon the Natural History of Religion* (1758) and Rousseau's *Discourses upon the Origin and Foundations of the Inequality among Mankind* (1762) (Solomon, "Robert Dodsley" 42).

Although Dodsley's frustrated genius as footman, his consequent championing of the rights of the common man, and his fierce patriotism are not really the subjects of this essay, this preface will prove useful for understanding the tone of the foregoing letters, for it conveys some feeling for the passionate temper of the man and the democratic themes he dearly espoused. It will suggest the degree of anger seething beneath the bookseller's letters to other privileged "tyrants" who, after denying Dodsley justice and honor, haughtily dismissed him with a reminder of his trade origins. The cool, rational prose of the letters belies the rage beneath. The consequent surface tension affords the letters' tone an extra depth and, at the same time, reveals the fiber and brilliant control of the master of Tully's Head.

Pope and the Letter to Warburton

William Warburton (1698–1779), soon to become bishop of Gloucester, had initially been quite friendly with Dodsley. In early April 1746, he wrote to offer the bookseller a review of John Brown's *Essay on Satire* (1745) for the new Tully's Head periodical *The Museum* (Dodsley, *Correspondence* 94–95). Even as late as 1751, when distressed with the insulting attack by Dodsley's author John Gilbert Cooper, Warburton chose to distinguish the publisher from the author: "Is there a new system of morality come out for the Wits & Poet's [*sic*] of the time! You are in the midst of them, and can tell. I believe you practice the old." Significantly, the more intimate expression "faithful" accompanies the usual formulaic closing to the disgruntled clergyman's letter.[11]

Cooper had been only one of the many antagonists nipping at the theologian's heels, and a late one at that. Since the publication of his *Divine*

Legation of Moses (1738), Warburton had been plagued by a host of critics; then when his edition of Shakespeare appeared in 1747, he was assaulted on still another front.[12] Amid all this controversy, the learned lumber to which he treated his critics was delivered with a supply of arrogance and pomposity that annoyed them.[13]

Alexander Pope had probably introduced Warburton to Dodsley sometime in the early 1740s. But exactly when the bookseller's relationship with Pope himself began is not clear, although it was certainly much earlier than Warburton's did. Pope's first recorded letter to Dodsley, in early 1733, when Dodsley was still serving as a footman in Whitehall, shows a familiarity that suggests an even earlier acquaintance with the aspiring young poet, perhaps implying that Pope had had a hand in the poems Dodsley had published a year or two earlier (Dodsley, *Correspondence* 65–66). Whatever the case, there is no doubt of Pope's offer of patronage in that letter of 1733. Here he not only agrees to read the manuscript of Dodsley's play *The Toy-shop* but also volunteers to recommend the piece to John Rich for a performance at Covent Garden. Before the play's production two years later, Pope's interim support is easily detected in the publication of three more Dodsley poems at the shop of Pope's own current publisher, Lawton Gilliver.[14] Whether Pope involved himself in Dodsley's later plays of 1737 and 1738 is not apparent, but certainly his patronage did not hurt the playwright's cause, for in 1738 Dodsley became the most popular playwright of the season, having three of his plays running on London stages within a single month.[15]

With a hundred-pound contribution from Pope and the author nights' profits from *The Toy-shop*, Dodsley opened a bookseller's shop in Pall Mall in 1735. To what extent Pope's assistance in setting up the shop stemmed from benevolence or from self-interest remains a moot point. David Foxon has speculated—and evidence from William Bowyer's printing ledgers partially bears him out—that after 1728 Pope had decided to act as his own publishing agent, dealing directly with printers and thereby preserving copyrights to himself.[16] Foxon suggests (102–4) that when copyrights Pope had sold to booksellers had run their fourteen-year term and reverted to the author, the poet had planned to publish a grand edition of his works from which he would reap a greater share of the profits. But in order to do so, of course, he needed a London bookseller to advertise, distribute, and sell the books, as well as an agent to register them at the Stationers' Company. Consequently, Foxon surmises, Pope had engaged young entrants to the book trade, who, unlike his former bargain-driving publishers Tonson and Lintot, would welcome the noted poet's business without demanding a share in the copyright.

That Dodsley had served this purpose is quite likely, for Pope's subsequent publications show him decreasing Gilliver's services and rerouting his business to Tully's Head. Accordingly, over the next eight years, Dodsley would publish eight volumes of Pope's works under his own imprint and four others in conjunction with other booksellers.[17] But even if this had been Pope's primary motivation, it precludes neither the likelihood of a growing respect for the young Dodsley's talents nor the inevitable personal relationship developing from their collaboration in putting these volumes through the press. From the outset, Pope had told William Duncombe that "the Author of the *Toy-shop* . . . has just set up as a Bookseller; and I doubt not, as he has more Sense, so will have more Honesty, than most of that Profession."[18] And as Ralph Straus suggests (60), Dodsley undoubtedly became a welcome guest at Pope's villa at Twickenham, where he probably met John Earl Radnor, later a "good friend," who occasionally franked the bookseller's letters (*Correspondence* 268–69).

While Warburton was not introduced to Pope until April 1740, he had begun to align himself with the poet in December 1738, when the first of his five letters defending Pope's *Essay on Man* was printed in the journal *The Works of the Learned*. The relationship quickly flourished with Warburton's much appreciated recommendations for the publication of both later editions of the *Dunciad* (1742, 1743), and it ultimately resulted in Pope's appointing Warburton his literary executor. Entrusted with Pope's "last corrections" to his canon, Warburton proceeded to prepare his "authoritative" edition of the poet's works, complete with his own commentary. The nine-volume collection eventually appeared in 1751. As Pope's friend and as the original publisher of several of the poet's works, Dodsley would likely have asked Warburton to sell him a share in the collected works, especially since Warburton had seen his way to sell shares to Andrew Millar and Somerset Draper, London booksellers who had no dealings with Pope. And indeed, Dodsley's letter acknowledges such an offer. Yet, even though Warburton had ignored the bid, Dodsley seems not to have abandoned hope during the flow of subsequent editions in the early 1750s, as the following pompous reprimand from Warburton testifies:

Decr 26 1755

Mr Dodsley

Let us not be misunderstood. When you came to me in Town, I told you, whenever I sold my whole property in Pope I would contrive if possible you should have some share. And I remember very well, as I found you disposed to understand this as a promise to let you have some share whenever I sold any, I set you right, & repeated to you again that my meaning was when I parted with the whole. For at that time, I had determined with my selfe to employ Mr Millar & Mr Draper in my concerns. I had my reasons on account of my knowledge of them, & affairs I have had with them. They had always done every thing to my satisfaction. And I must have things done my own way. On which account I sold, what I did sell to them, much cheaper than they bought of Mr Knapton.[19]

You will ask me then how I came to say I would contrive, if possible that you should have some share when I sold the whole? It was partly on your importunity; partly out of regard I have for your Brother here;[20] & partly because Mr Pope had a regard for you: tho', as I told you, I thought you had not been very regardfull of the memory of the man to whom you was so much obliged.

But as you mention Mr Millar in a complaining way, I must tell you, you do him much injury, to think you had any right to any part of that he bought of me or, of Mr Knapton. I chose him preferably to another: I chose him because I would have to do with no other but of my own appointment; and had he, (because you had told him of your willingness to be concerned with him in purchasing some share of Pope) let you have any which he purchased, without my knowledge & consent he had broke his word with me & violated his reputation. I am not a person to be bought & sold. Mr Knapton, who is an honest & a virtuous & a gratefull man, would have suffered me to be as much Master of the sale of his part of this property as if it had been my own. And it is with men of that Character only, that I hope I shall ever be concerned. You will do Mr Millar & me a justice, (a justice I must expect of you) to communicate the contents of this to him: and that if you have said any thing contrary to these contents (which in every part is exactly true) that you would own your selfe mistaken.

I am your very humble Servt

W. Warburton[21]

If a blind and enduring toadyism to Pope's aesthetic is what Warburton expected of Dodsley when he charged the bookseller with not having "been very regardfull of the memory of the man to whom you was so much obliged," Dodsley is probably guilty as charged. But it is to the bookseller's credit that by the mid-1740s he had already recognized a new poetic spirit emerging and began to publish poets and critics who challenged the artificialities of Pope's poetry and preferred less sophisticated and less stylized subjects and forms. For instance, William Melmoth ("Sir Thomas Fitzoborne"), amid lavish praise for Pope in his *Letters on Several Subjects* (1750), claimed that Pope "sometimes sacrifices simplicity to false ornament" (3d ed., Letter no. 41, pp. 201–5). Also, Thomas Warton's postscript to his *Observations on the Faerie Queen of Spenser* (1754) defended Lewis Theobald's *Shakespeare Restored* (1726), saying it merited "the thanks of genius and candor, not the satire of prejudice and ignorance [of Pope]." The poetry of Joseph and Thomas Warton, William Collins, William Shenstone, Edward Young, and Mark Akenside—Dodsley authors through the 1740s and 1750s—reflected the new poetic spirit in form and content.

Left unstated, and perhaps more galling to Warburton than Dodsley's admitting anti-Popeian "scribblers" to his press, were the attacks upon Warburton himself, attacks the clergyman associated with Dodsley authors. Dodsley had farmed out John Gilbert Cooper's *Cursory Remarks* to Mary Cooper for publication, but obviously Warburton knew its true source. Mary Cooper, Dodsley's frequent collaborator, had also published Thomas Edwards's *A Supplement to Mr. Warburton's Edition of Shakespeare* (1747), which poked fun at the "critic's" enhancing his reputation on Pope's shirttail. And it is not unlikely that Warburton had attributed to John Gilbert Cooper a corrosive assault by John Jackson.[22]

Nonetheless, Warburton's refusal to sell Dodsley a share in Pope's works quite understandably angered the bookseller, both for personal and business reasons. As Pope's personal friend for many years—something he claims in the present letter and Warburton allows in his December 26 letter—and as the poet's final choice among his several literary midwives, Dodsley would certainly have had a share from Pope himself, that is, if shares were to be sold at all. Surely Dodsley's benefactor, who recognized his bookseller "has more Sense, so will have more Honesty, than most of that Profession," would not have wished his protégé purposely excluded from the lucrative profits of his final legacy. Dodsley realized, then, that his participation in his friend's collected edition was being blocked by a clerical despot ("And I must have things done my own way"), by a man who had even once belittled Pope's genius.[23] This awareness must have been churning within the modest and fair-minded bookseller ever since Warburton's edition had first appeared, half a decade earlier.

Much to Dodsley's credit, however, his response, while it shows some heat, is completely rational, coolly challenging every turn of the autocrat's fabricated logic. When Warburton explains that he has refused Dodsley a share in Pope because the bookseller had published some "scribblers' " attacks on Pope, Dodsley implicitly reminds him of the nature of the commercial world by expressly pointing out that Andrew Millar, one of the booksellers Warburton regards as always having "done every thing to my satisfaction," was one time "guilty" of publishing a most malicious attack on Pope. The same is true, Dodsley urges, of Warburton's other "honest" and "virtuous" bookseller, John Knapton, who had published Dr. Sykes's attack on Warburton himself. The conclusion is inevitable: "What You have thought proper to make an objection against *me*, was not thought so in regard to *them*."

The heights of Warburton's haughtiness are no more evident than when he construes the bookseller's offer to purchase a share as an importunity for a favor. Warburton, overly conscious of sitting in the catbird's seat with shares of Pope to dole out, played the role of the general's lieutenant fully. He seems to have imagined that Dodsley stood daily in his levee, begging for a share. His patronizing pose is set in ludicrous relief by Dodsley's modest response that he had "never ask'd but once" and that had been at a "reasonable price."

Indeed Dodsley was never to have a share in Warburton's edition of Pope. This exchange seems to end their correspondence. But the failed negotiation with the notoriously pompous Warburton was probably to Dodsley's benefit in the end. Even the bishop's friend Richard Hurd thought Warburton's treatment of the bookseller had been excessive. Writing to William Mason on January 8, 1756, Hurd says, "With regard to [Warburton's] letters to D[odsley], I can readily believe that they are written with a frankness which to such a man might have been spar'd" (Hurd 22–23).

Cleone and the Letter to Garrick

When Dodsley had made the transition from lyrical footman to successful businessman in 1735, he did not give up writing; in fact, his list of credits after opening the doors of Tully's Head amounts to an enviable literary achievement. One of his works, *The Oeconomy of Human Life* (1750) has been judged, except for the Bible, by far the most printed book of the eighteenth century. It passed through no fewer than two hundred printings in the century; was translated into Danish, French, German, Hebrew, Italian, Latin, Portuguese, Russian, and Spanish; and prompted many imitators and parodies (Eddy 460).

Of all the works of various genres Dodsley turned out—poems, prose essays, fables, masques, pantomimes, songs, and moral maxims—he had a particular love for plays. Following the success of his own plays on the stage in 1737–38, he proceeded to amass a large collection of old English dramas from which he culled the contents of his twelve-volume *Select Collection of Old English Plays* (1744). Apparently his own early success on the stage spurred his fantasies well into middle age, and he seemed anxious to succeed in tragedy as he had earlier in comedy.

His first attempt at tragedy came sometime in 1753, when, taking the hint of a plot from Pope, he wrote out the initial version of *Cleone*.[24] In 1755 he submitted it to David Garrick, expecting his friend to accept it for performance at Drury Lane. But Garrick rejected it. Undaunted, Dodsley revised the tragedy with the help of friends several times through the mid-1750s, only to have Garrick reject it each time. Finally, in 1757, distraught with Garrick's continuing disapproval and armed with a letter of recommendation from Lord Chesterfield (*Correspondence* 318–19, 321–22), Dodsley turned to the less fashionable theater, Covent Garden, and to John Rich, the theater manager who had staged his first play, *The Toy-shop*, twenty-two years earlier.

When Rich finally scheduled a performance of the play the following year, Dodsley's now distinguished reputation as bookseller and patron of first-rate authors paid off, winning him considerable support to offset Garrick's purposeful attempts to see that the tragedy failed. Among other notables, Lord Chesterfield attended a rehearsal, even offering Dodsley advice regarding the actors' diction. Samuel Johnson, who referred to Dodsley as "my patron, Doddy" (Dodsley had published all of Johnson's major works to this point), also attended rehearsals, as well as the first performance. Although the house was not packed on opening night (December 2, 1758), *Cleone* drew huge applause, and the crowds continued to grow over twelve consecutive performances. Through Lord Bute's intercession, even the next king, George III, and other members of the royal family attended the sixth night (*Correspondence* 382). Dodsley thrilled to report to William Shenstone that he had sold two thousand copies of the play the first day and had printed another two thousand—an extraordinary printing by the day's standard (*Correspondence* 387). In short, *Cleone* succeeded beyond Dodsley's wildest hopes.

Dodsley received the following congratulatory note, doubtless much to his surprise, from Garrick on December 3, 1758, the morning after *Cleone*'s glorious debut:

Sunday Morn^g

Dear Sir

    I most sincerely congratulate You upon Your Success last Night—I heard with much concern, that some of y^r Friends, particularly Mr Melmoth were angry with me for playing the *Busy Body* against y^r Tragedy.[25] this I think is very hard upon Me, for I am certain that Your house was far from receiving any injury from Ours—however if You will call upon Me, & let me know, how I can support y^r Interest, without absolutely giving up my own, I will do it; for whatever You or y^r Friends may think I am most sincerely

Y^r Wellwisher
& hum^{bl} Ser^t
DG.[26]

[Garrick's Endorsement:] My first letter to Dodsley.

On the surface, Garrick's note seems innocent enough—sincere in its congratulations, perhaps even a generous acknowledgment of the theater manager's earlier misjudgment of *Cleone*'s potential. The only defensive note emerges in his attempt to allay the criticism of Dodsley's friends who had charged him with running Susannah Centlivre's *Busie Body* concurrently at Drury Lane. But as Garrick indicates, he could not give up his own interest to accommodate Dodsley. Business is business, and Dodsley, as a businessman, could be expected to understand that.

This is only how it seems. A closer review of the events leading up to the production of *Cleone* and, more particularly, those immediately surrounding it throws an entirely different cast on Garrick's "congratulatory" note; in fact, it shows Garrick to have been a singularly high-handed and hypocritical "Wellwisher."

Whatever the merit of *Cleone* as tragedy, certainly Garrick had misjudged its potential appeal to contemporary audiences when he finally rejected it for a performance at Drury Lane. But what is more important for present purposes, in the course of Garrick's various readings of the tragedy, he seemed to develop a prejudice toward the play that occasionally expressed itself in peevish sentiments toward its author. As early as October 1756 he wrote in response to one of Dodsley's petitions for the play: "You had been much deceived by your Friends. I cannot but think that I have behav'd to you with ye greatest sincerity and integrity, and I must flatter myself that I can judge almost as well as Mr Dodsley can write" (Dodsley, *Correspondence* 246). Despite Dodsley's continuing efforts to accommodate Garrick's criticisms and his drawing upon the advice of friends (eight critical commentaries in 1756 and 1757 alone; *Correspondence* 228 n. 2), Garrick continued to spurn each new submission. And if we can judge by a statement Dodsley made to Robert Lowth, Garrick's responses on these occasions were conveyed "with visible marks of unkindness and disgrace."

It is not surprising, then, that Dodsley began to look upon the theater mogul as a tyrant-king. Responding to Lowth's praise for his ode to the goddess of tragedy, *Melpomene*, published in September 1757, Dodsley regrets that, although he thought he had earned some favor with the goddess, "the King of her Country [Garrick], being informed by the said Cleone of my design on his favorite Melpomene, forbad my entrance into his Dominions on the pain of Damnation, deem'd my humble suit audacious and presuming, and dismiss'd poor Cleone from his presence with visible marks of unkindness and disgrace. Piqued at this repulse, I publish'd my Ode . . . to let the Tyrant see, tho' he scorn'd my offers, that the Lady had not disdained to admit me into some of her secret Misteries" (*Correspondence* 307). Dodsley had used the same haughty image of Garrick when writing to Moses Mendes the previous month: "The Tyrant, Sir, has refus'd my Tragedy! I leave you therefore to judge with what grace I can join with you in laughing at those who rail at him" (*Correspondence* 299).

If a disagreement regarding a play's quality—inevitably giving rise to harsh words between author and theater manager—constituted the total conflict between Dodsley and Garrick, we should not be surprised; the scenario is quite common. When the play Garrick had been able to throttle in his own "Country" was preparing for performance outside his "Dominions" at John Rich's Covent Garden, however, apparently second-guessing his own judgment, the "King" launched on a spiteful enterprise. Having put his reputation on the line with the town by condemning the acclaimed bookseller's play, Garrick resorted to hostile tactics to assure *Cleone*'s failure. As Dodsley reports to Shenstone, when Garrick learned of *Cleone*'s debut, he scheduled a new production of Susannah Centlivre's *Busie Body*—with himself playing the lead, Marplot, for the first time—to open the same night as *Cleone* (*Correspondence* 387). As Straus notes (228), when it was necessary to delay the performance of *Cleone* for a few nights, Garrick also delayed the first night of *Busie Body*. Garrick's connivance in this matter is transparent.

This was not all. The night before *Cleone* opened, Garrick attempted to sabotage the tragedy's premiere while making an appearance at a popular literary hangout, the Bedford Coffee House in Covent Garden. As the actress George Anne Bellamy vexingly blurted out to Dodsley when piqued with his annoying last-minute instructions for performing the role of Cleone on opening night: "Mr. Garrick had anticipated the damnation of it [*Cleone*], publicly, the preceding evening, at the Bedford Coffee-house, where he had declared, that it could not pass muster, as it was the very *worst* piece ever exhibited" (Bellamy 3: 109). The theater manager's campaign against *Cleone*, as well as the history of his early refusals of the manuscript, are reflected in Dodsley's present letter acknowledging Garrick's Sunday morning "congratulations." There Dodsley first reminds Garrick that he had not wanted to resort to Covent Garden; he had wanted his friend to produce the play at Drury Lane. One senses as much regret as rebuke in the letter's opening comment: "[I] could have wish'd You had thought proper to have put it in my power to have thank'd you for contributing towards it [*Cleone*'s success]." In short, had Garrick relented, they would now be celebrating a mutual triumph.

Deservedly, the principal thrust of Dodsley's rejoinder aims at the petty campaign Garrick conducted against the play in the last week before its opening. Garrick's maneuvering of *Busie Body*'s performance to coincide with that of *Cleone*, his own Bedford Coffee House "performance," and whatever other tactics he employed underlie Dodsley's charge of foul play: "the injury you have done me." Specifically, the author complains: "You have taken effectual care to nip its *Reputation* in the bud, by preventing ye Town, as far as lay in your power, from attending to it. . . . as to mine [reputation], you have certainly in this instance done all you could to lessen it."

Surpassing even the contemptibly dishonest congratulations, however, is Garrick's arrogant, patronizing air in the note. That Dodsley, aware of all Garrick's recent plotting, should be expected to swallow these preposterously false compliments, together with the denial of the manager's attempt to scuttle *Cleone*'s opening, is insulting enough; but that Garrick should assume the pose of a patron, inviting Dodsley to call on him to beg assistance for his play, is astonishing gall. The condescending suggestion was obviously calculated to enrage the playwright at the moment of his success and, at the same time, to call attention to the discrepancy between a success at Covent Garden and one at Drury Lane.

Once again, Dodsley shows himself the master of the situation, and his response to another aggrandizing tyrant is a model of control, reason, and wit: "As to my proposing any means in which you can now be of service to me, I hope you do not think that, after what has past, I can possibly bring my self to ask a favour of you. In short, if your behavior to me has been right, I see no cause you have to be concern'd about it; if wrong, why was it so?" Then Dodsley, cleverly and coolly, suggests the proper orientation for Garrick's feigned assistance, even hinting at a moral and professional responsibility: "I therefore leave it on your self to pursue what measure you may think most consistent with your own reputation." Even the letter's conclusion avoids the harshness and finality one might expect from such justified anger. As his letter began with a "regret" that the two friends failed to enjoy a mutual victory, so it concludes with a regret that Dodsley cannot "at present" subscribe himself with the usual cordiality. But ingeniously, Dodsley simultaneously heightens the regret and emphasizes Garrick's faithlessness by a visual trick. The regret is confined to the body of the text while the signature "Your friend and Servant" stands out in relief.

That *Cleone* had succeeded at all was a bitter enough pill for Garrick to swallow. But that Dodsley should manage such a clever response to his pretended congratulatory note amounted to a second victory, and Garrick knew it. He quickly fired off a sniveling, petulant retort, basely reminding the playwright of his humble trade origins by addressing him as "Master" and by expressing pleasure in being dismissed from such acquaintance. In short, he huffed off to the haughty heights of his Drury Lane castle.

[Wednesday, December 6, 1758]

Master Robert Dodsley.

When I first read Your peevish Answer to my well meant proposal to You, I was much disturb'd at it—but when I consider'd, that some minds cannot bear the smallest portion of Success, I most Sincerely pity'd You; and when I found in ye same letter, that You were graciously pleas'd to dismiss Me from y^r Acquaintance; I could not but confess so apparent an Obligation, & am wth due Acknowledgm^{ts}

Master Robert Dodsley
y^r most oblig'd
D.G [27]

[Garrick's Endorsement:] My Answer to Master Robt Dodsley.

Garrick was not yet finished. Piqued by the disagreeable exchange, he proceeded with another attack on *Cleone* that he had begun on its opening night. As Dodsley reports in a letter to Shenstone, Garrick had engaged the notorious Dr. John Hill to write a damning review of *Cleone*'s Saturday opening, which he proceeded to publish on the following Tuesday, "such was the industry exerted in prejudicing the Town against it," Dodsley says. "But he [Hill] did not miss his reward; Mr. Garrick brought on for him, some days afterward, the Farce call'd the Rout, which was damn'd the second Night" (*Correspondence* 392). In effect, despite Garrick's earlier claim that his judgment of *Cleone* had been "sincere & unprejudic'd" (*Correspondence* 291), his pride led him to wage a grubby crusade against the tragedy's success when it was finally submitted to the public for approval.

The Accomplishments in These Two Responses

These two Dodsley letters—to Warburton and to Garrick—have value for both the historian and the critic. Given Dodsley's humble origins and education, they show what native intelligence and industry were able to accomplish in a changing society, one in which vertical mobility was a real possibility, at least within the mercantile world. Dodsley's rise from mere footman to London's premiere publisher of *belles lettres* within a quarter of a century—one who rubbed shoulders with and counted among his friends the most significant men of the age—presages the democratic dream. Moreover, the letters reflect the social philosophy and code of life of a new breed of eighteenth-century man, one who not only valued innate worth above the prerogatives of social privilege but also passionately pursued that vision in his writings and publications. Supporting and regulating this enthusiasm, in Dodsley's case, were an honesty and a modesty that dealt respectfully but forthrightly with the deceitful and despotic, giving the present exchanges so much dignity and conviction.

As prose, the letters are exemplary demonstrations of epistolary finesse, exhibiting an unusually disciplined control of underlying anger and impatience. This mastery is abetted by a penetration, logic, and concision that creates a deceptive, rational surface calm, actually distracting readers from immediately sensing the degree of indignation below. The letters' energies and consequent surface tensions are felt only upon a disclosure of the circumstances motivating the letters' composition.

This is what we might expect of the man who opened his bookseller's shop under the sign of Marcus Tullius Cicero. Among the classics that dominate Dodsley's publication credits, Cicero was a favorite. During his lengthy career at Tully's Head, his most elaborate and expensive production was William Melmoth's edition of *The Letters of Cicero . . . to Several of his Friends* (1753). Dodsley's penchant for the epistolary was reflected even earlier in his very successful *The Preceptor: Containing a General Course of Education* (1748). Samuel Johnson's preface to *The Preceptor* urged that "this great Art [letter-writing] should be diligently taught." Mirroring the sentiment, Dodsley includes in *The Preceptor* a section entitled "On Writing Letters" that recommends a plan for letters "which rises like a well-contrived Building, beautiful, uniform, and regular" (107). The quality of the bookseller's letters to Warburton and Garrick did not come by chance.

NOTES

1. The Warburton letter printed later in this essay is that of "Tuesday." Since the date on Warburton's letter, Dec. 26, 1755, means that it was written on a Friday, Dodsley must be referring to the days on which he received the letters. Regrettably, the first letter, of "Monday," is missing.

2. This charge is alluded to in Warburton's letter printed below. For one of the "scribblers," see n. 12.

3. Dodsley here refers to Cooper, *Life of Socrates*. For the reader unfamiliar with the eighteenth-century book trade, it would be useful to know that the term *bookseller* in the period is roughly equivalent to the modern use of the term *publisher;* namely, a bookseller solicited manuscripts, contracted with authors, saw to the printing, advertising, binding, and distribution of such books, and, in his shop, sold almost exclusively the volumes he produced.

4. This letter is missing, and its content is unknown.

5. In 1749 Andrew Millar had published an edition of Bolingbroke's *Patriot King*, with an "Advertisement" by David Mallet, charging Pope with a breach of trust when the latter secretly printed 1,500 copies of the manuscript, which the author had given him merely for private circulation among mutual friends.

6. In 1744 John and Paul Knapton had published Arthur Ashley Sykes's attack on Warburton, *An Examination of Mr. Warburton's Account of the Conduct of the Ancient Legislators*.

7. Dodsley's letter is missing.

8. See the conclusion of Warburton's letter below.

9. Dodsley's issuing of Pope's works departed from normal publication procedures. First, as Pope's letters to the printer William Bowyer and Bowyer's own

ledgers testify, Pope had dealt directly with the printer, thereby circumventing the bookseller's traditional role of securing the printing and supplying proofs to the author, functions the bookseller provided even when he had not purchased a copyright but was merely acting as the author's agent. See Reginald Harvey Griffith, *Alexander Pope: A Bibliography. Pope's Own Writings* (London: Holland Press, 1962), 549, 556, 558; Keith Maslen, "Printing for the Author: From the Bowyer Printing Ledgers, 1710–1775," *Library*, 5th ser., 27 (1972): 305–6. In effect, despite the fact that the imprints for three of the Pope works published by Dodsley read "London: Printed for R. Dodsley, and sold by T. Cooper" and that the Stationers' registrations are entered as "Whole rights" in Dodsley's name, Pope—listed in Bowyer's ledgers as "customer"—apparently saw to everything except the volumes' advertising and sale. That Dodsley had indeed not managed to purchase any of Pope's copyrights (unless Pope had granted him some temporary right, which, as Foxon notes on 140, he had done in the case of Gilliver) is clear from this letter. Otherwise Warburton could not have deprived Dodsley of a share in the publication of his edition of the complete *Works*: Dodsley would have already owned a share.

10. When Thomas Gataker offered to mediate the falling out between Dodsley and Garrick that followed upon the theater manager's final rejection of *Cleone* in Sept. 1757, Dodsley wrote to Gataker on Nov. 4 that, if Garrick would give the tragedy a performance at Drury Lane, Dodsley would donate the author profits of the third night to the Society for the Encouragement of Arts, Manufactures, and Commerce (later the Royal Society of Arts); the profits of a sixth night to the Foundling Hospital; and those of the ninth night to a charity of Garrick's designation. In a letter to Garrick himself the same month, Dodsley offered to donate all profits to the forementioned society (*Correspondence* 306–7, 312–14).

11. Dodsley, *Correspondence* 141–42. In his *Life of Socrates* (1749), Cooper had charged that Warburton had been led astray by Aelian, a "Scrap-retailing Historian," and had promised more of the "renowned Mr. Warburton, whose great Sagacity I shall consider in the following notes" (54n).

12. In *Treatise on the Improvements Made in the Art of Criticism, Collected out of the Writings of a celebrated Hypercritic* (1748), John Jackson spoofed Warburton's attempt to show his learning in *Divine Legation*, saying the clergyman is not "literally an *Ass*, but only puts on the *Appearance* of one" (2–3). In his satire *Canons of Criticism . . . Being a Supplement to Mr. Warburton's Edition of Shakespeare* (1748), Thomas Edwards ridiculed the arrogant critical style of Warburton through twenty-five "canons": "He may alter any Passage of his Author, without reason and against the Copies; and then quote the passage so altered, as an authority for altering any other" (25). When Warburton's *Letter to the Viscount B———. Occasion'd by his Treatment of a Deceased Friend* (1749) tried to excuse Pope's earlier publication of Bolingbroke's *Patriot King*—a work the author had shared with Pope for only pri-

vate circulation—Bolingbroke's response was *A Familiar Epistle to the most Impudent Man Living* (1749).

13. Even Dr. William Stukely, Warburton's oldest friend, later regretted that success had made Warburton "fickle in friendships; haughty in his carriage: excessively greedy of flattery . . . [and that now] he looks down upon the whole world." Bodleian MS Eng Misc. e. 260, ff. 108–11, quoted in Peter Seary, *Lewis Theobald and the Editing of Shakespeare* (Oxford: Clarendon, 1990), 103–4. Edward Gibbon's judgment of Warburton was similar: "The real merit of Warburton was degraded by the pride and presumption with which he pronounced his infallible decrees . . . he lashed his antagonists without mercy or moderation"; *Memoirs of the Life of Edward Gibbon*, ed. G. B. Hill (London: Methuen, 1900), 178.

14. *The Modern Reasoners* (1734), *An Epistle to Mr. Pope, Occasion'd by his Essay on Man* (1734), *Beauty, or the Art of Charming* (1735).

15. *Sir John Cockle at Court* (Feb. 23) and *The King and the Miller of Mansfield* (Mar. 18 and 25), both at Drury Lane; and *The Toy-shop* (Mar. 20) at Covent Garden.

16. See n. 9.

17. *Works* (1735), with Knapton, Gilliver, and Brindley; *Second Epistle of the Second Book of Horace Imitated* (1737); *Letters* (1737), with Knapton, Gilliver, and Brindley; *The First Epistle of the First Book of Horace Imitated* (1737); *The Universal Prayer* (1738); *One Thousand Seven Hundred and Thirty Eight* (1738); *Poems* (1739), with Knapton, Gilliver, and Brindley; *Works*, vol. 2 (1739); *Works*, vol. 2, pt. 2 (1739); *Works . . . in Prose*, vol. 2(1739), with Knapton and Bathurst; *Works*, vol. 3, pt. 2(1742); *Verses on the Grotto at Twickenham* (1743).

18. May 6, 1735. *Correspondence of Alexander Pope*, ed. George Sherburn (Oxford: Clarendon, 1956), 3: 454.

19. The name of John Knapton, London bookseller, is often found in imprints together with his brother Paul's.

20. Dodsley's brother Isaac had been employed since 1741 as gardener to Ralph Allen of Bath. Warburton, having married Allen's niece, had apparently struck up some friendship with Isaac during his visits to Prior Park.

21. MS, Edinburgh University Library La. II. 153; Dodsley, *Correspondence* 212–14.

22. See nn. 11, 12; Dodsley, *Correspondence* 140–41.

23. In a letter to Matthew Cocanen, on Jan. 2, 1727, Warburton had accused Pope of borrowing "for want of genius"; John Nichols, *Illustrations of the Literary History of the Eighteenth Century* (London, 1817), 2: 195–98. Two years later, Warburton had attacked Pope's edition of Shakespeare in anonymous letters to the *Daily Journal* on Mar. 22 and Apr. 8 and 22, 1729. Still later, he had collaborated in the production of Lewis Theobald's edition of Shakespeare (1733), which regularly derided Pope's emendations.

24. In his preface to the printed edition of *Cleone*, Dodsley indicates that Pope encouraged him to expand an original three-act text into five acts, after admitting that Pope had burned his own attempt at a play on the subject.

25. William Melmoth, Dodsley's friend and author, had written the prologue to *Cleone*.

26. Victoria and Albert Museum MS F. 48 F. 7, ff. 1–2; Dodsley, *Correspondence* 381–82.

27. Victoria and Albert Museum MS F. 48 F. 7, ff. 5–6; Dodsley, *Correspondence* 384.

WORKS CITED

Bellamy, George Anne. *An Apology for the Life of George Anne Bellamy. Written by Herself*. 4 vols. London, 1785.

Cooper, John Gilbert. *Life of Socrates*. London, 1749.

Dodsley, Robert. *The Correspondence of Robert Dodsley, 1733–1764*. Ed. James E. Tierney. Cambridge: Cambridge UP, 1988.

———. *Miseries of Poverty*. London, 1731.

———. *The Preceptor: Containing a General Course of Education*. London, 1748.

———. *Rex et Pontifex*. London, 1745.

———. *Trifles*. London, 1745.

Eddy, Donald D. "Dodsley's *Oeconomy of Human Life*, 1750–1751." *Modern Philology* 85(1988): 460–79.

Foxon, David. *Pope and the Early Eighteenth-Century Book-Trade*. Rev. and ed. James McLaverty. Oxford: Clarendon, 1991.

Hurd, Richard. *The Correspondence of Richard Hurd and William Mason*. Ed. Leonard Whibley. Cambridge: Cambridge UP, 1932.

Pope, Alexander. *The Works of Alexander Pope, Esq. In Nine Volumes Complete. With his last Corrections, Additions and Improvements; as they were delivered to the Editor a little before his Death: together with the Commentaries and Notes of Mr. Warburton*. London: Printed for J. & P. Knapton, J. & R. Tonson and S. Draper, and C. Bathurst, 1751.

Solomon, Harry M., ed. *The King and the Miller of Mansfield*. Augustan Reprint Series 219. Los Angeles: William Andrews Clark Memorial Library, 1983.

———. "Robert Dodsley." *Dictionary of Literary Biography: Eighteenth-Century British Poets*. Ed. John Sitter. 1st ser. Vol. 95. Detroit: Bruccoli Clark Layman and Gale Research, 1990, 35–46.

———, ed. *The Toy-shop*. Augustan Reprint Series 218. Los Angeles: William Andrews Clark Memorial Library, 1983.

Straus, Ralph. *Robert Dodsley: Poet, Publisher & Playwright*. London: John Lane, 1910.

Edifying the Young Dog: Johnson's Letters to Boswell

Lance E. Wilcox

Samuel Johnson to James Boswell, December 8, 1763

DEAR SIR:

You are not to think yourself forgotten or criminally neglected that you have had yet no letter from me—I love to see my friends to hear from them to talk to them and to talk of them, but it is not without a considerable effort of resolution that I prevail upon myself to write. I would not however gratify my own indolence by the omission of any important duty or any office of real kindness.

To tell you that I am or am not well, that I have or have not been in the country, that I drank your health in the Room in which we sat last together and that your acquaintance continue to speak of you with their former kindness topicks with which those letters are commonly filled which are written only for the sake of writing I seldom shall think worth communication but if I can have it in my power to calm any harrassing disquiet to excite

Johnson to Boswell, Dec. 8, 1763, from Johnson, *Letters*, ed. Redford, 1: 237–40. In his 1952 edition of the *Letters*, R. W. Chapman used the text of this letter published in Boswell's *Life*; Redford, however, prints from the copy text used for the *Life* in Margaret Boswell's handwriting. Though there are no differences in wording between the two, the text printed by Chapman contains scores of commas not in Redford's text and manifests other changes in punctuation and spelling.

Johnson to Boswell, Sept. 7, 1782, from the manuscript of vol. 4 of Redford's edition, to be published in 1993. I would like to thank Professor Redford for his help and generosity in making the text of this letter available to me.

any virtuous desire to rectify any important opinion or fortify any generous resolution you need not doubt but I shall at least wish to prefer the pleasure of gratifying a friend much less esteemed than yourself before the gloomy calm of idle Vacancy. Whether I shall easily arrive at an exact punctuality of correspondance I cannot tell. I shall at present expect that you will receive this in return for two which I have had from you. The first indeed gave me an account so hopeless of the state of your mind that it hardly admitted or deserved an answer; by the second I was much better pleased and the pleasure will still be increased by such a narrative of the progress of your studys as may evince the continuence of an equal and rational application of your mind to some usefull enquiry.

You will perhaps wish to ask what Study I would recommend. I shall not speak of Theology because it ought not to be considered as a question whether you shall endeavour to know the will of God.

I shall therefore consider only such Studies as we are at liberty to pursue or to neglect, and of these I know not how you will make a better choice than by studying the civil Law as your father advises and the Ancient languages as you had determined for yourself; at least resolve while you remain in any setled residence to spend a certain number of hours every day amongst your Books. The dissipation of thought of which you complain is nothing more than the Vacillation of a mind suspended between different motives and changing its direction as any motive gains or loses Strength. If you can but kindle in your mind any strong desire, if you can but keep predominant any Wish for some particular excellence or attainment the Gusts of imagination will break away without any effect upon your conduct and commonly without any traces left upon the Memory.

There lurks perhaps in every human heart a desire of distinction which inclines every Man first to hope and then to believe that Nature has given him something peculiar to himself. This vanity makes one mind nurse aversions and another actuate desires till they rise by art much above their original state of power and as affectation in time improves to habit, they at last tyrannise over him who at first encouraged them only for Show. Every desire is a Viper in the Bosom who while he was chill was harmless but when warmth gave him strength exerted it in poison. You know a gentleman who when first he set his foot in the gay World as he prepared himself to whirl in the Vortex of pleasure imagined a total indifference and universal negligence to be the most agreable concomitants of Youth and the strongest indication of an airy temper and a quick apprehension. Vacant to every object and sensible of every impulse he thought that all appearance of diligence would deduct something from the reputation of Genius and hoped that he should appear to attain amidst all the ease of carelessness and all the tumult of diversion that knowledge and those accomplishments which Mortals of the common fabrick obtain only by mute abstraction and solitary drudgery. He tried this scheme of life awhile was made weary of it by his sence and his Virtue; he then wished to return to his Studies and finding long habits of idleness and pleasure harder to be cured than he expected still willing to retain his claim to some extraordinary prerogitives resolved the common consequences of irregularity into an unalterable decree of destiny and concluded that Nature had originally formed him incapable of rational employment.

Let all such fancys illusive and destructive be banished henceforward from your thoughts forever. Resolve and keep your resolution. Chuse and pursue your choice. If you spend this day in Study you will find yourself still more able to study tomorrow. Not that you are to expect that you shall at once obtain a compleat Victory. Depravity is not very easily overcome. Resolution will sometimes relax and diligence will sometimes be interrupted. But let no accidental surprize or deviation whether short or long dispose you to despondency. Consider these failings as incident to all Mankind, begin again where you left off and endeavour to avoid the Seducements that prevailed over you before.

This my Dear Boswell is advice which perhaps has been often given you, and given you without effect, but this advice if you will not take from others you must take from your own reflections, if you purpose to do the dutys of the station to which the Bounty of providence has called you.

Let me have a long letter from you as soon as you can. I hope you continue your journal and enrich it with many observations upon the country in which you reside. It will be a favour if you can get me any books in the Frisick Language and can enquire how the poor are maintained in the Seven Provinces. I am, Dear Sir, your most affectionate servant,

London, Dec. 8, 1763   Sam. Johnson

Samuel Johnson to James Boswell, September 7, 1782

DEAR SIR,

I have struggled through this year with so much infirmity of body, and such strong impressions of the fragility of life, that death, wherever it appears, fills me with melancholy; and I cannot hear without emotion, of the removal of any one, whom I have known, into another state.

Your father's death had every circumstance that could enable you to bear it; it was at a mature age, and it was expected; and as his general life had been pious, his thoughts had doubtless for many years past been turned upon eternity. That you did not find him sensible must doubtless grieve you; his disposition towards you was undoubtedly that of a kind, though not of a fond father. Kindness, at least actual, is in our power, but fondness is not; and if by negligence or imprudence you had extinguished his fondness, he could not at will rekindle it. Nothing then remained between you but mutual forgiveness of each other's faults, and mutual desire of each other's happiness.

I shall long to know his final disposition of his fortune.

You, dear Sir, have now a new station, and have therefore new cares, and new employments. Life, as Cowley seems to say, ought to resemble a well ordered poem; of which one rule generally received is, that the exordium should be simple, and should promise little. Begin your new course of life with the least show, and the least expence possible; you may at pleasure encrease both, but you cannot easily diminish them. Do not think your estate your own, while any man can call upon you for money which you cannot pay; therefore, begin with timorous parsimony. Let it be your first care not to be in any man's debt.

When the thoughts are extended to a future state, the present life seems hardly worthy of all those principles of conduct, and maxims of prudence, which one generation of men has transmitted to another; but upon a closer view, when it is perceived how much evil is produced, and how much good is impeded by embarrassment and distress, and how little room the expedients of poverty leave for the exercise of virtue; its sorrows manifest that the boundless importance of the next life, enforces some attention to the interests of this.[1]

Be kind to the old servants, and secure the kindness of the agents and factors; do not disgust them by asperity, or unwelcome gaiety, or apparent suspicion. From them you must learn the real state of your affairs, the characters of your tenants, and the value of your lands.

Make my compliments to Mrs. Boswell; I think her expectations from air and exercise are the best that she can form. I hope she will live long and happily.

I forget whether I told you that Rasay has been here; we dined cheerfully together. I entertained lately a young gentleman from Coriatachat.[2]

I received your letters only this morning. I am, dear Sir, yours, etc.

Sam. Johnson.

London, Sept. 7, 1782.

Wise Counsel for Young Adults

For over twenty years Samuel Johnson wrote letters to James Boswell in which he strove to foster and direct the moral development of his future biographer. His letters represent a remarkable, sustained effort of ethical pedagogy, during the course of which the two men moved from their original roles of teacher and disciple to the attainment of mature, adult friendship. In studying correspondences, we usually find that the personae assumed by writers within an exchange of letters develop first in face-to-face communications and are then carried over into the correspondence itself. In the case of Johnson and Boswell, however, we find their respective epistolary roles already in a sense foreshadowed by Johnson's public writings before the tumultuous meeting of the two men in May 1763.

Though unknown to Johnson, Boswell felt that the author of the *Rambler* had, in a way, been writing to him for years. By the time he met Johnson, Boswell writes, "I had for several years read his works with delight and instruction, and had the highest reverence for their authour, which had grown up in my fancy into a kind of mysterious veneration, by figuring to myself a state of solemn elevated abstraction, in which I supposed him to live in the immense metropolis of London" (1: 444–45). Boswell's absorption in these works stems in part from finding himself and his concerns vividly and specifically addressed by them. If we were to define the ideal implied reader of Johnson's works, we would create, in fact, a figure very like young James Boswell of Scotland. The reader most likely to benefit from "London," "The Vanity of Human Wishes," the *Rambler* essays, and *Rasselas* is a young adult just entering into life. As a moralist, Johnson seeks to intervene at the critical point of separation from parental protection. "It is into the hands of every young gentleman, and every young lady, too, that Johnson hopes *Rasselas* will fall. It is his version of a book of Advice to his Son, the son he never had" (Fussell 226). The same could be said of the moral essays and the verse satires.

When Johnson met his young readers in the flesh, he often adopted them as protégés, bestowing on them the encouragement and intellectual stimulation he himself had received years earlier from Gilbert Walmsley and Cornelius Ford.[3] Two years after meeting Boswell, Johnson told him, "I love the young dogs of this age," at once naming and acclaiming the breed. Well before meeting Boswell, thus, the Young Dog was already part of Johnson's personal gallery of character types, one of the standard figures in his social world. He had already drawn Bennet Langton, Topham Beauclerc, and George Strahan into Sage Counselor–Young Dog relationships and would add more to the list. In the relationship between Imlac and Rasselas, Johnson gave fictional representation to these roles, and he established them again between the persona and the implied reader of his essays. In reading Johnson's works, Boswell identified with the young adults so wisely counseled, and inevitably, upon reaching London, he sought out the author. The two men fell into their own mentor-protégé relationship shortly after their first meeting: "Finding [Johnson] in a placid humour, and wishing to avail myself of the opportunity which I fortunately had of consulting a sage . . . I opened my mind to him ingenuously, and gave him a little sketch of my life, to which he was pleased to listen with great attention. . . . Being at all times a curious examiner of the human mind, and pleased with an undisguised display of what had passed in it, he called to me with warmth, 'Give me your hand; I have taken a liking to you'" (Boswell 1: 468).

For the rest of the summer, until Boswell's departure for Utrecht on August 6, 1763, he listened to Johnson's conversation and sought his advice on personal matters. Part of the early success of Johnson and Boswell's friendship stems from the neatness with which each filled an already existing role in the other's usual cast of characters. In his life and writings Johnson played the Sage Counselor and readily adopted his Young Dogs.[4] Boswell, meanwhile, played the young wastrel searching for a wise and stable guide. The two met, assumed their roles in each other's "scripts," and for the next several years played these parts not only in face-to-face encounters but in their letters as well.

The First Letter

Johnson's very first letter to Boswell is one of the longest and finest he was ever to write to him. It is dated December 8, 1763, and was sent to Boswell in Utrecht. Boswell had elicited the letter with two of his own. These were, by his own account, letters such as a homesick child might write from camp. "I wrote to Johnson a plaintive and desponding letter, to which he paid no regard. Afterwards, when I had acquired a firmer tone of mind, I wrote him a second letter, expressing much anxiety to hear from him" (1: 547).

Johnson's letter begins, as so many of his do, with a caveat not to take his tardiness as a correspondent as a mark of disfavor. He admits to being a slow and reluctant letter writer, though at the same time he notes one reliable, if curious, motivation to correspond: "I would not . . . gratify my own indolence by the omission of any important duty or any office of real kindness." Though Johnson gets little pleasure from writing, he accepts the responsibility to do so on ethical grounds. He develops these grounds in the second paragraph, in which he establishes the epistolary relationship he expects with Boswell. He rules out immediately the prospect of his writing purely social, conversational letters, "letters . . . which are written only for the sake of writing." Instead, he proposes a correspondence dedicated entirely to Boswell's personal improvement. He will write whenever he is able "to calm any harrassing disquiet to excite any virtuous desire to rectify any important opinion or fortify any generous resolution." These sound more like goals for the *Rambler*s than for private letters, and the results are predictable. Redford writes that "Johnson's letters usually resemble a moral essay that has been cursorily adjusted to the identity of the recipient" (207–8). Though this does not fairly characterize Johnson's letters as a whole, it certainly captures the flavor of his correspondence with Boswell.[5] The role Johnson proposes to play in these letters is largely pedagogical. This is not to be a correspondence between friends or even equals. Johnson shows little intention here of revealing anything about himself, his life, or his activities and interests. And since the implied readers of Johnson's writings had always been, in a sense, the young Boswells of the world, Johnson's letters to him are even more "cursorily adjusted to the identity of the recipient" than usual.[6] If *Rasselas* is, as Fussell suggests, Johnson's book of advice to his son, then his first letter to Boswell proposes a correspondence not unlike that of Chesterfield's to Philip Stanhope.

Implied in this pedagogical stance is the right to judge Boswell's performances as reported or reflected in his letters. Johnson reads Boswell's letters as something like the confessions of a young parishioner or as term papers from a student in the school of life and responds with praise or blame accordingly. Of the two letters he received from Boswell, Johnson writes: "The first indeed gave me an account so hopeless of the state of your mind that it hardly admitted or deserved an answer; by the second I was much better pleased." Johnson then proceeds to coach Boswell on his third assignment: "[My] pleasure will still be increased by such a narrative of the progress of your studys as may evince the continuence of an equal and rational application of your mind to some usefull enquiry." The asymmetry in the relationship between the two men becomes dramatically clear if we try to imagine Boswell writing to Johnson in such terms.

Still in schoolmaster dress, Johnson goes on to respond to an earlier request of Boswell's for a curriculum of study to follow while on the Continent. Johnson recommends a characteristic mix of theology, civil law, and ancient languages.[7] But as the rest of the paragraph makes clear, the selection of subjects itself does not really get to the root of Boswell's problem as Johnson understands it.

In his long fifth paragraph, Johnson finally arrives at the heart of what he has to say to his young friend. The paragraph begins with the even, sweeping cadences, precise abstractions, and live verbs of the best *Rambler*s: "There lurks perhaps in every human heart a desire of distinction which inclines every Man first to hope and then to believe that Nature has given him something peculiar to himself." The combination of these cadences with these beliefs is as distinctive as a signature. Boswell would certainly recognize—with how much pride and delight we can imagine—the voice of the author he had so long admired. He would also realize, however, that these comments were hardly Johnson's way of making conversation; their application to his own case is clearly imminent. Master in his letters of a wide range of prose styles, Johnson here robes himself in the grave, judicious rhetoric of his *Rambler* essays, effectively putting the young Boswell on notice that what follows is serious moral exhortation. He is, as it were, clearing his throat and deepening his voice. He presents the portrait of a vain, capricious young man launching into all the vacuous tumult of Vanity Fair, while still hoping, through some magical process or other, to gain knowledge. The strategic third person—"You know a gentleman who"—rather than accusing Boswell directly, compels him to apply the description to his own case and to pronounce his own guilt. The phrase "mute abstraction and solitary drudgery," furthermore, reflects Johnson's sense of his own work as a scholar ("a writer of dictionaries; a harmless drudge") and registers his solidarity with the "Mortals of the common fabrick" whom he sees Boswell as trying to impress if not show up.

If this were the whole story, Boswell's case might well appear hopeless, but fortunately it is not. Johnson reminds Boswell that he already at some level knows better than to continue in this manner: "He tried this scheme of life awhile was made weary of it by his sence and his Virtue; he then wished to return to his Studies and finding long habits of idleness and pleasure harder to be cured than he expected still willing to retain his claim to some extraordinary prerogitives resolved the common consequences of irregularity into an unalterable decree of destiny and concluded that Nature had originally formed him incapable of rational employment." We hear in the last line what must be the echo of Boswell's two earlier letters to Johnson. He is depressed, at loose ends, dissipated, and, finding himself unable to crack his books, bemoans his destiny as a genius manqué. And here is the main point of contact—and conflict—between Boswell's letters and Johnson's. Boswell paints himself as a tragic, romantic figure: a blighted genius, incapable of productive, sustained intellectual effort. Johnson redraws this supine, pastel portrait in the hard-edged pen and ink of ethical judgment. Boswell is not accursed; he is just lazy. Worse yet, he is vain. These are not the tragic strokes of fate; they are bad habits, and he had better change them. As Alkon notes, Johnson consistently opposes any notion of psychological determinism: "By acquiescing to any such scheme of 'moral predestination,' an individual can find a ready excuse for giving up all pretense of self-control and, instead of trying to guide his own conduct, can merely allow himself to be swayed by desires welling up capriciously within his mind or excited from without" (25). This is precisely what Johnson accuses Boswell of doing. Boswell has come to believe himself formed by "Nature . . . incapable of rational employment." He has therefore abandoned any attempt to order his existence and has allowed himself to remain anarchically "sensible of every impulse."

Johnson's purpose, however, is not so much to induce guilt in Boswell
as to offer him hope. It is precisely because Boswell's problems are of his
own making that he can fix them. Boswell bids for a romantic loftiness
of mind at the price of tragic impotence. Johnson offers him humiliation,
embarrassment, repentance—and a happy, productive life. Boswell wishes
to "retain his claim to some extraordinary prerogitives" even if it means
despair. Johnson bids him accept his place among "Mortals of the common
fabrick," confess the "common consequences of irregularity," and pursue
his studies one book, one page, at a time. If Boswell does this, Johnson tells
him, "the Gusts of imagination will break away without any effect upon
your conduct and commonly without any traces left upon the Memory."

In the broadest philosophical terms, the shift Johnson seeks here and
throughout his letters to provoke in Boswell's life is that from the aesthetic to the ethical sphere of existence, very much as these were depicted
in the next century in Søren Kierkegaard's *Either/Or*. The entire correspondence, beginning with this first letter, can be read as a long-standing
dispute between the two friends concerning the sort of man James Boswell
will become. As indirectly reflected even in this letter, Boswell continually
seeks to present himself as a dashing, romantic figure, as Corsican Boswell,
ladies' man, cavalier, defender of the Stuarts, member of the literati, genius
laboring under the dark star of his untoward fate—every inch the aesthete
of Kierkegaard's imagining. Johnson, meanwhile, labors to construct a
characterization of Boswell that is grounded on more solid, ethical deter-
minants, in hopes that Boswell will recognize its superiority and adopt it as
his own.[8]

A central conflict between the aesthetic and ethical spheres is what one
does with, or makes of, time. For the aesthete, for the Byronic (or Bos-
wellian) romantic, time is the brilliant moment, the evanescent flash of
intense experience. For Johnson, as representative par excellence of the
ethical sphere, time is both the moment of decision and the medium in
which one constructs one's life. The aim of the ethicist is to acquire some
consistency, some stability of action and effort from one day to the next,
and thus to move forward, or, as the English idiom so aptly expresses it, to
make something of oneself. Kierkegaard writes: "What [the ethicist] works
for is continuity" (230). Put another way: "The person who lives ethically
has a memory of his life . . . the person who lives esthetically does not have
it at all" (230).

Johnson urges, as does Kierkegaard, a decisive, energetic choice, followed by continuity of direction and effort. If Boswell "can but kindle in [his] mind any strong desire, if [he] can but keep predominant any Wish for some particular excellence or attainment," he will be saved. Having presented his Hogarthian portrait of Boswell, Johnson bluntly exhorts him: "Resolve and keep your resolution. Chuse and pursue your choice." Johnson wants Boswell to see himself as master of his fate, as agent rather than patient, and to direct his life consciously and steadily toward a specific goal. This is why Johnson asks to see in Boswell's next letter evidence of "the continuence of an equal and rational application of your mind to some usefull enquiry." *Rational* and *usefull* are, of course, key terms of approbation for Johnson in any case, but at least as significant here is his stress on "continuence of . . . application." Such continuance implies the steady, deliberate, internally directed assumption and daily resumption of some enduring project. Though Johnson suggests theology, law, and ancient languages for Boswell's curriculum, the choices themselves are less important than the steadiness with which Boswell pursues them. "At least resolve while you remain in any setled residence to spend a certain number of hours every day amongst your Books."

Johnson construes Boswell's predicament not as victimization by fate but as a struggle for self-control, a struggle involving ups and downs certainly, but promising triumph if Boswell will only will success with sufficient energy and persistence. The terms of this exhortation reflect its ethical grounding: on the one side, *resolution, diligence,* and *victory;* on the other, *depravity, deviation, seducements, failings,* and *despondency.* All of these implicitly refer to a struggle of the will, a battle for self-control, either carried to virtuous success or lapsing in culpable defeat.

Johnson paints a sufficiently heroic picture of ethical struggle but in a fashion that denies Boswell any "extraordinary prerogitives." The heroism of the ethical life results in no aristocracy, no special glamor; its struggles are "incident to all Mankind." If Boswell is to succeed in his studies, he will have to accept the "mute abstraction and solitary drudgery" with which "Mortals of the common fabrick" advance in knowledge. To win control of his life, he will have to relinquish his romantic claims to "something peculiar to himself" and understand himself more in his continuities with humanity than in his precious eccentricities. In short, he will have to curb his vanity.[9]

A person living in the ethical sphere, finally, construes the world not primarily in terms of experiences but in terms of duties and responsibilities. "The person who lives ethically sees tasks everywhere" (Kierkegaard 251). The duties of the ethical life are always already given in one's actual life circumstances. Simply by entering the ethical sphere, one receives one's life more profoundly by receiving it as a field for ethical action. "The individual sees this, his actual concretion, as task, as goal, as objective" (251). His situation reveals itself to him as more than a collection of historical accidents; it reveals itself as Providence, as eternally valid duty and blessing.

Before Boswell's departure for Utrecht, Johnson was already leading him to interpret his position as a future Scots laird as a special providence implying specific ethical responsibilities. Johnson "was pleased to listen to a particular account which I gave him of my family, and of its hereditary estate . . . recommending, at the same time, a liberal kindness to the tenantry, as people over whom the proprietor was placed by Providence" (Boswell 1: 535). Johnson recurs to precisely the same notion toward the end of his first letter to Boswell. Concerning the suggestions he has given, Johnson writes: "But this advice if you will not take from others you must take from your own reflections, if you purpose to do the dutys of the station to which the Bounty of providence has called you."

The Intervening Correspondence

For the next twenty-one years, until Johnson's last letter to Boswell in November 1784, their correspondence reflects the history of this clash between the claims of the aesthetic and ethical spheres in the life of James Boswell. In his first letter Johnson effectively presents two different Boswells: the actual despairing aesthete and the potential vigorous ethicist. Over time, Johnson fleshes out the picture of the Ethical Boswell he hopes to see the Young Dog become. The Boswell of Johnson's designing is, not surprisingly, a married man; a resident of his native Scotland (if possible, on his ancestral estate); a dutiful, even affectionate, son on good terms with his admittedly difficult father; a steady, practicing lawyer; the author of scholarly works on the Scots Middle Ages; a serious Christian; and in time, as we will see, the prudent and kindly laird of Auchinleck. Through all of this, Johnson makes no attempt to reshape Boswell into a radically new or different self; he builds consistently on the interests, temperament, and background Boswell brings as his providential legacy. Johnson leaves the given, natural Boswell intact, merely presenting Boswell an image of himself as he would be were he to direct and assess his acts by ethical standards.

To some degree, of course, such a transformation actually occurs. In time Boswell does marry, settle in Scotland, and practice law. As he tells John Wilkes in 1772, explaining why he will not visit Wilkes in jail, "I am a Scotch laird and a Scotch lawyer and a Scotch married man. It would not be decent" (Brady 9). If Boswell never really grows close to his father, he at least gives him less objective cause for complaint, and though he never does write the feudal history of Scotland, he at least outgrows his early pose of Corsican Boswell, to Johnson's undoubted relief. That the transformation is never complete and stable we also know. Despite his attempt to live in the ethical sphere, Boswell frequently lapses into the follies and vices of his younger days, slipping away from his family to fraternize with the literati, libertines, and stage girls of London. Still, Boswell does resemble more and more over time the model of him presented in Johnson's letters, with the result that the relationship between the two men changes as well.

Johnson willingly establishes Sage Counselor–Young Dog relationships with the young men around him, but always with the goal of dissolving this relationship in the full, mutual respect of genuine adult friendship. Though the essentially pedagogical cast of the December 8, 1763, letter precludes such a friendship, Johnson hopes to establish one whenever Boswell proves sufficiently mature. The maturity required by Johnson, however, entails adoption of an ethical view of life.[10] Once again Johnson's sense of such matters finds expression in Kierkegaard: "The absolute condition for friendship is unity in a lifeview. . . . The lifeview in which one is united must be a positive view. . . . But a positive view of life is unimaginable unless it has an ethical element in it. . . . So the ethical element in the lifeview becomes the essential point of departure for friendship, and not until friendship is looked at in this way does it gain meaning and beauty" (319–21).

To see how such a friendship would reflect in Johnson's letters, we need look no further than those he wrote to Mrs. Thrale, a woman Johnson accepted as a mature adult from the beginning. What we find when we do this, interestingly enough, is gossip, comedy, banter. His letters to Mrs. Thrale are brisk and funny, skipping lightly from topic to topic, reveling in gossip of petty quarrels, absurd happenings, and even budding romances. As Redford notes, in his letters to Mrs. Thrale Johnson "attempts on most occasions to recreate the warm inconsequentiality, the private allusiveness, and the darting fragmentations of candid oral discourse" (217). The letters have, to be sure, their more serious moments—on the death of Henry Thrale, for example, or on the night of Johnson's stroke—but their general tone is chatty, whimsical, and relaxed. They are precisely the social letters "written only for the sake of writing" that Johnson refuses at the outset to write to Boswell, and it is Mrs. Thrale's ethical maturity that makes them possible. When writing to Mrs. Thrale, Johnson feels no pedagogical responsibility. Mrs. Thrale does not need his moral tutelage. He is free to relax and play.

Grundy shares the current high opinion of Johnson's letters to Mrs. Thrale on the grounds that they are "the most epistolary," that they make the best use of the "techniques of spontaneity" by which a letter mimics spoken conversation (220–21). And she shrewdly guesses that of the letters Johnson writes to Boswell "we should expect the best to be written after the shared experience of the Scottish journey," which indeed they are, if in fact letters are to be judged by their "epistolarity" (220). By the time of their Scotland jaunt, in the late summer and fall of 1773, Boswell had known Johnson for a decade and had become the respectable figure he describes for Wilkes, living in the ethical sphere and thus capable of real friendship with Johnson. "As a lawyer and settled married man," writes Brady, "Boswell was as near Johnson's equal as he would become" (33). The journey itself gave Johnson the opportunity to observe Boswell for three months at close quarters against his most socially rooted background. He watched Boswell living with his wife and children, visiting his father on his hereditary estate, conversing with friends and scholars in Edinburgh, and exploring his native land. Boswell, for his part, appears to have been on his best behavior throughout. As a result, Johnson's letters to Boswell following their tour do strongly resemble those to Mrs. Thrale. They flit from topic to topic with the same quickness, and they accentuate the privacy of their own discourse by referring overwhelmingly to incidents and persons familiar to the two men alone. As a result, the letters from this period require flurries of footnotes for their explication and may never be of major interest to critics reading letters "as literature." They are, in fact, too successful as purely personal communications to invite general anthologizing.[11]

The 1782 Letter

A central turning point in Boswell's adult life came at the end of August 1782, when Boswell was forty-one. His father, Alexander Boswell, died, leaving James the laird of Auchinleck. Boswell immediately dispatched a number of letters announcing the event, one of them to Johnson. Johnson, with rare promptness, returned an answer the day he received it (September 7, 1782), responding both to the death itself and to Boswell's new life as Scots laird. Nineteen years stand between this letter and the first one Johnson wrote to him, and though Johnson still has much sage counsel to offer, the tone is markedly gentler, more respectful: man-to-man rather than man-to-boy.

The letter is not, obviously, "written for the sake of writing." Johnson attempts in the writing of it to perform two "offices of real kindness": to console and to advise. The consolatory function of the letter presents Johnson with an especially ticklish problem of tact, in that he himself did not like Alexander and knew that Boswell's own feelings toward his cold, imperious father were mixed at best.[12] Johnson begins his letter, thus, with a statement of his own reaction to the news of Alexander's death that is at once touchingly personal and strangely oblique: "I have struggled through this year with so much infirmity of body, and such strong impressions of the fragility of life, that death, wherever it appears, fills me with melancholy; and I cannot hear without emotion, of the removal of any one, whom I have known, into another state." The statement is already more self-revelatory than anything in the letter of 1763. Johnson confesses here to discomforts both physical and emotional. As condolence, however, the statement represents a curious compromise between the sharing of sorrow required by the occasion and Johnson's refusal to pretend grief over Alexander's death per se. Since any pretense of personal sorrow for Boswell's father would be disingenuous, Johnson chooses to share a different grief, though one still prompted by his death. He does not grieve for Alexander; he grieves for himself. Nearly seventy-three and in ill health, the news of anyone's death reminds him of his own mortality, and it is this that "fills [him] with melancholy."

Johnson continues in a more standard consolatory vein by suggesting to Boswell the comforting realities of his situation: "Your father's death . . . was at a mature age, and it was expected." Though Johnson would, of course, consider it presumptuous to promise the salvation of anyone, he does offer what evidence he can that Alexander's eternal condition will be happy. Alexander Boswell had sufficient time to prepare himself for his final judgment, and he could be trusted to have had the sobriety and foresight to do so.[13] Johnson's offer of this particular kind of comfort in itself assumes a mature Christian as his reader.

When Boswell received the news of his father's fatal collapse, he rushed to see him but found him already sunk into unconsciousness. In closing the consolatory portion of his letter, Johnson acknowledges the pain this must have caused Boswell and then follows up with a remarkably matter-of-fact assessment of the relationship between father and son: "His disposition towards you was undoubtedly that of a kind, though not of a fond father. . . . and if by negligence or imprudence you had extinguished his fondness, he could not at will rekindle it." Boswell knows perfectly well that he "extinguished" his father's "fondness" in part by his "negligence or imprudence" and does not need anyone pretending otherwise. Johnson, for his part, respects Boswell too much to palliate or dismiss his sense of guilt as illusory. Not to take Boswell's guilt seriously, even at its most painful, would be to deprive him of the dignity of an ethical being. On the other hand, Johnson hardly engages in chastisement. The rest of the passage is quiet, reflective, and suggests a future less of self-recrimination than of calm forgiveness and acceptance. Johnson leads Boswell through sorrow, disappointment, and guilt—and beyond them. With exquisite tact, he is helping Boswell lay his father's ghost. Significantly, Johnson follows this passage with an inquiry into the "disposition of [Alexander's] fortune" and then immediately launches into his discussion of Boswell's new life. The laird is dead; long live the laird.

The three succeeding paragraphs are given over to advice rather than consolation. As Johnson sees it, Alexander's death represents for Boswell one further separation from the parent, and he again takes the opportunity to guide him in the initial direction of his new life. The paragraphs represent Johnson's nearest approach to the pedagogical mode of his earliest letters, engaging in moral exhortation and theological reflection with the goal of encouraging in Boswell the attitudes and actions of a responsible, kindly Scots laird. But his advice, by contrast to that of his first letter, seems less personal and more generic. Johnson is not attacking Boswell's characteristic vices; he is offering advice worth hearing by any inheritor of a new estate. Johnson, in fact, addresses Boswell in these paragraphs as a man needing less to be instructed than reminded.

As an ethicist, Johnson highlights the duties and responsibilities of Boswell's changed situation rather than its new experiences: "You, dear Sir, have now a new station, and have therefore new cares, and new employments." Boswell is to ask not what Auchinleck can do for him, but what he can do for Auchinleck. Nor does Johnson any longer direct Boswell to his books; he is no longer tutoring a young student but advising a man of affairs. Boswell, Johnson insists, must remember that his estate represents not just the property of one man but the interests and livelihood of many. He encourages a social rather than a purely individualistic understanding of Boswell's new status: "Be kind to the old servants, and secure the kindness of the agents and factors." Johnson had from his first letter encouraged Boswell to take seriously "the duties of the station to which the bounty of Providence has called you," one of these being "a liberal kindness to the tenantry." He reminds Boswell of these duties here at the very start of his tenure as laird.

Johnson's first concern, however, is simply that Boswell not lose the farm through his careless enjoyment of it. Now that Boswell has possession, his first duty is to keep possession. Johnson uses a literary reference to illustrate the principle involved: "Life, as Cowley seems to say, ought to resemble a well ordered poem; of which one rule generally received is, that the exordium should be simple, and should promise little." And as the characteristic movement of Johnson's mind is always from principle to application, Boswell would expect something like the homily that actually follows: "Begin your new course of life with the least show, and the least expence possible. . . . Let it be your first care not to be in any man's debt." Stylistically, the passage is striking for its simplicity and plainness. This is not the "Johnsonian" style of Wimsatt's analysis, the style that makes almost any page of the *Rambler* immediately recognizable. It is, however, characteristic of Johnson's letters.

In the next sentence, by contrast, Johnson shifts suddenly into his famous marmoreal prose. The structure and rhythm of this sentence are quintessentially "Johnsonian." The architecture of the sentence places in parallel two conceptual possibilities, one specious and the other sound: "When the thoughts are extended . . . the present life seems . . . but . . . when it is perceived . . . its sorrows manifest that. . . ." Though Conception A leads to falsehood, Conception B leads to truth. Within this larger structure, Johnson deploys several of his characteristic doublets: "principles of conduct, and maxims of prudence"; "how much evil is produced, and how much good is impeded"; "expedients of poverty" versus "exercise of virtue"; "the . . . importance of the next life" and "the interests of this."

The idea of this paragraph could, obviously, be stated more simply. Johnson wonders how Boswell will accept "maxims of prudence" in a consolatory letter (Is this any time to think of money?), and he moves to forestall such a reaction. It may seem trivial or even callous to discuss finances in the face of death, but as he goes on to suggest, mortality itself makes such considerations necessary. Our salvation depends on our integrity and generosity, and how we manage our possessions influences these profoundly. From Franklin a similar insight produces a homely parable of empty purses standing not upright, and from Wesley the lively injunction "Make all you can, save all you can, give all you can." From Johnson the insight evokes a one-sentence *Rambler*.

What the two paragraphs demonstrate, appearing so close together, is that in the case of Samuel Johnson, the style is not the man; the style is the persona. That is, the style represents a deliberate rhetorical choice the writer makes in order to accomplish specific ends—a role not a self, a costume not a body, something he can put on and take off at will. The earlier paragraph, more typical of Johnson's epistolary prose, is direct, plain, natural, and in second person: addressed to "you." But as if worrying that he has intruded too quickly with his counsel, he suddenly pulls his focus back away from Boswell to take a longer and more spacious view.

As a result, the latter paragraph is written in Johnson's vintage *Rambler* style, his characteristic medium for reflecting on the eternal verities. The paragraph represents in two senses an apology for the one preceding. It represents in its earlier phrases an apology in the usual sense, asking pardon for mentioning a sensitive matter. The latter half is apology as formal defense, explaining why the discussion of such matters is necessary nevertheless. And here Johnson the man vanishes entirely behind the impersonal grandeur that marks this passage. The prose here is a stately *vox celeste,* formal and majestic, not so much addressing Boswell as towering impersonally above both Boswell and Johnson. This is no longer Johnson speaking in his own person; it is a kind of moral ventriloquism, with Johnson rendering the ultimate principles of ethical reality into their nearest English equivalents. In his earliest letter to Boswell, Johnson used this prose to drive Boswell into an awareness of his spiritual condition under the Eye of Omniscience. Here, having warned his friend to watch his spending, he shifts to his *Rambler* voice to enforce, as if from above, the theological necessity of such caution.

Then, having done so, Johnson drops just as suddenly back into his standard, disarmingly ordinary epistolary prose for the rest of the letter. "Be kind to old servants" and so on. He makes his "compliments to Mrs. Boswell," as he always does, delighting to address Boswell as paterfamilias, and he offers his best wishes for the recovery of his wife's health: "I hope she will live long and happily." He then quickly winds up his letter with the purely social chitchat he had refused Boswell at the start of their correspondence. The paragraph is hardly memorable, but it would interest Boswell, and it reflects what is most typical of Johnson's letters to his adult friends: "I forget whether I told you that Rasay has been here; we dined cheerfully together. I entertained lately a young gentleman from Coriatachat."

Whoever wishes to analyze these sentences "as literature" is welcome to try. They are, in Grundy's phrase, perfectly "epistolary," perfectly representative of the "techniques of spontaneity" that mimic conversational speech ("I forgot whether I told you"), but they are also, to be frank, perfectly forgettable. They represent not exhortation but mere private news, not improvement but friendship. And what they suggest, when set against the background of the rest of Johnson's correspondence, is that, in however shaky and uncertain a fashion, the Young Dog has finally grown up.

NOTES

1. Chapman prints "it grows manifest" instead of "its sorrows manifest," incorporating a change in the 1793 edition of Boswell's *Life*, which, however, he admits may or may not have any authority. Redford prints the original 1791 reading.

2. Chapman prints "Corrichatachin," again incorporating a change from the 1793 edition of Boswell's *Life*. Redford, in printing "Coriatachat," follows the 1791 edition.

3. Bate (45–86) is especially sensitive to what the friendship of these older, successful men of the world meant to Johnson.

4. "There is no doubt that in daily life as well as in writing [Johnson] attempted to act the part of the 'wise man'" (Damrosch 100).

5. By actual count, only a small portion of Johnson's complete collected letters would "resemble a moral essay." A great number are scrappy memos, brief notes, and business correspondence. Of the more fully developed letters, the plurality are

to Mrs. Thrale and are, as Redford demonstrates in detail, the furthest things from *Ramblers*. For all that, essayistic letters certainly are more common in Johnson's correspondence than in most writers', and they are striking when they appear. Their very distinctiveness, perhaps, makes them seem more abundant than they really are.

6. Early in the twentieth century, phenomenologist Max Scheler described what he called the "pedagogical attitude." By contrast with full, mutual love between equals, the pedagogical attitude seeks to change the other qualitatively. It endeavors "actually to 'raise' the value of its object, either by merely wishing its betterment, or by actively willing and trying to secure this, as when we seek to 'better' a person or help them in any way to secure a higher value" (157).

7. Johnson had already on one occasion expatiated at length on Boswell's curriculum, only to have Boswell "recollect with admiration an animating blaze of eloquence, which rouzed every intellectual power in me to the highest pitch, but must have dazzled me so much, that my memory could not preserve the substance of his discourse" (1: 533).

8. It is striking that in *Either/Or*, Kierkegaard's own fictional representative of the ethical sphere, Judge William, expresses his convictions in a pair of long letters, through which he too tries to convert a young aesthete to the ethical life. The aesthete, by contrast, is revealed only inadvertently by private journals and an assortment of unpublished essays. Kierkegaard's choice of forms itself suggests something of the egoism and isolation of the aesthetic life compared with the concrete interpersonal concerns of the ethical.

9. Defining oneself by one's peculiarities is, according to Kierkegaard, of the essence in living in the aesthetic sphere. "Insofar as the esthetic individual, with 'esthetic earnestness,' sets a task for his life, it is really the task of becoming absorbed in his own accidental traits, of becoming an individual whose equal in paradoxicality and irregularity has never been seen, of becoming a caricature of a human being" (261). That such a project frequently absorbed Boswell's energies even a cursory reading of his journal will suggest.

10. Kierkegaard's Judge William expresses the same wish toward the end of one of his letters to his aesthete friend: "So accept my greeting, take my friendship, for although, strictly speaking, I dare not describe our relationship this way, I nevertheless hope that my young friend may some day be so much older that I shall dare to use this word legitimately" (332).

11. The celebrated letter to Chesterfield, by contrast, positively invites anthologizing by its public, "open" quality. Johnson's willingness to dictate the letter to Boswell and Chesterfield's willingness to leave it open on his table both suggest that the men understood this to be a document in a public quarrel. This open, public quality, however, also makes the letter one of the least typical that Johnson wrote.

12. Boswell's journal records his reaction to watching by his father's bed the night before his death: "Wept; for alas! there was not affection between us" (Brady 226).

13. As it happens, Johnson's confidence in Alexander's piety appears to have been misplaced. According to Alexander's physician, Dr. Thomas Gillespie, the old laird in his final years "showed no more signs of religion than a stock or a stone" (Brady 224).

WORKS CITED

Alkon, Paul K. *Samuel Johnson and Moral Discipline*. Evanston, Ill.: Northwestern UP, 1967.

Bate, Walter Jackson. *Samuel Johnson*. New York: Harcourt, 1975.

Boswell, James. *Boswell's Life of Johnson*. Ed. George Birkbeck Hill, rev. L. F. Powell. 6 vols. Oxford: Clarendon, 1934–50.

Brady, Frank. *James Boswell: The Later Years*. New York: McGraw, 1984.

Damrosch, Leopold, Jr. *Samuel Johnson and the Tragic Sense*. Princeton: Princeton UP, 1972.

Fussell, Paul. *Samuel Johnson and the Life of Writing*. New York: Norton, 1971.

Grundy, Isobel. "The Techniques of Spontaneity: Johnson's Developing Epistolary Style." *Johnson after Two Hundred Years*. Ed. Paul J. Korshin. Philadelphia: U of Pennsylvania P, 1986. 211–24.

Johnson, Samuel. *The Letters of Samuel Johnson*. Ed. Bruce Redford. 3 vols. to date. Princeton: Princeton UP, 1992–.

———. *The Letters of Samuel Johnson, with Mrs. Thrale's Genuine Letters to Him*. Ed. R. W. Chapman. 3 vols. Oxford: Clarendon, 1952.

Kierkegaard, Søren. *Either/Or: Part II*. Trans. and ed. Howard V. Hong and Edna H. Hong. Princeton: Princeton UP, 1987.

Redford, Bruce. *The Converse of the Pen: Acts of Intimacy in the Eighteenth-Century Familiar Letter*. Chicago: U of Chicago P, 1986.

Scheler, Max. *The Nature of Sympathy*. Trans. Peter Heath. Hamden, Conn.: Archon Books, 1970.

Wimsatt, W. K., Jr. *The Prose Style of Samuel Johnson*. New Haven: Yale UP, 1941.

The Paradox of the Actress: Morality, Profession, and Behavior in Two Letters by Denis Diderot

Emita B. Hill

Denis Diderot to Mademoiselle Jodin, August 21, 1765

J'ai lu, Mademoiselle, la lettre que vous avez écrite à mad^e votre mère. Les sentiments de tendresse, de dévouement et de respect dont elle est remplie ne m'ont point surpris. Vous êtes un enfant malheureux, mais vous êtes un enfant bien né. Puisque vous avez reçu de la nature une âme honnête, connaissez tout le prix du don qu'elle vous a fait, et ne souffrez pas que rien l'avilisse.

Je ne suis pas un pédant; je me garderai bien de vous demander une sorte de vertus presque incompatibles avec l'état que vous avez choisi, et que des femmes du monde, que je n'en estime ni ne méprise davantage pour cela, conservent rarement au sein de l'opulence et loin des séductions de toute espèce dont vous êtes environnée. Le vice vient au devant de vous; elles vont au devant du vice. Mais songez qu'une femme n'acquiert le droit de se défaire des lisières que l'opinion attache à son sexe que par des talents supérieurs et les qualités d'esprit et de coeur les plus distinguées. Il faut mille vertus réelles pour couvrir un vice imaginaire. Plus vous accorderez à vos goûts, plus vous devez être attentive sur le choix des objets.

On reproche rarement à une femme son attachement pour un homme

Diderot to Mlle Jodin, Aug. 21, 1765, from Diderot, *Correspondance* 5: 100–105; Diderot to Mlle Jodin, Nov. 1765, from Diderot, *Correspondance* 5: 201–4.

d'un mérite reconnu. Si vous n'osez avouer celui que vous aurez préféré, c'est que vous vous en mépriserez vous-même, et quand on a du mépris pour soi, il est rare qu'on échappe au mépris des autres. Vous voyez que, pour un homme qu'on compte entre les philosophes, mes principes ne sont pas austères: c'est qu'il seroit ridicule de proposer à une femme de théâtre la morale des Capucines du Marais.

Travaillez surtout à perfectionner votre talent; le plus misérable état, à mon sens, est celui d'une actrice médiocre.

Je ne sçais pas si les applaudissements du public sont très flatteurs, surtout pour celle que sa naissance et son éducation avoient moins destinée à les recevoir qu'à les accorder, mais je sçais que ses dédains ne doivent être que plus insupportables pour elle. Je vous ai peu entendue, mais j'ai cru vous reconnoître une grande qualité, qu'on peut simuler peut-être à force d'art et d'étude, mais qui ne s'acquiert pas; une âme qui s'aliène, qui s'affecte profondément, qui se transporte sur les lieux, qui est telle ou telle, qui voit et qui parle à tel ou tel personnage. J'ai été satisfait lorsque, au sortir d'un mouvement violent, vous paroissiez revenir de fort loin et reconnoître à peine l'endroit d'où vous n'étiez pas sortie et les objets qui vous environnoient.

Acquérez de la grâce et de la liberté, rendez toute votre action simple, naturelle et facile.

Une des plus fortes satires de notre genre dramatique, c'est le besoin que l'acteur a du miroir. N'ayez point d'apprêt ni de miroir, connoissez la bienséance de votre rôle et n'allez point au delà. Le moins de gestes que vous pourrez; le geste fréquent nuit à l'énergie, et détruit la noblesse. C'est le visage, ce sont les yeux, c'est tout le corps qui doit avoir du mouvement, et non les bras. Savoir rendre un endroit passionné, c'est presque ne rien savoir. Le poëte est pour moitié dans l'effet. Attachez-vous aux scènes tranquilles; ce sont les plus difficiles; c'est là qu'une actrice montre du goût, de l'esprit, de la finesse, du jugement, de la délicatesse quand elle en a. Etudiez les accents des passions; chaque passion a les siens, et ils sont si puissants qu'ils me pénètrent presque sans le secours de la parole. C'est la langue primitive de la nature. Le sens d'un beau vers n'est pas à la portée de tous; mais tous sont affectés d'un long soupir tiré douloureusement du fond des entrailles; des bras élevés, des yeux tournés vers le ciel, des sons inarticulés, une voix faible et plaintive, voilà ce qui touche, émeut et trouble toutes les âmes. Je voudrois bien que vous eussiez vu Garrick jouer le rôle d'un père qui a laissé tomber son enfant dans un puits. Il n'y a point de maxime que nos poëtes aient plus oubliée que celle qui dit que les grandes douleurs sont muettes. Souvenez-vous en pour eux, afin de pallier par votre jeu l'impertinence de leurs tirades. Il ne tiendra qu'à vous de faire plus d'effet par le silence que par leurs beaux discours.

Voilà bien des choses, et pas un mot du véritable sujet de ma lettre. Il s'agit, mademoiselle, de votre maman. C'est, je crois, la plus infortunée créature que je connoisse. Votre père la croyoit insensible à tout événement; il ne la connoissoit pas assez. Elle a été désolée de se séparer de vous, et il s'en falloit bien qu'elle fût remise de sa peine lorsqu'elle a eu à supporter un autre événement fâcheux. Vous me connoissez, vous sçavez qu'aucun motif, quelque honnête qu'on pût le supposer, ne me feroit dire une chose qui ne seroit pas dans la plus exacte vérité. Prenez donc à la lettre ce que vous allez apprendre.

Elle étoit sortie; pendant son absence on a crocheté sa porte et on l'a volée. On lui a laissé ses nippes, heureusement; mais on a pris ce qu'elle avoit d'argent, ses couverts et sa montre. Elle en a ressenti un violent chagrin, et elle en est vraiment changée. Dans la détresse où elle s'est trouvée, elle s'est adressé à tous ceux en qui elle a espéré trouver de l'amitié et de la commisération. Mais vous avez appris par vous même combien ces sentiments sont rares, économes et peu durables, sans compter qu'il y a, surtout en ceux qui ne sont pas faits à la misère, une pudeur qui les retient et qui ne cède qu'à l'extrême besoin.

Votre mère est faite autant que personne pour sentir toute cette répugnance. Il est impossible que les modiques secours qui lui viennent puissent la soutenir. Nous lui avons offert notre table pour tous les jours et nous l'avons fait, je crois, d'assez bonne grâce pour qu'elle n'ait point souffert à l'accepter. Mais la nourriture, quoique le plus pressant des besoins, n'est pas le seul qu'on ait. Il seroit bien dur qu'on ne lui eût laissé ses nippes que pour s'en défaire. Elle luttera le plus qu'elle pourra, mais cette lutte est pénible; elle ne dure guère qu'aux dépens de la santé, et vous êtes trop bonne pour ne pas la prévenir ou la faire cesser. Voilà le moment de lui prouver la sincérité des protestations que vous lui avez faites en la quittant.

Il m'a semblé que mon estime ne vous étoit pas indifférente. Songez, mademoiselle, que je vais vous juger; et ce n'est pas, je crois, mettre cette estime à trop haut prix que de l'attacher aux procédés que vous aurez avec votre mère, surtout dans une circonstance telle que celle-ci. Si vous avez résolu de la secourir, comme vous le devez, ne la laissez pas attendre. Ce qui n'est que d'humanité pour nous est de premier devoir pour vous; il ne faut pas qu'on dise que, sur les planches et dans la chaire, l'acteur et le docteur de Sorbonne sont également soigneux de recommander le bien, et habiles à se dispenser de le faire.

J'ai le droit par mon âge, par mon expérience, l'amitié qui me lioit avec monsieur votre père, et l'intéret que j'ai toujours pris à vous, d'espérer que les conseils que je vous donnerai sur votre conduite et votre caractère ne seront point mal pris. Vous êtes violente; on se tient à distance de la violence, c'est le défaut le plus contraire à votre sexe, qui est complaisant, tendre et doux. Vous êtes vaine; si la vanité n'est pas fondée, elle fait rire. Si l'on mérite en effet toute la préférence qu'on s'accorde à soi même, on humilie les autres, on les offense. Je ne permets de sentir et de montrer ce qu'on vaut, que quand les autres l'oublient jusqu'à nous manquer. Il n'y a que ceux qui sont petits qui se lèvent toujours sur la pointe des pieds.

J'ai peur que vous ne respectiez pas assez la vérité dans vos discours. Mademoiselle, soyez vraie, faites vous en l'habitude; je ne permets le mensonge qu'au sot et au méchant; à celui-ci pour se masquer, à l'autre pour suppléer à l'esprit qui lui manque. N'ayez ni détours, ni finesses, ni ruses. Ne trompez personne; la femme trompeuse se trompe la première. Si vous avez un petit caractère, vous n'aurez jamais qu'un petit jeu. Le philosophe qui manque de religion, ne peut avoir trop de moeurs. L'actrice, qui a contre ses moeurs l'opinion qu'on a conçue de son état, ne sçaurait trop s'observer et se montrer élevée. Vous êtes négligente et dissipatrice; un moment de négligence peut coûter cher, le tems amène toujours le châtiment du dissipateur.

Pardonnez à mon amitié ces réflexions sévères. Vous n'entendrez que trop la voix de la flatterie. Je vous souhaite tout succès.

Je vous salue et finis sans fadeur et sans compliment.

DIDEROT

(I have read, mademoiselle, the letter you wrote your mother. I was not surprised by the sentiments of tenderness, respect, and devotion that fill it. You are an unfortunate child, but wellborn. Since nature gave you an open-minded and fair character, recognize the true value of this gift, and do not permit anything to demean it.

I am not a strict moralist; I would never ask of you the kind of virtue that is practically incompatible with your chosen profession, and that women in society, whom I neither admire nor scorn any more for this fact, rarely conserve even while living in the lap of luxury and far from the many kinds of temptations that surround you. Vice seeks you out; they seek out vice. But remember that a woman only earns the right to free herself from the limits public opinion assigns to her sex through outstanding talents and through noteworthy qualities of heart and mind. One needs a thousand real virtues to offset an imagined vice. The more you give in to your desires, the more careful you must be in choosing the objects of them.

People rarely criticize a woman for loving a man of recognized merit. If you dare not admit to the person you have chosen, that means you will despise yourself for that choice, and when someone loses respect for herself, she rarely retains the respect of others. You can see that for a man considered a *philosophe,* my principles are not austere: that's because it would be ridiculous to recommend to an actress the morals of the Capucine nuns in the Marais.

Above all, work at perfecting your art; in my opinion, the lowest status is that of a mediocre actress.

I don't know whether the applause of the public is very flattering, especially for a woman whose birth and education had destined her rather to bestow than to receive applause, but I do know that public disdain must be even more intolerable for that person. I have not seen much of your acting, but I have thought I saw in you a fine quality that perhaps can be simulated through art and study, but cannot truly be acquired if it is not innate; this consists of a spirit that can distance itself, can be deeply moved, can bridge time and space becoming this or that, seeing and speaking to this or that character. I was gratified when, after a violent scene, you seemed to come back from far away and scarcely to recognize the place you had not in fact left or the objects surrounding you.

Seek to acquire grace and freedom, make your acting simple, natural, and effortless.

One of the strongest satires of our current acting tribe is the actor's need for a mirror. You should not rely on makeup or mirrors; know what is appropriate to your role and do not exceed it. Make as few gestures as possible; gestures often take away from your energy and undermine the nobility of the part. Your face, your eyes, your entire body, and not your arms, must move. To know how to render a passionate scene is to know almost nothing. Half the credit belongs to the poet. Work on quiet scenes; these are the most difficult; it is in these that an actress can show her taste, her intelligence, her subtlety, her judgment, her delicacy, if she possesses these. Study the accents of passion; each passion has its own, and they are so powerful that I respond to them almost without the help of words. This is the primitive language of nature. The meaning of a fine line of poetry is not accessible to everyone; but all are moved by a long sigh drawn painfully from the depth of your bowels; by raised arms, eyes turned skyward, inarticulate sounds, a weak, plaintive voice. These are what touch, stir, and disturb all souls. I wish you could have seen Garrick play the part of a father who had let his son fall into a well. There is no maxim more forgotten by our poets than that the greatest sorrows are mute. You must remember what they have forgotten, in order to remedy by your acting the irrelevance of their declamations. It's up to you to be more eloquent through your silence than through their fine lines.

Here I've discussed many subjects and not said a word yet of the true subject of my letter. Mademoiselle, it's about your mother. I believe her to be the most unhappy creature I know. Your father believed her indifferent to whatever happened; he didn't know her well enough. She has been distraught at the separation from you and had no sooner recovered from that pain than she had to endure another unfortunate event. You know me, you know that no motive, however honest it might appear, would make me say something that is not strictly true. Take literally, therefore, what you are about to learn.

She had gone out; during her absence someone forced open her door and robbed her. They left her clothes, fortunately, but took all the money she had, her silverware, and her watch. She was violently distressed and is no longer herself. In her distress she has turned to everyone from whom she could expect friendship and commiseration. But you have experienced for yourself how rare, parsimonious, and ephemeral these feelings are, without adding that there exists, especially in people unfamiliar with poverty, a kind of modesty that holds them back from asking for help and that is only conquered when their need becomes extreme.

Your mother, as much as anyone, feels this distaste. The minimal help she has received cannot possibly sustain her. We have offered to share our meals with her on a daily basis and did so, I believe, in such a tactful way that she has had no embarrassment in accepting. But while food is the most pressing of needs, it is not the only one. It would be very painful if the thieves had left her her clothes only to have her forced to sell them. She will resist as much as she can, but such a struggle is painful; if it lasts it will harm her health, and you are too kind not to ward this off or put an end to it. This is the moment for you to prove to her the sincerity of the feelings you expressed to her when you left.

I have believed that you are not indifferent to my good opinion of you. Consider, mademoiselle, that I will be judging you; I do not believe that it sets this good opinion at too high a price if I make it depend on the conduct you will have with your mother, especially in such circumstances. If you have decided to rescue her from her poverty, as you should, don't force her to wait. What is simple humanity for us is a primary obligation for you. Don't let it be said that the actor onstage and the Sorbonne professor from his exalted chair are equally careful to recommend good deeds and equally skillful at excusing themselves from performing them.

My age, my experience, the friendship I had with your father, and the interest I have always had in you give me the right to hope that the advice I will give you on your conduct and your character will not be taken amiss. You have a violent temper. People distance themselves from violence; it is the most inappropriate defect for someone of your sex, which should be pleasing, tender, and gentle. You are vain; if vanity is not well founded, it provokes laughter. If one deserves in fact all one's self-bestowed admiration, it demeans and offends others. I only permit people to feel and declare their value when others undervalue it to the point of lacking in respect. Only short people go about always standing on tiptoes.

I fear that you are not always strictly truthful in what you say. Mademoiselle, be true, make a habit of it; I only permit lies to a fool and a wicked man; to the latter to mask what he is, to the former to make up for the wit he lacks. Do not be devious or subtle or crafty. Do not deceive anyone; a deceitful woman deceives herself first of all. If your own character is petty, your acting will always be petty. The *philosophe* who lacks religious faith needs even stricter morals. The actress, already believed to lack morals because of the public judgment of her profession, cannot be too careful about her behavior and must show herself to be above criticism. You are careless and fond of pleasure. One moment of inattention can cost you dear; time always brings about retribution for the pleasure seekers.

Please forgive a friend these sobering reflections. You will hear all too often more flattering voices. I wish you every success.

I greet you and end my letter without empty compliments.)

Denis Diderot to Mademoiselle Jodin, November 1765

Ce n'est pas vous, Mademoiselle, qui pouviez vous offenser de ma lettre; mais c'étoit peut-être madame votre mère. En y regardant d'un peu plus près, vous auriez deviné que je n'insistois d'une manière si pressante sur le besoin qu'elle avoit de vos secours, que pour ne vous laisser aucun doute sur la vérité de son accident. Ces secours sont arrivés fort à tems, et je suis bien aise de voir que votre âme a conservé sa sensibilité et son honnêteté, en dépit de l'épiderme de votre état, dont je ferois le plus grand cas si ceux qui s'y engagent avoient seulement la moitié autant de moeurs qu'il exige de talents.

Mademoiselle, puisque vous avez eu le bonheur d'intéresser un homme habile et sensé, aussi propre à vous conseiller sur votre jeu que sur votre conduite, écoutez le, ménagez le, dédommagez le du désagrément de son rôle par tous les égards et toute la docilité possibles.

Je me réjouis très sincèrement de vos premiers succès; mais songez que vous ne les devez en partie qu'au peu de goût de vos spectateurs. Ne vous laissez pas enyvrer par des applaudissements de si peu de valeur. Ce n'est pas à vos tristes Polonais, ce n'est pas aux barbares qu'il faut plaire. C'est aux Athéniens.

Tous les petits repentirs dont vos emportements ont été suivis devroient bien vous apprendre à les modérer. Ne faites rien qui puisse vous rendre méprisable. Avec un maintien honnête, décent, réservé, le propos d'une fille d'éducation, on écarte de soi toutes ces familiarités insultantes que l'opinion malheureusement trop bien fondée qu'on a d'une comédienne, ne manque presque jamais d'appeler à elle, surtout de la part des étourdis et des gens mal élevés qui ne sont rares en aucun endroit du monde.

Faites-vous la réputation d'une bonne et honnête créature. Je veux bien qu'on vous applaudisse, mais j'aimerois encore mieux qu'on pressentît que vous étiez destinée à autre chose qu'à monter sur des tréteaux, et que, sans trop savoir la suite d'événements fâcheux qui vous a conduite là, on vous en plaignit.

Les grands éclats de rire, la gaîté immodérée, les propos libres, marquent la mauvaise éducation, la corruption des moeurs, et ne manquent presque jamais d'avilir. Se manquer à soi même, c'est autoriser les autres à nous imiter. Vous ne pouvez être trop scrupuleuse sur le choix des personnes que vous recevez avec quelque assiduité. Jugez de ce qu'on pense en général de la femme de théâtre par le petit nombre de ceux à qui il est permis de la fréquenter sans s'exposer à de mauvais discours. Ne soyez contente de vous que quand les mères pourront voir leurs fils vous saluer sans conséquence. Ne croyez pas que votre conduite dans la société soit indifférente à vos succès au théâtre. On applaudit à regret à celle qu'on hait ou qu'on méprise.

Economisez; ne faites rien sans avoir l'argent à la main; il vous en coûtera moins, et vous ne serez jamais sollicitée par des dettes criardes à faire des sottises.

Vous vous époumonnerez toute votre vie sur les planches, si vous ne pensez pas de bonne heure que vous êtes faite pour autre chose. Je ne suis pas difficile; je serai content de vous si vous ne faites rien qui contrarie votre bonheur réel. La fantaisie du moment a bien sa douceur; qui est-ce qui ne le sait pas? Mais elle a des suites amères qu'on s'épargne par de petits sacrifices, quand on n'est pas une folle.

Bonjour, mademoiselle; portez-vous bien; soyez sage si vous pouvez; si vous ne pouvez l'être, ayez au moins le courage de supporter le châtiment du désordre.

Perfectionnez-vous. Attachez-vous aux scènes tranquilles, il n'y a que celles-là qui soient difficiles. Défaites-vous de ces hoquets habituels qu'on voudrait vous faire prendre pour des accents d'entrailles, et qui ne sont qu'un mauvais technique, déplaisant, fatigant, un tic aussi insupportable sur la scène qu'il le seroit en société. N'ayez aucune inquiétude sur nos sentiments pour madame votre mère; nous sommes disposés à la servir en toute occasion.

Saluez de ma part l'homme intrépide qui a bien voulu se charger de la dure et pénible corvée de vous diriger. Que Dieu lui en conserve la patience. Je n'ai pas voulu laisser partir ces lettres, que madame votre mère m'a remises, sans un petit [mot] qui vous montrât l'intérêt que je prens à votre sort. Quand je ne me soucierai plus de vous, je ne prendrai plus la liberté de vous parler durement; et si je vous écris encore, je finirai mes lettres avec toutes les politesses accoutumées.

(Mademoiselle, you certainly could not take offense at my letter, but perhaps your mother could. On reading it carefully, you doubtless guessed that if I dwelled so insistently on her need for your help, it was only to remove any doubt you might have about the reality of her plight. Your help arrived in time, and I am pleased to see that your spirit has kept its sensitivity and decency in spite of the thick skin attributed to people in your profession, whom I would hold in high esteem if they had even half as many morals as they do talent.

Mademoiselle, since you have been privileged to arouse the interest of a sensible and talented man, as ready to counsel you on your acting as on your conduct, listen to him, take good care of him, compensate him for the down side of his role by showing him every mark of courtesy and respect.

I am genuinely delighted at your first triumphs; but remember that you owe them in part to your audience's lack of taste. Do not allow yourself to be carried away by applause of such little value. It is not these sorry Poles, it is not the barbarians, it is the Athenians you must please.

All the little attacks of repentance that have followed your tantrums should teach you to control them. Do nothing that could earn you any scorn. If you behave with honesty, decency, and reserve and speak as an educated woman, you will protect yourself from all the insulting familiarities that the unfortunately too well-founded opinion people have of an actress never fails to attract to her, especially on the part of the scatterbrained or ill-bred people found everywhere in the world.

Earn for yourself the reputation of being honest and well behaved. I want you to get applause, but I would prefer it if people would feel intuitively that you were destined for something better than the stage and, without any clear knowledge of the unfortunate events that led you there, those people would feel sorry for you.

Great bursts of laughter, unbridled gaiety, vulgar remarks, are signs of lack of breeding and of corrupt behavior and never fail to debase one. To be untrue to oneself is to allow others to do the same. You cannot be too careful in your choice of the people you see frequently and with pleasure. You can judge for yourself how public opinion sees the actress by the small number of people permitted to frequent her without laying themselves open for slander. Be pleased with yourself only when mothers can see their sons talk to you without worrying. Do not think that your behavior in society has no bearing on your success in the theater. People are reluctant to applaud someone they dislike or scorn.

Save your money. Undertake nothing without having the money in hand. It will be easier for you, and you will never be pushed through unmanageable debts into committing acts you will regret.

You will spend your whole life shouting your lungs out on the stage if you don't realize early on that you are made for other things. I'm not hard to please; I will be satisfied so long as you do nothing contrary to your real happiness. The fantasy of the moment has true sweetness; who doesn't recognize that? But it is followed by bitter consequences that you can spare yourself through small sacrifices, if you are not too foolish.

Good day, mademoiselle; stay in good health; behave wisely if you can; if you can't, then at least have the courage to bear the punishment brought on by your folly.

Work at perfecting your art. Concentrate on the tranquil scenes; these are the only difficult ones. Eliminate those constant hiccoughs that people would have you believe are the accents of passion and that are no more than bad technique, unpleasant to watch, tiresome, a tic just as unwelcome onstage as in society. Have no worries about our feelings for your mother; we remain committed to helping her at all times.

Please give my greetings to the intrepid man who has taken on the demanding and painful task of being responsible for you. May God preserve his patience. I didn't want to send off these letters that your mother gave me without a little note to demonstrate to you the interest I take in your future. If in future I were to lose interest in you, I would no longer take the liberty of speaking so severely; if I still wrote you anyway, I would finish my letters with the usual polite greetings.)

Diderot's correspondence was slower than that of his contemporaries Voltaire and Rousseau to receive scholarly attention and editing, as, too, were his complete works. Long underestimated as a writer, recognized primarily for his work as prime mover of the French *Encyclopédie*, Diderot was neglected as late as the first third of this century. This neglect stemmed in large part from the fact that many of his best works were still unknown. Diderot left his novels and his most provocative philosophical works— and, of course, all his personal correspondence—unpublished during his lifetime, in order to protect himself from the wrath of the censor, from the real danger of imprisonment (he was incarcerated in 1749 for four months in the prison at Vincennes for one of his early writings), and from worse threats.

Unlike Voltaire, who fled Paris to the relative safety of his castle at Ferney on the Swiss border, Diderot chose to remain fully exposed in Paris, where he dedicated many years of his life to completing the *Encyclopédie* even after the authorities banned it and forbade his continued work on it. The manuscripts of many of Diderot's works remained inaccessible until the middle of the twentieth century. What editions existed were faulty, based on carelessly executed copies of copies. Curiously enough, the most extensive collection of manuscripts available to editors until recently was the collection made for Catherine the Great of Russia and held in the Hermitage library in St. Petersburg. These were not supposed to be copied—

the copies were made "under the table" by an entrepreneurial Frenchman visiting Russia on unrelated business—whence came some of the blatant inaccuracies. Needless to say, once those hastily made copies were in France the various publishers undertaking to reproduce them did not admit to their origin and most certainly could not check them for accuracy. Various stories were manufactured regarding the provenance of the manuscripts. In fact, most of the original manuscripts and many of the better scribal copies reviewed by Diderot himself languished in the attic of one of his descendants.

All this, of course, has now been rectified. The story of the recovery of the extraordinary cache of manuscripts known as the *Fonds Vandeul*— Vandeul being the patronym of Diderot's son-in-law—its careful removal first to Widener Library at Harvard for microfilming and inventorying, and then its return to France and its entry into the Bibliothèque Nationale has been told and retold, first by Herbert Dieckmann in 1951, in the preface to his *Inventaire*, and most recently and far more completely by Jane Dieckmann.[1]

Credit for this belongs to Herbert Dieckmann, whose patience and perhaps also whose charm persuaded the reluctant heirs finally to release the long-withheld papers to him personally. Among the *Fonds Vandeul* manuscripts were hundreds of letters, beginning with letters to Diderot's future wife, Antoinette Champion, in 1742 when Diderot was twenty-nine and ending a few months before his death in 1784.

The best complete current edition of Diderot's letters, although flawed from too-hasty execution—some letters occur more than once, some are misdated or misattributed with respect to the intended recipient—was a labor of love begun by Georges Roth in 1955 after he retired from active teaching. For fifteen years Roth worked alone, producing the first twelve volumes of what would eventually fill sixteen volumes of letters, many of them not included in earlier editions. Roth's work was completed in 1970 with the assistance of Jean Varloot. Until his recent retirement Varloot was the general editor of the Edition Nationale of Diderot's complete works, which will replace Roth's and all other earlier editions of Diderot's correspondence. This latest edition, drawing on the premier Diderot scholars of many continents, is the first to have full access to the *Fonds Vandeul* as well as to the collection of manuscripts in Russia. While numerous volumes are published, the remaining volumes of correspondence are still in preparation.

According to Roth, Diderot's son-in-law tried to gather together the makings of a complete correspondence immediately after Diderot's death, only to be turned down by many of Diderot's friends who claimed not to have kept their originals. Only a handful of letters is included in the various nineteenth-century editions (not surprising since so many major texts are also missing, their existence unknown to the editors), although one series, 139 of the letters to Diderot's mistress, Sophie Volland, was reproduced in 1831 from copies of the manuscripts in St. Petersburg.

The twenty-volume edition of Diderot's works prepared late in the nineteenth century by Jean Assézat and Maurice Tourneux that held pride of place until Dieckmann unearthed the *Fonds Vandeul* and that served all *dix-huitièmistes,* including the present writer, through the early 1960s included almost three hundred letters by Diderot. In 1939, as letters held in regional libraries or archives or by private collectors continued to surface, Lester Crocker estimated that over six hundred letters were extant. In fact, we now have almost six hundred letters to Sophie alone.

By the time Georges Roth determined to embark on his edition of Diderot's complete letters in 1955, he had the inestimable advantage of being able to consult the manuscripts of the *Fonds Vandeul,* now available in the Bibliothèque Nationale thanks to Herbert Dieckmann. Even with this advantage, however, Roth's edition has omissions and errors. Diderot's handwriting is tiny, almost indecipherable to the uninitiated. Moreover, many manuscripts, in particular the hundreds of pages of the exchange of letters between Diderot and Falconet, were obscured by passages obliterated and also passages inserted, making the choice of text as well as the simple reading of it very difficult. Also, of course, many letters were still undiscovered in private collections or unexplored libraries.

Nonetheless, Roth's sixteen-volume edition was a Herculean labor, light years ahead of its predecessors, and introduced scholars and casual readers for the first time to the delights of Diderot's chatty, witty, thoughtful, poignant, and at all times idiosyncratic personal correspondence and to the cast of characters who peopled his private universe—philosophers, artists, actors, friends and family from his provincial home in Langres, friends and loved ones in sophisticated Paris.

Herbert Dieckmann, in a brilliant essay written in 1959, "Diderot et son lecteur," analyzed Diderot's apparent need to dialogue, to have a reader or an interlocutor whom he could address in the first person and for whom he could frame the story he was telling or the idea he was communicating.

Usually this was a real reader—his friend Melchior Grimm, his mistress Sophie—but failing that, an invented reader for whom he invented responses to keep the dialogue going (*Cinq Leçons* 2–39).

Georges Roth's edition is especially valuable to the nonspecialist because of the background material Roth painstakingly supplied. He introduced each correspondent with a biographical note, situating him or her in Diderot's universe and in the society of the particular year or years of the correspondence. When possible, he included at least fragments of the letters from these correspondents that had triggered Diderot's letters to them. In the one instance of the correspondence with Falconet—an exchange that Diderot and Falconet both considered publishable after extensive editing (so extensive that Diderot gave up on achieving it and ultimately forbade the publication)—Roth includes the entire text of Falconet's letters. Unfortunately, the letters Diderot's admirers would perhaps most have liked to read, those written by his mistress of many decades, Sophie Volland, are missing, doubtless destroyed in a misguided attempt by her relatives to protect her reputation. Diderot corresponded with many women and clearly shone in feminine society, whether that of Sophie and her sisters or of the more worldly women in the philosophical circles. His letters to Sophie are among the most thoughtful and provocative he wrote. Unlike his correspondence with many other women and also with men to whom he related as *philosophe* or as mentor, Diderot's letters to Sophie are free of pedantry or of any suggestion of patronizing. Clearly, Diderot respected her as an intellectual equal and as a woman of spirit, even though she could never fully defy her mother or the conventions of their society. Sophie's letters to Diderot, given his estimate of her character and intelligence, are a great loss.

The most extensive and best known of Diderot's correspondences are his letters to Sophie, his exchange with Falconet, and his letters to Grimm. In many instances the letters to Grimm provide almost companion pieces to the letters to his mistress as he rhetorically embraced and shared with these two, his dearest male and dearest female friends, his concerns, his activities, his encounters, his ambitions. He was more often separated from Sophie than from Grimm—her family spent most summers away from Paris—but when Grimm is traveling in Germany or Switzerland and Sophie is also away, the content of the letters to both friends is almost identical. The reader unacquainted with Diderot cannot do better than to read the letters to Sophie or to Grimm. A selection of the former are available in a recent English translation by Peter France. They contain elements of all Diderot's written works on art, philosophy, politics, morals, theater, music, and contemporary society. They include many of the plots that appear either as independent short stories or as digressions within longer narrative works such as *Jacques le fataliste*, and they contain Diderot's summaries and critiques of many of the plays he saw, the books he read, and the conversations he held.

Rather than these well-known correspondences, however, I have selected for the purposes of this essay the first two letters from a lesser-known series of twenty-two letters written to Mademoiselle Marie-Magdeleine Jodin, an aspiring actress young enough to be Diderot's daughter. She was the daughter of a former contributor to the *Encyclopédie*, a Swiss watchmaker then deceased.[2] In his notes introducing this correspondence, Georges Roth writes: "Marie-Magdeleine Jodin n'a pas laissé de trace dans les fastes de l'art dramatique. Sa modeste notoriété tient tout entière à ce qu'elle a été, moralement sinon juridiquement, la pupille d'un homme célèbre" (Diderot, *Correspondance* 5: 97). Diderot, in other words, conferred immortality on her and saved her from oblivion, as he did so many of his other contemporaries who catch our attention only because they once held his. Diderot's letters to Mademoiselle Jodin did not, unfortunately, find their way into the *Fonds Vandeul*. Neither the originals nor any copies were in the family's collections. A private collector, Alfred Dupont, at one point owned nineteen, but when he sold his collection, the Bibliothèque Nationale did not purchase them, and they are now dispersed among many purchasers. Fortunately, however, Georges Roth in the twentieth century and Jean Assézat and Maurice Tourneux, Diderot's coeditors in the late nineteenth century, were able to consult the originals and reproduce them.

This correspondence began in 1765 at a time when Diderot was heavily engaged in thinking and writing about the arts, not only the theater, about which he wrote to the young actress, but also music and the visual arts. As it happened, Sophie Volland was absent from Paris for nine long months starting in May 1765, which may have contributed to his concentrated work. Moreover, the final ten volumes of the *Encyclopédie* were completed in 1765, relieving Diderot of the burden he had carried for fifteen years.

Diderot considered himself an expert not only on the theater, but also on painting, sculpture, enamel-working, and other arts. He did not hesitate to advise Falconet how to sculpt, Boucher how to paint, and of course Rousseau and others how to write. He critiqued not only Mademoiselle Jodin's acting but also that of established stars like Mademoiselle Clairon or David Garrick. Since 1759 he had been serving as art critic for the *Correspondance littéraire*, a manuscript newsletter edited by Grimm that circulated to most of the crowned heads of Europe outside France. He had been reviewing the works exhibited in the biennial expositions at the Louvre, at first relying on the guidance of his artist friends, especially Falconet, but by 1765 feeling confident of his own critical judgment. In fact, he wrote proudly to Sophie during her long absence in 1765 that the *Salon* of that year's exposition was "certainly the best thing I have done since I began to cultivate letters" (*Correspondance* 5: 167).

His involvement with the theater was lifelong. He had frequented the theater (and, he suggests to Sophie, also frequented actresses) when first he arrived in Paris as a young man from the provinces. He wrote about the theater in his earliest novel, the erotic *Bijoux indiscrets*, written in 1748, taking his protagonists to a play, imagining them ignorant of theater and therefore observing the scene before them as though the action and the players were real people. By 1765 he considered himself both a playwright (he wrote three plays) and an expert theoretician and critic of playwriting and of acting. He considered Garrick, whom he greatly admired, a personal friend and attributed some of his theories about acting in his best-known theoretical work, *Le Paradoxe sur le comédien*, to Garrick, although the great English actor clearly disagreed with the attribution. David Garrick and his wife had sojourned in Paris in the spring of 1765, and the first letter we have from Diderot to Mademoiselle Jodin is dated from August of that year.

The letters to Mademoiselle Jodin coincide also with Diderot's exchange of letters with Falconet, begun while both men were in Paris and continued when Falconet traveled to Russia in 1766 to create the statue of Peter the Great commissioned by Catherine. This correspondence was in the form of a debate, entitled by the two authors *Le Pour et le contre*, and presented the different conceptions held by the two friends about the artist, his nature, his commitment to his art, his ambition, his morality, his desire or lack of desire to achieve immortality through his art.

The two dominant themes in Diderot's letters to Mademoiselle Jodin are major themes throughout his writings: art and morality, or, more specifically, the artist's profession and the artist's—here the actress's—morality. Diderot's best-known work, *Le Neveu de Rameau*, presents the disturbing case of a wholly immoral but talented individual hungry for artistic achievement and fame. The moderately talented nephew of an indisputably great artist, he is, to his sorrow and frustration, fully aware of his limitations. In Diderot's first letter to Mademoiselle Jodin he writes: "In my opinion, the lowest status is that of a mediocre actress." He also suggests a correlation between her personal self and her performance: "If your own character is petty, your acting will always be petty."[3]

This first letter, from August 1765, consists of fourteen paragraphs. Of these, seven address Mademoiselle Jodin's personal character and behavior. Four address her acting abilities and the actor's profession generally. The remainder of this first letter—the central three paragraphs and also the real occasion for the letter—concerns Mademoiselle Jodin's mother, who has just been robbed by burglars. Since Diderot's aim in informing Mademoiselle Jodin of this misfortune is to stimulate the appropriate filial response, to urge her to send money to her mother, these paragraphs also fit into the category of personal behavior or morality, although they are not necessarily related to her being an actress, only the daughter of a woman in need.

In fact, once he has laid out in two paragraphs the essential facts of the burglary and robbery of Madame Jodin and her need for assistance from her daughter, Diderot takes the opportunity to stress the importance of charity and expounds on how to give and also how difficult it is to receive. He presents himself and Madame Diderot as model givers, generous but delicate at the same time, taking care to offer in such a way that the needy individual, here Madame Jodin, cannot take offense. He reminds Mademoiselle Jodin that he is a *philosophe* and also that he is acting toward her as her father's friend whose esteem she should desire and hope to earn. "Il m'a semblé que mon estime ne vous étoit pas indifférente," he says, and, again, "Je vais vous juger." And he proceeds to lecture her on her reputedly "violent" character, unbecoming to a woman, and on her vanity. His tone, as he generalizes about human frailty and folly, resembles that of La Rochefoucauld's *Maximes* or of La Bruyère's *Caractères*: "Je ne permets le mensonge qu'au sot et au méchant; à celui-ci pour se masquer, à l'autre pour suppléer à l'esprit qui lui manque." In these letters as well as in his best-known novel, *Le Neveu de Rameau*, Diderot demonstrates his direct descent from these seventeenth-century moralists and from Montaigne in the sixteenth century.

The second letter, written two months later, after Mademoiselle Jodin has responded as Diderot would have wished with timely aid for her mother, again focuses on the profession and also the personal behavior of the actor—this time with the two themes so closely intertwined that it is difficult to separate them and would be foolish to attempt it. The relationship here to Diderot's depiction of Rameau's nephew is even more apparent. Diderot would like to believe that moral character and artistic integrity and excellence are related. At the same time he is aware that actors and artists in general are unpredictable, often capricious, if not actively immoral like the nephew. In a letter to Sophie in January 1766, reflecting on the behavior of another actress, Mademoiselle Arnou, he writes:

> Les poètes, les artistes, toute cette famille là est si bizarre, si singulière, si ennemie de toute lisière, que le maître de la maison devroit les y laisser faire, courir, se heurter, se casser le nez, se relever, rire, crier, pleurer, sans s'en apercevoir. Ce sont commes des arbres qu'on trouve sur son chemin; on se blesse le pié contre une racine qui sort de terre; mais il n'y a qu'à frotter le bout de son pié, lever la main et cueillir quelques uns des fruits délicieux qui pendent à l'arbre et qui sont offerts à tous. (*Correspondance* 6: 35)[4]

The same image of the spreading tree occurs in *Le Neveu de Rameau* in a discussion of the great Rameau, the uncle, who was a bad husband, father, and friend but whose music has enriched humanity. The broader theme of the artist and posterity is of course central to the correspondence with Falconet. These are constants in Diderot's preoccupation with art and artists, so it is not surprising that they occur also in the letters to Mademoiselle Jodin.

But in the letters to Mademoiselle Jodin Diderot's concern about her behavior takes a more practical turn. She is a young woman, the daughter of a former colleague. He knows her mother. His concern is for her behavior and for her reputation. He reminds her in almost every paragraph that the reputation of an actress, no matter how careful her behavior, is tarnished if not wholly wicked. Actors and actresses in eighteenth-century France were excommunicated and refused burial in holy ground. Actresses were regarded as little more than prostitutes, albeit glamorous ones, greatly sought after by young men as mistresses but unfit to become wives and mothers.

Curiously, Diderot's advice to Mademoiselle Jodin in this context is to rely on the man who is currently her lover both to guide her personal conduct and to improve her acting skills.[5] We do not know whether Diderot was in fact acquainted with this man—the son of a Danish diplomat and a count—or whether he simply attributed worthy qualities to him as "a sensible and talented man" and "an intrepid man" because he had chosen to become Mademoiselle Jodin's lover and protector. "Listen to him," he advises, "take good care of him, compensate him for the down side of his role by showing him every mark of courtesy and respect."

Here again, a letter to Sophie written in the same month as Diderot's first letter to Mademoiselle Jodin echoes this recommendation, but for a reason that is highly unflattering to womankind, namely, that women tend to parrot their male companion and have no independent ideas of their own.

> Qu'il est essentiel à une femme de s'attacher un homme de sens! Vous n'êtes pour la plupart que ce qu'il nous plaît que vous soyez; et voilà la raison pour laquelle celles qui sont à beaucoup d'hommes ne sont rien. Leur caractère, ainsi que leur ramage, est fait de pièces et de morceaux, et un homme de goût qui s'amuseroit à les étudier restitueroit à chacun ce qui lui appartient. L'idée qui leur vient le matin désigneroit souvent celui avec qui elles ont passé la nuit. (*Correspondance* 5: 90)[6]

While Diderot says plainly to Mademoiselle Jodin that he cannot hold her as an actress to the same moral standards as women not of that profession, nonetheless there is a standard even for actresses. He exhorts her, again in a fatherly tone, to watch her behavior and also the appearances that might occasion any criticism of her behavior. His famous letter to his daughter on the occasion of her marriage in 1772 echoes the same concern with appearances to sustain or mar a woman's good reputation: "On a le droit de juger les femmes sur les apparences, et s'il y a quelques personnes d'une justice assez rigoureuse pour n'en pas user et pour mieux aimer accorder le titre de vertueuse à une libertine que de l'ôter à une femme sage, c'est une grâce qu'ils vous font" (*Correspondance* 12: 123).[7]

Diderot also gives his daughter advice with respect to her husband that resembles his advice to Mademoiselle Jodin with respect to her lover, namely, that she should model her behavior on his and show him every consideration: "Il a du sens et de la raison. . . . Vous ne sauriez montrer trop d'estime pour votre mari." He also advises her, although unlike Mademoiselle Jodin she is an amateur, not a professional, artist, to practice her music and value her skill: "Ne négligez pas votre talent. C'est le seul côté par lequel vous puissiez peut-être vous distinguer sans qu'il vous en coûte aucun sacrifice essentiel." A scant month later a disabused father confides to Grimm how little his son-in-law deserved Angélique's consideration: "Mon ami, j'ai donné ma fille à un personnage moitié grave et moitié freluquet" (*Correspondance* 12: 178).

With respect to her art, he stresses to Mademoiselle Jodin the value of simplicity, of respecting nature (a treacherous concept in the eighteenth century needing redefinition by each writer using it),[8] of understanding the use of gesture—subtle rather than exaggerated gesture—reminding her again that "the greatest sorrows are mute." He had written three years earlier, in an essay paying tribute to the realism of Samuel Richardson, that "a gesture is sometimes as sublime as words." He warns her against mannerisms, flamboyance, the tragic hiccough. Diderot was highly critical of actors who declaimed and whose gestures were exaggerated. He advises Mademoiselle Jodin to "study the accents of passion . . . they are so powerful that I respond to them almost without the help of words. This is the primitive language of nature."

Readers familiar with Diderot's *Paradoxe sur le comédien* will note that some of what he writes to Mademoiselle Jodin runs counter to the theories he later developed in that work. Diderot applauds her for apparently losing herself in her role, for having or appearing to have "a spirit that . . . can be deeply moved, can bridge time and space becoming this or that." In the *Paradoxe* Diderot says the opposite, that the "comédien de nature" is unpredictable, excellent one day, detestable the next, vulnerable to his personal ups and downs, his health, his romantic life, and that the great actor on the contrary should be "un spectateur froid et tranquille," able to move the audience precisely because he or she is unmoved and therefore able to calculate the nuances of his performance and also replicate those nuances at every performance. This is not the place or the time to go further into Diderot's great *Paradoxe*, the subject of commentary by numerous actors and critics and to which the Edition Nationale of Diderot's complete works has devoted an entire volume. My more modest purpose here is simply to introduce the reader to Diderot's letters and to demonstrate that many of Diderot's constants on art, on the artist, and in particular on the theater and the actor's profession and role in society are present even in this limited series of letters to Marie-Magdeleine Jodin, as they are in some of his better-known works.

Finally, I draw the reader's attention to the persona of Diderot himself as he presents it in these letters. He is the *philosophe* par excellence and often uses this term to describe himself, including in these two letters "pour un homme qu'on compte entre les philosophes." The closest translations for *philosophe* are "man of letters," "humanist," or "renaissance man" and not the cognate "philosopher." He is of course the great encyclopedist compiling and also writing articles that attempt to span all the branches of learning. In the 1750 prospectus to that enterprise, Diderot once again uses the image of a tree, this time to illustrate the interrelationship of the arts and sciences. He is the moralist, the *MOI* who plays straight man to the tortured but amusing nephew of Rameau. He is a sober father figure who claims the right to offer advice to Mademoiselle Jodin through "my age, my experience, the friendship I had with your father, and the interest I have always had in you." Diderot's general correspondence provides countless examples of incidents in which he intervened with advice and sometimes— as is also the case with Mademoiselle Jodin's unfortunate mother—with tangible assistance for friends and even for friends of friends. This was a man who had to feel used, useful, generous, and who obviously believed that this gave him license to dispense advice and criticism without giving offense. An extraordinary example concerns a young, presumably penniless writer named Glénat, whom he supplied with work copying manuscripts and who, in fact, turned out to have been working against Diderot as a spy in the employ of the censor during the full four years that Diderot had been his benefactor (*Correspondance* 4: 157).

While Diderot concludes his first letter to Mademoiselle Jodin apologetically, "Please forgive a friend these sobering reflections," he has abandoned all tentativeness by the second letter and challenges the young woman to satisfy him and justify his interest. Still, he claims to be a benevolent mentor, "not hard to please," and concludes this letter by saying that his severity and his interest are in direct relationship and that "if in future I were to lose interest in you, I would no longer take the liberty of speaking so severely." This persona of the friend, sage, and counselor to persons in trouble was clearly very congenial to Diderot. In his letters to Mademoiselle Jodin as in all his letters, Denis Diderot comes across to us, the third-party readers listening in two centuries later, as warmhearted, generous, impulsive, effusive, a marvelous conversationalist and storyteller, a man who by his own avowal lacks the dispassionate nature he believes appropriate to the genius or great artist in any field.

Art, morality, the relationship between the two in the work of art and in the artist's character, family and family obligations, friendship and the obligations that carries, love and lovers, the advantages for a young woman of having a protector and the obligations that imposes on her as on him— all of these themes are present here. Through the narrow framework of these two first letters to a young actress whom Diderot knew only slightly and who was performing on a stage in Warsaw where he could not see her act, I hope to have provided readers unfamiliar with Denis Diderot with an entrée to his complete correspondence and to have sparked the desire in them to become better acquainted with this extraordinary man.

The letter form was obviously very congenial to Diderot as a way of expressing his ideas on any given subject, including such controversial ones as religion, sexuality, morality, and evolution. In addition to the genuinely personal letters written by Diderot, a number of his other works carry *letter* in the title, most notably the *Lettre sur les Aveugles* and the *Lettres sur les Sourds et Muets*. Others, including the lengthy pieces of art criticism known as the *Salons* are cast in the form of letters to his friend Melchior Grimm. In addition, some of his short stories and one of his novels are partly epistolary. *La Religieuse*, cast as memoirs by a young nun, is preceded by a set of letters, half genuine, half composed by Diderot, who had engaged a friend in what the latter took to be a real correspondence, not knowing that the young woman with whom he was corresponding was in fact the creature of Diderot's fertile imagination.

Letters, then, for Diderot, are not only the best way to make the acquaintance of the man but also an excellent medium through which to approach his entire opus.

NOTES

1. Jane Dieckmann told the story in 1984 at a Parisian *table ronde* of Diderot's editors in honor of the bicentennial of Diderot's death.

2. Jean Jodin, born in 1713, the same year as Diderot, in Geneva after his Protestant father took refuge there, moved back to France in 1733. His daughter was born in Paris in 1741. A skilled watchmaker, he contributed to the *Encyclopédie* and published several scientific papers including *Les Echappemens à repos comparés aux échappemens à recul* (Paris, 1754). He died in 1761, four years before the first letter we have from Diderot to Mlle Jodin.

3. The fear of mediocrity that haunts Rameau's nephew and also Diderot's concern with immoral behavior and with personal reputation are already present in his discussion about acting in his *Second Entretiens* following his play, *Le Fils naturel*, in 1757: "Il n'y a que la médiocrité qui donne du dégoût au théâtre; et, dans quelque état que ce soit, que les mauvaises moeurs qui déshonorent."

4. "Poets, artists, all that breed, are so bizarre, so odd, so opposed to any restraint, that the master of the house should let them behave, run about, knock into each other, break their noses, get up again, laugh, shout, weep, without taking

any notice of them. They are like some trees that cross your path; you can stumble and hurt your foot on a root that grows up out of the ground, but there is nothing to do except rub your foot and then raise your hand to pluck some of the delicious fruits hanging from the tree for all to enjoy."

5. Mlle Jodin's protector was Count Werner von Schulenburg, either the son or the nephew of the Danish general Jean-Mathias von Schulenburg, according to Roth's notes on this letter, based upon a thesis written in Poland in 1951 by Karyna Wierzbicka and dealing with the history of theater in Warsaw.

6. "How essential it is for a woman to attract a man of good sense! Most of you [women] are nothing but what we want you to be, and that's why women who belong to many men have no identity. Their character, like their chatter, is composed of bits and pieces, and a man with taste and perception who amused himself by studying them could attribute to each man the piece that came from him. Their first idea in the morning would often allow you to identify the man with whom they spent the night."

7. "A woman can legitimately be judged by appearances, and if you find people so rigorously fair as not to do so and to prefer rather to accord the title of virtuous to a woman who does not deserve it than deny it to a woman who does, then this is a favor that they are giving you."

8. For this idea see the monumental thesis by Ehrard.

WORKS CITED

Diderot, Denis. *Correspondance*. Ed. Georges Roth and Jean Varloot. 16 vols. Paris: Minuit, 1955–70.

————. *Oeuvres complètes*. Ed. Herbert Dieckmann and Jean Varloot. 33 vols. to date. Paris: Hermann, 1975–.

Dieckmann, Herbert. *Cinq Leçons sur Diderot*. Publications romanes et françaises 64. Geneva: Droz, 1959.

————. *Inventaire du fonds Vandeul, et inédits de Diderot*. Geneva: Droz, 1951.

Ehrard, Jean. *L'Idée de Nature en France dans la première moitié du XVIIIe siècle*. 2 vols. Paris: SEVPEN, 1963.

France, Peter, trans. *Diderot's Letters to Sophie Volland: A Selection*. London: Oxford UP, 1972.

Krakeur, Lester G. *La Correspondance de Diderot, son intérêt documentaire, psychologique et littéraire*. New York: Kingsley, 1939.

Prose and Power in Two Letters by Jane Austen

Susan C. Whealler

Jane Austen to Cassandra Austen, November 3, 1813

Godmersham Park Wednesday Novr 3^d.

MY DEAREST CASSANDRA

I will keep this celebrated Birthday by writing to you, & as my pen seems inclined to write large I will put my lines very close together.—I had but just time to enjoy your Letter yesterday before Edward & I set off in the Chair for Cant^y—& I allowed him to hear the cheif of it as we went along. We rejoice sincerely in Henry's gaining ground as he does, & hope there will be weather for him to get out every day this week, as the likeliest way of making him equal to what he plans for the next.—If he is tolerably well, the going into Oxfordshire will make him better, by making him happier.—Can it be, that I have not given you the minutiae of Edward's plans?—See here they are—To go to Wrotham on Saturday ye 13th, spend Sunday there, & be in Town on Monday to dinner, & if agreable to Henry, spend one whole day with him—which day is likely to be Tuesday, & so go down to Chawton on Wednesday.—But now, I cannot be quite easy without staying a little while with Henry, unless he wishes it otherwise;— his illness & the dull time of year together make me feel that it would be horrible of me not to offer to remain with him—& therefore, unless you know of any objection, I wish you would tell him with my best Love that

Jane Austen to Cassandra Austen, Nov. 3, 1813, from Austen, *Letters*, no. 90; Jane Austen to Cassandra Austen, Nov. 6, 1813, from Austen, *Letters*, no. 91.

I shall be most happy to spend 10 days or a fortnight in Henrietta S^r—if he will accept me. I do not offer more than a fortnight because I shall then have been some time from home, but it will be a great pleasure to be with him, as it always is.—I have the less regret & scruple on your account, because I shall see you for a day and a half, & because you will have Edward for at least a week.—My scheme is to take Bookham in my way home for a few days & my hope that Henry will be so good as to send me some part of the way thither. I have a most kind repetition of Mrs. Cooke's two or three dozen Invitations, with the offer of meeting me anywhere in one of her airings.—Fanny's cold is much better. By dosing & keeping her room on Sunday, she got rid of the worst of it, but I am rather afraid of what this day may do for her; she is gone to Cant^y with Miss Clewes, Liz. & Ma. and it is but roughish weather for any one in a tender state.—Miss Clewes has been going to Cant^y ever since her return, & it is now just accomplishing. Edward & I had a delightful morn^g for our Drive *there,* I enjoyed it thoroughly, but the Day turned off before we were ready, & we came home in some rain & the apprehension of a great deal. It has not done us any harm however.—He went to inspect the Gaol, as a visiting Magistrate, & took me with him.—I was gratified—& went through all the feelings which People must go through—I think in visiting such a Building.—We paid no other visits—only walked about snugly together & shopp'd.—I bought a Concert Ticket & a sprig of flowers for my old age.—To vary the subject from Gay to Grave with inimitable address I shall now tell you something of the Bath party—& still a Bath party they are, for a fit of the Gout came on last week.—The accounts of Lady B. are as good as can be under such a circumstance, Dr. P.—says it appears a good sort of Gout, & her spirits are better than usual, but as to her coming away, it is of course all uncertainty.—I have very little doubt of Edward's going down to Bath, if they have not left it when he is in Hampshire; if he does, he will go on from Steventon, & then return direct to London, without coming back to Chawton.—This detention does not suit his feelings.—It may be rather a good thing however that Dr. P. should see Lady B. with the Gout on her. Harriot was quite wishing for it.—The day seems to improve. I wish my pen would too.—Sweet Mr. Ogle. I dare say he sees all the Panoramas for nothing, has free-admittance everywhere; he is so delightful!—Now, you need not see anybody else.—I am glad to hear of our being likely to have a peep at Charles & Fanny at Christmas, but do not force poor Cass. to stay if she hates it.—You have done very right as to Mrs. F.A.—Your tidings of S & S. give me pleasure. I have never seen it advertised.—Harriot, in a Letter to Fanny today, enquires whether they sell Cloths for Pelisses at Bedford House—& if they do, will be very much obliged to you to desire them to send her down Patterns, with the Width & Prices—they may go from Charing Cross almost any day in the week—but if it is a *ready money* house it will not do, for the Bru of feu the Archbishop says she cannot pay for it immediately.—Fanny & I suspect they do not deal in the Article.— The Sherers I beleive are now really going to go, Joseph has had a Bed here the two last nights & I do not know whether this is not the day of moving. Mrs. Sherer called yesterday to take leave. The weather looks worse again.—We dine at Chilham Castle tomorrow, & I expect to find some amusement; but more from the Concert the next day, as I am sure of seeing several that I want to see. We are to meet a party from Goodnestone, Lady B. Miss Hawley & Lucy Foote—& I am to meet Mrs. Harrison, & we are to talk about Ben & Anna. 'My dear Mrs. Harrison, I shall say, I am afraid the young Man has some of your Family Madness—& though there often appears to be something of Madness in Anna too, I think she inherits more of it from her Mother's family than from ours.'—That is what I shall say—& I think she will find it difficult to answer me.—I took up your letter again to Refresh me, being somewhat tired; & was struck with the prettiness of the hand; it is really a very pretty hand now & then—so small & so neat!—I wish I could get as much into a sheet of paper.—Another time I will take two days to make a Letter in; it is fatiguing to write a whole long one at once. I hope to hear from you again on Sunday & again on friday, the day before we move.—On Monday I suppose you will be going to Streatham, to see quiet Mr. Hill & eat very bad Baker's bread.—A fall in Bread by the bye. I hope my Mother's Bill next week will shew it. I have had a very comfortable Letter from her, one of her foolscap sheets quite full of little home news.—Anna was there the first of the two Days—. An Anna sent away & an Anna fetched are different things.—This will be an excellent time for Ben to pay his visit—now that we, the formidables, are absent. I did not mean to eat, but Mr. Johncock has brought in the Tray, so I must.—I am all alone. Edward is gone into his Woods.—At this present time I have five Tables, Eight & twenty Chairs & two fires all to myself.—Miss Clewes is to be invited to go to the Concert with us, there will be my Brother's place & ticket for her, as he cannot go. He & the other connections of the Cages are to meet at Milgate that very day, to consult about a proposed alteration of the Maidstone road, in which the Cages are very much interested. Sir Brook comes here in the morn^g, & they are to be joined by Mr. Deedes at Ashford.—The loss of the Concert will be no great evil to the Squire.—We shall be a party of three ladies therefore—& to meet three Ladies.—What a convenient Carriage Henry's is, to his friends in general!—Who has it next?—I am glad William's going is voluntary, & on no worse grounds. An inclination for the Country is a venial fault.—He has more of Cowper than of Johnson in him, fonder of Tame Hares & Blank verse than of the full tide of human Existence at Charing Cross.—Oh! I have more of such sweet flattery from Miss Sharp!—She is an excellent kind friend. I am read & admired in Ireland too.—There is a Mrs. Fletcher, the wife of a Judge, an old Lady & very good & very clever, who is all curiosity to know about me—what I am like & so forth—. I am not known to her by *name* however. This comes through Mrs. Carrick, not through Mrs. Gore—You are quite out there.—I do not despair of having my picture in the Exhibition at last—all white & red, with my Head on one Side;—or perhaps I may marry young Mr. D'arblay.—I suppose in the meantime I shall owe dear Henry a great deal of Money for Printing &c.—I hope Mrs. Fletcher will indulge herself with S & S.—If I *am* to stay in H. S^t & if you should be writing home soon I wish you w^d be so good as to give a hint of it—for I am not likely to write there again these 10 days, having written yesterday.

Fanny has set her heart upon it's being a Mr. Brett who is going to marry a Miss Dora Best of this Country. I dare say Henry has no objection. Pray, where did the Boys sleep?—

The Deedes' come here on Monday to stay till friday—so that we shall end with a flourish the last Canto.—They bring Isabella & one of the Grown ups—& will come in for a Cant^y Ball on Thursday. I shall be glad to see them.—Mrs. Deedes & I must talk rationally together I suppose.

Edward does not write to Henry, because of my writing so often. God bless you. I shall be so glad to see you again, & I wish you many happy returns of this Day.—Poor Lord Howard! How he does cry about it!—

Y^{rs} very truly

J.A.

Jane Austen to Cassandra Austen, November 6, 1813

Saturday Novr 6—Godmersham Park

MY DEAREST CASSANDRA

Having half an hour before breakfast—(very snug, in my own room, lovely morn^g, excellent fire, fancy me) I will give you some account of the last two days. And yet, what is there to be told? I shall get foolishly minute unless I cut the matter short.—We met only the Brittons at Chilham Castle, besides a Mr. & Mrs. Osborne & a Miss Lee staying in the House, & were only 14 altogether. My B^r & Fanny thought it the pleasantest party they had ever known there & I was very well entertained by bits & scraps.—I had long wanted to see Dr. Britton, & his wife amuses me very much with her affected refinement & elegance.—Miss Lee I found very conversible; she admires Crabbe as she ought.—She is at an age of reason, ten years older than myself at least. She was at the famous Ball at Chilham Castle, so of course you remember her.—By the bye, as I must leave off being young, I find many Douceurs in being a sort of Chaperone for I am put on the Sofa near the Fire & can drink as much wine as I like. We had Music in the Even^g, Fanny & Miss Wildman played, & Mr. James Wildman sat close by & listened, or pretended to listen.—Yesterday was a day of dissipation all through, first came Sir Brook to dissipate us before breakfast—then there was a call from Mr. Sherer, then a regular morn^g visit from Lady Honeywood in her way home from Eastwell—then Sir Brook & Edward set off—then we dined (5 in number) at ½ past 4—then we had coffee, & at 6 Miss Clewes, Fanny & I draved away. We had a beautiful night for our frisks.—We were earlier than we need have been, but after a time Lady B. & her two companions appeared, we had kept places for them & there we sat, all six in a row, under a side wall, I between Lucy Foote & Miss Clewes.—Lady B. was much what I expected, I could not determine whether she was rather handsome or very plain.—I liked her, for being in a hurry to have the Concert over & get away, & for getting away at last with a great deal of decision & promtness, not waiting to compliment & dawdle & fuss about seeing *dear Fanny,* who was half the even^g in another part of the room with her friends the Plumptres. I am growing too minute, so I will go to Breakfast.

When the Concert was over, Mrs. Harrison & I found each other out & had a very comfortable little complimentary friendly chat. She is a sweet

Woman, still quite a sweet Woman in herself, & so like her Sister!—I could almost have thought I was speaking to Mrs. Lefroy.—She introduced me to her Daughter, whom I think pretty, but most dutifully inferior to la Mere Beauté. The Faggs & the Hammonds were there, Wm Hammond the only young Man of renown. *Miss* looked very handsome, but I prefer her little, smiling, flirting Sister Julia.—I was just introduced at last to Mary Plumptre, but should hardly know her again. She was delighted with *me* however, good enthusiastic Soul!—And Lady B. found me handsomer than she expected, so you see I am not so very bad as you might think for.— It was 12 before we reached home. We were all dog-tired, but pretty well to-day, Miss Clewes says she has not caught cold, & Fanny's does not seem worse. I was so tired that I began to wonder how I should get through the Ball next Thursday, but there will be so much more variety then in walking about, & probably so much less heat that perhaps I may not feel it more. My China Crape is still kept for the Ball. Enough of the Concert.— I had a Letter from Mary Yesterday. They travelled down to Cheltenham last Monday very safely & are certainly to be there a month. Bath is still Bath. The H. Bridges' must quit them early next week, & Louisa seems not quite to despair of their all moving together, but to those who see at a distance there appears no chance of it.—Dr. Parry does not want to keep Lady B. at Bath when she can once move. That is lucky.—You will see poor Mr. Evelyn's death. Since I wrote last, my 2^d Edit. has stared me in the face.—Mary tells me that Eliza means to buy it. I wish she may. It can hardly depend upon any more Fyfield Estates.—I cannot help hoping that *many* will feel themselves obliged to buy it. I shall not mind imagining it a disagreable Duty to them, so as they do it. Mary heard before she left home, that it was very much admired at Cheltenham, & that it was given to Miss Hamilton. It is pleasant to have such a respectable Writer named. I cannot tire *you* I am sure on this subject, or I would apologise.—What weather! & what news!—We have enough to do to admire them both.—I hope you derive your full share of enjoyment from each.

I have extended my Lights and increased my acquaintance a good deal within these two days. Lady Honeywood, you know;—I did not sit near enough to be a perfect Judge, but I thought her extremely pretty & her manners have all the recommendations of ease & goodhumour & unaffect-edness;—& going about with 4 Horses, & nicely dressed herself—she is altogether a perfect sort of Woman.—Oh! & I saw Mr. Gipps last night— the useful Mr. Gipps, whose attentions came in as acceptably to us in hand-ing us to the Carriage, for want of a better Man, as they did to Emma Plumptre.—I thought him rather a goodlooking little Man.—I long for your Letter tomorrow, particularly that I may know my fate as to London. My first wish is that Henry sh^d really chuse what he likes best; I shall certainly not be sorry if he does not want me.—Morning church tomorrow.— I shall come back with impatient feelings. The Sherers are gone, but the Pagets are not come, we shall therefore have Mr. S. again. Mr. Paget acts like an unsteady Man. Dr. Mant however gives him a very good Character; what is wrong is to be imputed to the Lady.—I dare say the House likes Female Government.—I have a nice long Black & red Letter from Charles, but not communicating much that I did not know. There is some chance of a good Ball next week, as far as Females go. Lady Bridges may perhaps be there with some Knatchbulls.—Mrs. Harrison perhaps with Miss Oxenden & the Miss Papillons—& if Mrs. Harrison, then Lady Fagg will come. The shades of Evening are descending & I resume my interesting Narrative. Sir Brook & my Brother came back about 4, & Sir Brook almost immediately set forward again for Goodnestone.—We are to have Edwd B. tomorrow, to pay us another Sunday's visit—the last, for more reasons than one; they all come home on the same day that we go.—The Deedes' do not come till Tuesday. Sophia is to be the Comer. She is a disputable Beauty that I want much to see. Lady Eliz. Hatton & Annamaria called here this morn^g;—Yes, they called,—but I do not think I can say anything more about them. They came & they sat & they went.—*Sunday*—Dearest Henry! What a turn he has for being ill! & what a thing Bile is!—This attack has probably been brought on in part by his previous confinement & anxiety;—but however it came, I hope it is going fast, & that you will be able to send a very good account of him on Tuesday.—As I hear on Wednesday, of course I shall not expect to hear again on friday. Perhaps a Letter to Wrotham would not have an ill effect. We are to be off on Saturday before the Post comes in, as Edward takes his own Horses all the way. He talks of 9 o'clock. We shall bait at Lenham. Excellent sweetness of you to send me such a nice long Letter;—it made its appearance, with one from my Mother, soon after I & my impatient feelings walked in.—How glad I am that I did what I did!—I was only afraid that *you* might think the offer superfluous, but you have set my heart at ease.—Tell Henry that I *will* stay with him, let it be ever so disagreable to him. Oh! dear me!—I have not time or paper for half that I want to say.—There have been two Letters from Oxford, one from George yesterday. They got there very safely,

Edwd two hours behind the Coach, having lost his way in leaving London.
George writes cheerfully & quietly—hopes to have Utterson's rooms soon,
went to Lecture on wednesday, states some of his expences, and concludes
with saying, 'I am afraid I shall be poor.'—I am glad he thinks about it so
soon.—I beleive there is no private Tutor yet chosen, but my Brother is
to hear from Edwd on the subject shortly.—You, & Mrs. H. & Catherine
& Alethea going about together in Henry's carriage seeing sights!—I am
not used to the idea of it yet. All that you are to see of Streatham, seen
already!—Your Streatham & my Bookham may go hang.—The prospect
of being taken down to Chawton by Henry, perfects the plan to me.—
I was in hopes of your seeing some illuminations, & you *have* seen them.
'I thought you would came, and you *did* came.' I am sorry *he* is not to
came from the Baltic sooner.—Poor Mary!—My Brother has a Letter from
Louisa today, of an unwelcome nature;—they are to spend the winter at
Bath.—It was just decided on.—Dr. Parry wished it,—not from thinking
the Water necessary to Lady B.—but that he might be better able to judge
how far his Treatment of her, which is totally different from anything she
had been used to—is right; & I suppose he will not mind having a few more
of her Ladyship's guineas.—His system is a Lowering one. He took twelve
ounces of Blood from her when the Gout appeared, & forbids wine &c.—
Hitherto, the plan agrees with her.—*She* is very well satisfied to stay, but
it is a sore disappointment to Louisa & Fanny.—

The H. Bridges leave them on Tuesday, & they mean to move into a
smaller House. You may guess how Edward feels.—There can be no doubt
of his going to Bath now;—I should not wonder if he brought Fanny Cage
back with him.—You shall hear from me once more, some day or other.

Yours very affec:^ly   J.A.

We do not like Mr. Hampson's scheme.

The Critical Discussion of Jane Austen's Letters

In *Northanger Abbey* Henry Tilney explains to Catherine Morland that "the
usual style of letter-writing among women is faultless, except in three particulars," which he identifies as "a general deficiency of subject, a total
inattention to stops, and a very frequent ignorance of grammar" (27). In

this critique of women's letters Austen seems to have anticipated the way in which her own personal letters would be received. While no one has attacked her heavy reliance on dashes or her repeated misspellings, criticism of her subject matter, with very few exceptions, has been consistently severe.[1]

In 1867 Jane Austen's niece Caroline Austen expressed what might at best be described as indifference toward her aunt's correspondence: "There is nothing in those letters which *I* have seen that would be acceptable to the public—They were very well expressed, and they must have been very interesting to those who received them—but they detailed chiefly home and family events: and she seldom committed herself *even* to an opinion—so that to strangers they could be *no* transcript of her mind—they would not feel that they knew her any the better for having read them—" (cited in Modert xxv).

In the twentieth century, criticism of Austen's letters flourished with R. W. Chapman's publication of the complete collection. In *Essays by Divers Hands*, H. W. Garrod described Austen's letters as "a desert of trivialities punctuated by occasional oases of clever malice" (cited in Austen, *Letters* xlii). A review in the *Times Literary Supplement* of R. W. Chapman's edition, while praising Chapman's scholarly work, echoed Garrod's evaluation, proclaiming that "triviality varied by touches of ill breeding and of sententiousness, characterizes these letters as a whole." The reviewer, later identified as E. M. Forster, concluded that because they were "temporary" and "local," the letters are valuable only as a family record (822).

Even Chapman admitted in *Jane Austen: Facts and Problems* that those who have enjoyed Austen's novels "opened the letters with high hopes of entertainment, only to find them made up of family news, mostly commonplace and largely meaningless." He urges the reader to put "himself" in the role of Cassandra Austen. "Then it all becomes interesting enough to be read with attention; and as we attend, we are rewarded by the turn of a phrase; we catch an inflection, or share an emotion." If the reader is not amused, "he shall remember that he had no right to expect family gossip to be very amusing" (104).

Added recently to the discussion of Austen's extant letters is the debate over the nature of letters that may no longer exist, if in fact they ever did. Austenian lore tells us that Cassandra Austen destroyed—by burning completely or clipping lines from—many of her sister's letters in an effort to protect the author's reputation and the family's privacy. Support for this belief comes from Mary Augusta Austen-Leigh, who stated in *Personal Aspects of Jane Austen* that Cassandra Austen "kept *only* those [letters] which she considered so totally devoid of general interest that it was impossible anyone should, at any time, contemplate their publication" (cited in Modert xxvi). Several suggestions have been made about the nature of what may have been destroyed. R. W. Chapman and others have assumed that Cassandra burned letters concerning the two sisters' love lives. Janet Todd also comments on the sisterly censoring that "shielded" Austen from public knowledge of her personal life and her thoughts: "The little that is left, the harmless residue, gives nothing much away" (396). Feminist critics have often used the report of destroyed letters to help position Austen in the feminist controversy of the end of the eighteenth century. For instance, Margaret Kirkham argues that Cassandra Austen "subjected [the letters] to a good deal of censorship" that "may well have been designed to expunge from the record evidence of her sister's interest in matters of a more public nature" (*Jane Austen* 61).[2]

Recently, Jo Modert, in the introduction to her facsimile edition of Austen's letters, has argued that Cassandra Austen, in fact, did not destroy her sister's letters; rather, she saved them and eventually divided them among friends and family members before her own death. Losses may have occurred after the dispersal, but Cassandra could not be blamed for that (see esp. xx–xxii). For over one hundred years Austen scholars have pilloried Cassandra Austen for censoring her sister's letters and have lamented the loss of "the greater portion" of those letters. And for at least the past fifty years critics have debated the nature of letters that may not exist. The question is why, especially when the extant letters have drawn so much attack. The answer to this question resides both in the reasons we read letters of well-known literary figures and in the nature of Jane Austen's letters. Studies in epistolarity and autobiography say that we turn to the private letters of a literary figure to find biographical information about his or her life, opinions, mind, emotions, and psyche. We look for material that will inform the literature. We look for details of the figure's quality of life and manner of living. We look for a reaffirmation of what we already believe to be true about that person.[3] We look for a "portrait" of the figure. In a letter from one of Jane Austen's nieces, Louisa Knight, to another, Fanny Knight, is the following expression of this desire to know more about Austen—her looks and her life—and of the confidence that even one letter could reveal it: "Lady Campbell is . . . a most ardent admirer and enthusiasic lover of

Aunt Jane's works. . . . When she heard that I was her niece she was in extasies. 'My dear, is it possible, are you Jane Austen's niece? that I should never have known that before!—come and tell me about her—do you remember her? was she pretty? wasn't she pretty? Oh, if I could have seen her. . . . Oh! write and ask [Fanny] if she can only send me *one* of her own real letters, and tell me any and every particular she may know about her life, self, everything, I should be so delighted!' " (cited in Modert xxiii).

For many critics not even the 156 letters R. W. Chapman published have provided a satisfactory portrait of Jane Austen. They do not reveal "every particular . . . about her life, self, everything," nor do they discuss the novels at length, and so critics enumerate their deficiencies. Like Cassandra's sketch of Jane Austen, her only authentic portrait, which has frustrated so many viewers, the letters disappoint those who turn to them for a definitive "life" or for narrative theory.[4] Unlike other literary figures who wrote letters with an eye toward their being collected, circulated, and published, Jane Austen wrote her letters for a very restricted audience, and as a result they have a decidedly domestic and private, although not personal, nature. They are full of references to and descriptions of people we cannot—and largely do not want to—identify today. There are jokes and allusions that family members may have enjoyed but that we pass over without recognition. There are multitudes of everyday details: the cost of fabric and food, menus and attendance at parties, changes in fashion, health complaints of family and friends, problems with domestic help, gardening, home repair. This "desert" of family gossip is simply not what some readers are seeking and not what they expect from a novelist of Austen's reputation and ability. In the criticism of the letters, disappointed expectations are clear. Sounding like Henry Tilney in his lecture to Catherine Morland, Forster remarks, "She has not enough subject-matter on which to exercise her powers. . . . She takes no account of politics or religion, and none of the war except when it brings prize-money to her brothers" (822). Austen's nephew James Edward Austen-Leigh warned readers not to "expect too much from" Austen's letters. While their style may be pleasant, "the materials may be thought inferior to the execution, for they treat only the details of domestic life. There is in them no notice of politics or public events; scarcely any discussions of literature, or other subjects of general interest" (57).

Like the collection itself, which is faulted for what it does not contain, the subjects of the letters are faulted for not being something different, something other than domestic, something "of more general interest." And yet, studies of letters and of women's writing tell us that women's letters are often private and domestic, that they serve the function of gossip, and that they dignify the details of everyday life by rendering that life with minute particularities (Spacks, *Gossip* 69–78). To criticize Austen's letters for not satisfying "general interest" with discussions of war, politics, and literature is to deny what they do discuss. To say that she lacked subject matter is simply to ignore the subject matter she did choose. And to refer to the letters' gossip as a "desert" is to fail to acknowledge the purpose of Austen's gossip. Far from being trivial and meaningless, Jane Austen's letters compose a significant narrative of power, both public and private.[5] Power is public when it allows one to control others and to control one's own public life in society; it is private when it governs one's interior life, the way one responds emotionally and intellectually to society. Through Austen's treatment of her most frequent subjects—travel and money—she conveys her understanding of the location and application of public power in her society. The letters themselves and the act of writing them—the act of narrating her life through an epistolary self (or selves) to an absent imagined audience—are simultaneously a subversion of that public power and a demonstration of her private power. That her audience is almost always her most intimate friend and sister, Cassandra, a woman who shared her experiences and her position in the larger public world as well as the private world of their family, intensifies the subversive nature of Austen's letters.

In the past two decades a great number of studies have described the position of women in the eighteenth and nineteenth centuries, and many have examined the ways in which society affected Jane Austen as a novelist.[6] Very few have analyzed the effects of society on Jane Austen as a letter writer.[7] While many of the facts of Austen's letters, their composition, and their audiences are known, the subjects of these letters and what those subjects reveal about Austen and her society have not yet been explored thoroughly. The two letters at the beginning of this essay, written three days apart in November 1813, exhibit typical treatment of Austen's most common subjects and indicate her attitudes toward them. Her choice of subjects, her thematic treatment of them, and her attitudes reveal her sensitivity to the degree to which public power controlled her. Finally, the letters demonstrate the various ways in which Austen typically exerted her own private power in letter writing.

Themes, Subjects, and Concerns of the Two Letters

Many subjects recur in Austen's letters: travel, family, health, money, and fashion are just a few. Some of these topics, such as family and travel, appear in virtually every letter because they are the motivation for the letters. Because Austen is temporarily separated from one or more members of her family, she writes to maintain contact and to share news. In the two letters written in November 1813, Austen has traveled to visit her brother Edward at his home in Godmersham Park while her sister Cassandra has traveled to the home of their brother Henry in London. To keep her sister, as well as Henry, up to date on the health and activities of the Godmersham party, Austen writes. Thus, travel causes the letters to be written. Austen's treatment of travel as a subject for comment and observation, however, reveals her understanding of public power and her response to it.

The same is true of one other common subject, money. A frequent topic of gossip, it provided amusing material for letters that were usually read aloud: "Legacies are very wholesome diet" (*Letters*, no. 50). Discussions of money, however, are also inseparable from discussions of public power. In a society such as Austen's, where money was passed from generation to generation through males, where it could not be easily earned by females, and where it was tied so strongly to class, it was imbued with additional power. Related to the subject of money, for Austen, were other common topics such as health and fashion, but money and travel are the topics that provide the most telling evidence of Austen's insights into the governing, public powers of her society, both her society at large and the smaller society of her family.[8]

In Jane Austen's letters of November 3 and 6, 1813, we see a striking example of her treatment of the power of travel, specifically the ability to determine one's own location as well as the location of others. Spanning the two letters is the question of whether Austen should go to visit her brother Henry once Cassandra leaves him. As these letters and all other letters by Austen make clear, the decision of whether to travel was never based on her desires. Instead, it was based on the needs and convenience of some other person, almost without fail a male family member. On November 3 she writes Cassandra, "But now, I cannot be quite easy without staying a little while with Henry, unless he wishes it otherwise;—his illness & the dull time of year together make me feel that it would be horrible of me

not to offer to remain with him." Comparing the tone of this passage with
that which follows—"I wish you would tell him with my best Love that I
shall be most happy to spend 10 days or a fortnight in Henrietta S^t—if he
will accept me"—it is obvious that the former was intended for Cassandra's
eyes only and that the latter was written to be read aloud to Henry. It is
clear too from the comparison that Austen's travel depended on Henry's,
or some other brother's, wanting her and on her feeling of obligation to
give him what he wanted. This is not to imply that Austen did not love
her brothers. On the contrary, the Austen family seems to have been a very
close one, and her fondness for her brothers, especially Henry, is apparent
in her letters. When Austen writes that "it will be a great pleasure to be
with [Henry], as it always is," her sincerity is not to be doubted, but at
the same time her letters convey her understanding that her brother commanded all the power of mobility, the power to summon or reject. The
location of power is made clear again in the following letter when Austen
writes Cassandra, "I long for your Letter tomorrow, particularly that I may
know my fate as to London. My first wish is that Henry sh^d really chuse
what he likes best; I shall certainly not be sorry if he does not want me."
The question is finally settled when Cassandra's letter arrives from London,
and Austen responds, "Tell Henry that I *will* stay with him, let it be ever
so disagreable to him." Again, the two passages seem to be written for
different audiences, the first for Cassandra, who shared her sister's "fate"
of traveling when a brother required her or supplied the opportunity, and
the second for Henry, who, with the other brothers, controlled their travel
and, therefore, their physical location.

Austen's choice of the word *fate* is particularly telling, for travel was
something that happened to her rather than something that she controlled.
Like so many of her own and other fictional heroines, Austen appears physically passive, having no power to determine her own location.[9] In fact, she
so completely lacks power that on November 3 she describes her own travel
arrangements as "Edward's plans." For all the "minutiae" she provides, she
neglects to mention that she will be traveling with Edward, which only
becomes obvious when she says that although Edward plans to "spend one
whole day" with Henry, she will not feel right "without staying a little
while" in London. Edward also carries her along on a trip to Canterbury:
"He went to inspect the Gaol, as a visiting Magistrate, & took me with
him.—I was gratified." Her expression of gratitude may be interpreted as
ironic, or it may be read seriously, that she was grateful for the experience

or the drive, but we should not miss the point that Austen makes clear with her wording: Edward *took* her, exercising all the power.

Austen was quite aware of her position and her dependence on her brothers. Like Fanny Price in *Mansfield Park* who is sent to Portsmouth and cannot return to Mansfield Park until she is needed and sent for, Austen was without power over her movement, and therefore, she was denied a choice of location. Her very place in the world was determined by men, as her letters show repeatedly. For example, on September 18, 1796, she writes Cassandra about the "Doubt & Deliberation" she has faced in trying to visit her friends the Pearsons. "Edward has been so good as to promise to take me to Greenwich," and "my Father will be so good as to fetch home his prodigal Daughter from Town, I hope, unless he wishes me to walk the Hospitals, Enter at the Temple, or mount Guard at St. James." To Cassandra, who shares her restrictions, Austen comments on the inevitability of her dependence on her brother and father for travel arrangements by suggesting three ridiculous alternatives. She also mocks the reasons for this dependence: "For if the Pearsons were not at home, I should inevitably fall a Sacrifice to the arts of some fat Woman who would make me drunk with Small Beer," a scene reminiscent of Hogarth's and Defoe's fictional worlds, but not Austen's (*Letters*, no. 7).

The Austen's move to Bath in 1801 is always discussed at length in Jane Austen's biographies, for it was the first time, at the age of twenty-five, she lived anywhere other than Steventon. Family history tells us that when Austen heard that they were to move, she fainted. Whether the story is true or not, there is no question that her father's decision to relocate the family was a shock and a hardship to her. She writes to Cassandra, "I get more & more reconciled to the idea of our removal. We have lived long enough in this Neighbourhood, the Basingstoke balls are certainly on the decline. . . . It must not be generally known however that I am not sacrificing a great deal in quitting the Country" (*Letters*, no. 29). Her desire to appear "reconciled" may have been an attempt to talk both herself and Cassandra into accepting their fate, but in later letters, it is clear that this relocation, which was imposed on her, never suited her. Upon arriving in Bath in 1801 she writes, "The first view of Bath in fine weather does not answer my expectations; I think I see more distinctly through rain. The sun was got behind everything, and the appearance of the place from the top of Kingsdown was all vapour, shadow, smoke, and confusion" (*Letters*, no. 35). Seven years later she reminds Cassandra, "It will be two years tomorrow since we left Bath for Clifton, with what happy feelings of Escape" (*Letters*, no. 54). Just like the move to Bath, Austen's "escape" and her settling finally at Chawton were controlled by the men in her family. The power of the father and brothers is understandable, for they were to provide the housing, but at the same time, Austen was quite conscious that movement was beyond her control. Whether it was relocating the family home or going to a ball, she traveled at the convenience of men.

On June 15, 1808, she describes a situation much like the one in the letters of November 1813: "I should have preferred a rather longer stay here certainly, but there is not prospect of any later conveyance for me. . . . I shall at any rate be glad not to be obliged to be an incumbrance on those who have brought me here, for, as James has no horse, I must feel in their carriage that I am taking his place. We were rather crowded yesterday, though it does not become me to say so, as I and my boa were of the party" (*Letters*, no. 51). At another time she shares a similar discomfort with her sister: "I shall be sorry to pass the door at Seale without calling, but it must be so— & I shall be nearer to Bookham than I c^d wish, in going [with Edward] from Dorking to Guilford—but till I have a travelling purse of my own, I must submit to such things" (*Letters*, no. 53).

Austen's letters frequently account for the movements of her brothers and other men, and the two letters printed here illustrate this: "Edward is gone into his Woods"; "Sir Brook comes here in the morn^g, & they are to be joined by Mr. Deedes at Ashford"; "first came Sir Brook to dissipate us before breakfast . . . then Sir Brook & Edward set off." They also record the movements of women who, remarkably, have power over their own mobility. For instance, Austen contrasts her own powerless condition to that of Lady B., whom she admires "for getting away [from the concert] at last with a great deal of decision & promtness, not waiting to compliment & dawdle & fuss." She also comments that Lady Honeywood's "going about with 4 Horses" is part of what makes her "altogether a perfect sort of Woman." Both women control their own movement, a power that Austen deems worthy of notice and praise. On November 3, 1813, she comments on Henry's "convenient Carriage," which he makes available to "his friends in general," and three days later she exclaims, "You, & Mrs. H. & Catherine & Alethea going about together in Henry's carriage seeing sights!—I am not used to the idea of it yet." The unusual opportunity to travel without a brother, like the ability to leave a concert with "decision & promtness," surprises Austen. And yet it is clear that Henry has given the power to his sister only temporarily by making the carriage available. He still remains in control, for just a few sentences later Austen refers to "being taken down to Chawton by Henry."

Despite her dependent state, Austen has her own ideas for traveling. On November 3 she writes, "My scheme is to take Bookham in my way home for a few days & my hope that Henry will be so good as to send me some part of the way thither." But her plan is only a "scheme," an attempt to subvert the governing power, a wish to accomplish her own desires, and by the next letter, it has been changed. She writes, "My Bookham may go hang," because Henry will take her directly home to Chawton. For Henry's ears, she adds, "The prospect of being taken down to Chawton by Henry, perfects the plan to me," but significantly, because it now conforms to what Henry wants, it is a "plan," no longer a "scheme."

Related to travel is money, for money eases travel; even women with money find travel within their power. On November 3 Austen writes Cassandra that if Henry can send her "some part of the way thither," she can visit with her friend Mrs. Cooke, who has issued "two or three dozen Invitations, with the offer of meeting me anywhere in one of her airings." Like Lady Honeywood, the "perfect sort of Woman" who has her own horses, Mrs. Cooke has money enough to allow her independent movement.

Money, of course, allows all kinds of conveniences to those who can wield its power, and for Jane Austen who had very little of it, it had a tremendous fascination. Her letters are full of references to money. They tell the exact amounts spent on fabric, ribbon, livestock, books, food, furniture, and lodging. They estimate the amount others spend on clothes, as well as the amount they inherit. Time and again, they speculate on her own impoverished and dependent future, while at the same time commenting on the income and expenses related to her novels. When Austen writes on November 3, "perhaps I may marry young Mr. D'arblay.—I suppose in the meantime I shall owe dear Henry a great deal of Money for Printing &c.," she shows her knowledge of the usual and limited ways in which women may come to have money, by marrying into it or by receiving it from their families, as well as her knowledge that in both cases, access to this form of power is available only through men. At thirty-seven, Austen jokes with her sister about marriage to "young Mr. D'arblay," who is only nineteen, and about the possibility of having money. She also jokes in the second letter about her more likely fate of remaining dependent "Aunt Jane." "As I must leave off being young, I find many Douceurs in being a sort of

Chaperone for I am put on the Sofa near the Fire & can drink as much wine as I like." Despite the jokes, however, she is resigned to the fact that she "shall owe dear Henry a great deal." Just as Henry and her other brothers controlled her movement and location, they also controlled her finances, and as a result, Austen and her sister had to depend on them for where they lived as well as for how they lived. Only through her publishing could Austen make any money of her own, but her brothers made that enterprise possible by providing the initial investment for printing and by making the initial contacts with the publishing world. Thus, by exerting her own private power through writing novels, she created what she could sell, but finally the sales were dependent on the public power of men.

Austen did not come from a wealthy family, or even a financially secure one. One brother, Edward, became well-off but only because his parents sent him to live with his uncle and aunt whose last name, Knight, and estate, Godmersham Park, he eventually acquired.[10] With the death of her father in 1805, Jane Austen, her mother, and her sister were reduced to an annual income of around £210, and the brothers added enough annually to this to raise it to a modest £450 (Honan 213–14). Because a sum was not settled on Mrs. Austen but rather contributions were given each year from four different sources, the Austen women were always conscious of their dependence on their family, the brothers as well as others with money. With Cassandra as audience, Austen expressed her annoyance and indignation at the differences between those who had and those who did not have money and power. For her sister's amusement and her own relief she worked her sharp wit on those who exerted this power over them. On April 21, 1805, Austen reports that her Aunt Perrot "is in a great hurry to pay me for my Cap, but cannot find in her heart to give me good money." Instead she offers to buy her niece a ticket to the Grand Sydney-Garden Breakfast. "This offer I shall of course decline; & all the service she will render me therefore, is to put it out of my power to go at all." Her aunt's financial control forces Austen into exercising one of her only public powers, the power of refusal. While she acknowledges the necessity of relying on relatives for financial security, she is annoyed and embarrassed nonetheless. She continues her letter, "I thought it was of the first consequence to avoid anything that might seem a slight to them. I shall be glad when it is over, & hope to have no necessity for having so many dear friends at once again" (*Letters*, no. 44).

This sensitivity to the power of money is evident throughout her letters, and it ranges from the smallest of subjects to the most significant. On January 7, 1807, Austen informs Cassandra that their mother has been going over her accounts for the year. "Frank too has been settling his accounts and making calculations, and each party feels quite equal to our present expenses; but much increase of house-rent would not do for either" (*Letters*, no. 48). On November 3, 1813, she remarks on "a fall in Bread by the bye. I hope my Mother's Bill next week will shew it." On November 6, 1813, she praises her nephew George for his early consideration of economics. George writes of his living expenses at Oxford and closes by "saying, 'I am afraid I shall be poor.'" Austen remarks, "I am glad he thinks about it so soon," implying that as a second son, George had best concern himself with money as soon as possible so that he can avoid the restricted, dependent position in which Austen and her sister find themselves.

Unlike most women of her time, Austen found a way of making money, a way of gaining some degree of public power. Henry Austen's "Biographical Notice" explains that she "became an authoress entirely from taste and inclination. Neither the hope of fame nor profit mixed with her early motives" (6). Austen's letters, however, frequently mention the income from her novels and her desire to increase it. For instance, on November 3, 1813, she expresses the wish that Mrs. Fletcher, "an old Lady & very good & very clever, who is all curiosity to know about me," will "indulge herself with S & S." Three days later she brings up the subject of sales again. "Mary tells me that Eliza means to buy [*Sense and Sensibility*]. I wish she may. . . . I cannot help hoping that *many* will feel themselves obliged to buy it. I shall not mind imagining it a disagreable Duty to them, so as they do it." While conscious that some people would find this focus on money and sales inappropriate and unfeminine, Austen knows that Cassandra does not mind hearing about it, and so she adds, "I cannot tire *you* I am sure on this subject, or I would apologise." From this letter it is clear that the two sisters shared the understanding that money controlled where and how they lived and that their lack of it put them in unalterably subservient positions.

Not all of the letters detailing income are written to Cassandra. One is to Martha Lloyd, a lifelong friend who lived with the Austen women for years and finally married Frank Austen: "P. & P. is sold.—Egerton [Austen's publisher] gives £110 for it.—I would rather have had £150, but we could not both be pleased, & I am not at all surprised that he should not chuse to hazard so much.—It's being sold will I hope be a great saving of Trouble to Henry, & therefore must be welcome to me" (*Letters*, no. 74.1). Because

Martha Lloyd has been like a family member to her, Austen provides the details of the sale, and perhaps because she is a woman who also lacks public power, Austen comments that in the financial arrangement the man, not she, was "pleased."

Austen shares her understanding of the role of money with her niece Fanny Knight in several letters, perhaps as a way of educating her in the ways of the world Fanny will soon enter. On November 18, 1814, she writes, "You will be glad to hear that the first Edit: of M.P. is all sold.— Your Uncle Henry is rather wanting me to come to Town, to settle about a 2ᵈ Edit: . . . I am very greedy & want to make the most of it;—but as you are much above caring about money, I shall not plague you with any particulars" (*Letters*, no. 103). A few days later she adds that "it is not settled yet whether I *do* hazard a 2ᵈ Edition. . . . People are more ready to borrow & praise, than to buy—which I cannot wonder at;—but tho' I like praise as well as anybody, I like what Edward calls *Pewter* too" (*Letters*, no. 106). Perhaps Austen felt obliged to inform Fanny of the power of money in a way that her father, Edward, had not, and so by describing her feelings about earning money in Edward's own terms, Austen shows her niece that the power of money, while usually reserved for men, affects women's lives too. This point is made more directly in a later letter when Austen connects money to marriage: "Single women have a dreadful propensity for being poor—which is one very strong argument in favour of Matrimony" (*Letters*, no. 141). Marriage is, she says, one of the only ways a woman can protect herself from economic hardship, a lesson so central to her understanding of the world that it is conveyed in each of her novels, as well as many of her letters. If one cannot "marry young Mr. D'arblay," then one is fated to be like Miss Bates or "Poor Mrs. Stent" whose lot it is "to be always in the way . . . unequal to anything & unwelcome to everybody" (*Letters*, no. 44). This complete lack of power, the inability to choose one's own surroundings and to determine when and how one travels, can be avoided only by having money, and that can occur only with the consent and assistance of men.

Writing novels and publishing them allowed Austen some degree of participation in the public realm of power. Through publishing, she earned some power that would not have been hers otherwise, and by accounting for her income in her letters, she was expressing both astonishment and pride in the accomplishment. "I have now therefore written myself into £250— which only makes me long for more," she writes her brother Frank (*Letters*, no. 81). These earnings, however, would not have been possible without the help of her brothers, as she freely admits on several occasions. Thus, the public power is tempered by the knowledge of its rising from a male influence.

Denied the public power of free movement and any significant power from money, Austen exercised the only true power open to her—writing. More than her novels, her letters are symbols of that power and vehicles for expressing her private power. Like gossip, a form of power for the publicly powerless (Spacks, *Gossip* 4–5), letters allow those without public control to comment on those in control. These comments do not affect the power structure (the brothers do not change their travel plans, for instance, when Austen writes that she would prefer something different), but they provide the powerless with a feeling of control. Ironically, this control comes in part from the mobility her letters provide Austen. As they move freely about the country, going where she cannot, they create a sense of independence, not physical but psychic and private. This private sense of control, as well as the constant and contrasting knowledge of subordination, is frequently expressed in Austen's letters.

The November 3, 1813, letter opens with Austen's expression of private power, over her pen and over her brother Edward: "As my pen seems inclined to write large I will put my lines very close together," Austen playfully begins, exerting control over the strong-willed pen by manipulating the space within which it can move. In the context of her comments on male control over her life, it is tempting to read the comment ironically: Austen will control her pen at least, if nothing else. She continues by telling Cassandra that she received her letter just before leaving with Edward for a drive to Canterbury. "I allowed him to hear the cheif of it as we went along," she says, indicating that she maintained control over the correspondence, "allowing" Edward only that information she wanted him to have. The letter closes with a similar statement of control over information and writing: "Edward does not write to Henry, because of my writing so often." Thus, while the letters are written to be shared and read aloud, any information that is exchanged between the two family groups is filtered through the sisters. Similar acts of filtering are evident in other letters to Cassandra—"I have borne the arrival of your Letter today extremely well; anybody might have thought it was giving me pleasure" (*Letters*, no. 133)—and to her niece Fanny Knight, with whom Austen exchanged letters containing secrets not meant to be shared with others. On November 18, 1814, having received a packet of sheet music from Fanny with a letter secreted inside,

Austen replied, "Your sending the Music was an admirable Device, it made everything easy, & I do not know how I could have accounted for the parcel otherwise; for tho' your dear Papa [Austen's brother Edward] most conscientiously hunted about till he found me alone in the Din^g-parlour . . . I do not think anything was suspected." Later she urges Fanny to "write *something* that may do to be read or told" (*Letters*, no. 106). Writing again to Fanny in 1817 she says, "Do not be surprised at finding Uncle Henry acquainted with my having another [novel] ready for publication. I could not say No when he asked me, but he knows nothing more of it" (*Letters*, no. 142).

Austen made the filtering of information easier by providing two discourses in many of her letters, one for the addressee, almost always a woman, and another for a larger audience to whom the letter might be read.[11] The two sample letters from November 1813 demonstrate how Austen weaves the two together, thereby making her private feelings known ("I shall certainly not be sorry if he does not want me") but providing material for public consumption as well ("Tell Henry that I *will* stay with him, let it be ever so disagreable to him"). The parallel discourses also comment on the tension between what should be done and what Austen wants to do, between what she must do and what she knows she cannot do, between the public obligation and the private desire. On November 3, 1813, for instance, Austen tells Cassandra that she plans to meet Mrs. Harrison, the aunt of Ben Lefroy, the man her niece Anna eventually married, and she describes the conversation she would like to have: " 'My dear Mrs. Harrison, I shall say, I am afraid the young Man has some of your Family Madness—& though there often appears to be something of Madness in Anna too, I think she inherits more of it from her Mother's family than from ours.'—That is what I shall say—& I think she will find it difficult to answer me." The next letter reports on the actual exchange, "a very comfortable little complimentary friendly chat." Austen found Mrs. Harrison "a sweet Woman, still quite a sweet Woman in herself" and announced plans to see her again at a ball the following week. The forum of the private letter allowed Austen the power to describe at length what she would like or what would amuse her. By using parallel discourses she juxtaposed that with what she in fact did. Not all letters develop both discourses so separately and distinctly. On November 3, 1813, for instance, Austen merges the two discourses neatly in one sentence: "Mrs. Deedes & I must talk rationally together I suppose."

Austen's private power resides in part in the minute details of domestic life. If her brothers control Austen's location, she attends to the details that affect that location. Thus, her letters purposefully overflow with the particulars of her life as she essentially names all the things over which she has control. A passage such as the following shows Austen reeling through a list of details under "Female Government": "I wonder whether the Ink bottle has been filled.—Does Butcher's meat keep up at the same price? and is not Bread lower than 2/6.—Mary's blue gown!" (*Letters*, no. 87). When Austen writes her sister, "You know how interesting the purchase of a spongecake is to me" (*Letters*, no. 51) or "I bought some Japan ink . . . and next week shall begin my operations on my hat, on which you know my principal hopes of happiness depend" (*Letters*, no. 10), she is not sending news to share with the family but laying claim to areas over which she has power.

Austen claims minutiae as the subject matter with which to fill her letters, and she asks for the same from her correspondents. "I long to know whether you are buying stockings or what you are doing" (*Letters*, no. 89), she writes Cassandra, requesting a description of the trivial details that give meaning to domestic life. Knowing that with all the particulars, she can vicariously participate in an event, she writes, "I shall be extremely anxious to hear the Event of your Ball, & shall hope to receive so long & so minute an account of every particular that I shall be tired of reading it" (*Letters*, no. 5). She compliments Cassandra on her handwriting, "so small & so neat!—I wish I could get as much into a sheet of paper" (*Letters*, no. 90). Sometimes she worries that she is getting "foolishly minute" or "growing too minute" (*Letters*, no. 91) and cuts herself off, but she does not leave off being minute, only "too minute." In addition to itemizing areas of private control, the details serve to connect her with the absent, the major objective of personal letter writing. Offering and requesting the smallest details of everyday life, Austen uses the letters to transcend the physical distance between herself and her audience. The particulars allow the reader to imagine the daily routine, the ball, the drive, and the conversation that he or she has missed. Thus, the letters are a private way to regain some control over the distance that has been imposed between Austen and her reader, most often her sister. While they may not be in control of their locations, through letters they can achieve emotional and intellectual closeness and at least temporarily suspend the separation.

One of Austen's most common techniques for controlling distance in her letters is the precise establishment of the setting in which she writes. In her November 6, 1813, letter she begins, "Having half an hour before breakfast—(very snug, in my own room, lovely morn^g, excellent fire, fancy me) I will give you some account of the last two days." Such an introductory framing device allows her reader to envision Austen in the act of writing, almost in the act of speaking. In her novels, Austen carefully locates her characters, using position and movement to heighten a scene's dramatic effect. In her letters, she employs a similar strategy, describing spatial arrangements of both people and objects to give the reader a sense of the place and event. For instance, of the party at Chilham Castle Austen writes, "We had Music in the Even^g, Fanny & Miss Wildman played, & Mr. James Wildman sat close by & listened, or pretended to listen." At a concert the next night, "there we sat, all six in a row, under a side wall, I between Lucy Foote & Miss Clewes." When she mentions letter writing, however, most often the settings are private, a luxury for Austen who had so little control over her own location. She wrote on November 3, 1813, "I am all alone. . . . At this present time I have five Tables, Eight & twenty Chairs & two fires all to myself." This privacy contributes to the sense of private power, as Austen conveys when she writes, "I am now alone in the Library, Mistress of all I survey" (*Letters*, no. 84).

This expression of power, however, is undercut with Austen's humorous reference to William Cowper's "Verses, Supposed to be written by Alexander Selkirk, during his solitary abode in the island of Juan Fernandez," which begins, "I am monarch of all I survey." Austen's paraphrasing of the line is both playful and self-mocking. While Cowper's poem describes the misery of solitude, Austen's letter reflects her delight in her privacy. It also acknowledges, however, the limitations of her power, which is exerted only in solitude and when writing. When Austen continues, "at least I may say so & repeat the whole poem if I like it, without offence to anybody," she recognizes that at Godmersham she enjoys only that solitude and space allowed her by others, like Fanny Price at Mansfield Park.

This humor, whether directed toward herself or toward another, is another device that Austen uses to reduce the distance between herself and her reader. Because humor assumes that the reader and writer share similar opinions, it, like gossip, aligns the reader and writer and allows them to feel some degree of power over the subject of the joke. Austen works her humor on a variety of topics, but she directs it most frequently toward other women. These women may have been perceived as safe targets for humor, for they often had as little public power as Austen did. Austen's letters have often been attacked for their abusive tone, and indeed some of her comments are blunt, more surprising than humorous. She is not unaware of her tone and how it might appear to others, however, as she acknowledges to both her sister and her brother Frank. To Cassandra she writes of the imminent death of Mrs. Lloyd, the mother of their friend Martha, and says, "The Nonsense I have been writing in this and in my last letter, seems out of place at such a time; but I will not mind it, it will do you no harm, & nobody else will be attacked by it" (*Letters*, no. 43). For Frank, who is aboard the HMS *Elephant* in the Baltic, she describes Mrs. Edward Bridges, who is "a poor Honey—the sort of woman who gives me the idea of being determined never to be well—& who likes her spasms & nervousness & the consequence they give her, better than anything else.—This is an ill-natured sentiment to send all over the Baltic!" (*Letters*, no. 85). She recognizes her tone and questions the propriety of her comments, but she does not restrain her observation and humor, for they are among her arsenal of expressions of private power. In fact, the mere act of saying what one should not say—that Charles Powlett's wife "is discovered to be everything that the Neighbourhood could wish her, silly & cross as well as extravagant" (*Letters*, no. 14)—while recognizing that one should not say it is an expression of power.

Often the humorous observations in Austen's letters have the ring of her character descriptions in her novels, making these statements among the most often cited in studies of the letters. In comments such as "Lady B. was much what I expected, I could not determine whether she was rather handsome or very plain," "I was just introduced at last to Mary Plumptre, but should hardly know her again. She was delighted with *me* however, good enthusiastic Soul!" and "She is a disputable Beauty that I want much to see" (*Letters*, no. 91), Austen employs the ironic pairing that is one of the hallmarks of her novels. Just as the novels' irony aligns the reader with the narrator, so the letters' irony assumes that the reader would share Austen's opinions of the people she has met. Throughout the letters the ironic tone and humorous characterization amuse the reader and unite him or her with Austen across the distance.

Private Power

Austen's letters have largely been dismissed or diminished by critics who have expected something other than what is in them. Looking for letters that were written for publication or for letters that were written by men or by those who occupied the mainstream of power and society, critics have found Austen's letters tedious and trivial. These letters, however, function as a narrative of a private life of a woman who was removed from the realm of public power and aware of the distances and differences between herself and those who commanded that power. The individual letters identify the areas in which she lacked public power, and they chronicle her attempts to exert private control over certain parts of her life. Read as a whole, the collection of the letters demonstrates the greatest power Austen had, the private power to describe and comment on the public world of power in which she could not partake, while at the same time defining her own realm of power. As a humorous, insightful, sometimes acid narrative, Austen's letters set in contrast the subjects of travel and money, which eluded her control, and the powerful fact of her letter writing. "My interesting Narrative" she calls her November 6, 1813, letter to Cassandra, although the topics are not politics and war. Austen's letters are "quite full of little home news," which fixes her readers and herself in time and space, demonstrating the control she was capable of exerting with her private power.

NOTES

1. One notable exception is Henry Austen's sentimental "Biographical Notice," in which he says, "The style of her familiar correspondence was in all respects the same as that of her novels. Every thing came finished from her pen; for on all subjects she had ideas as clear as her expressions were well chosen. It is not hazarding too much to say that she never dispatched a note or letter unworthy of publication" (8).

2. In *Jane Austen* and her earlier article "The Austen Portraits and the Received Biography," Kirkham argues not only that Austen was aware of the feminist controversy at the end of the eighteenth century but also that she responded to it in her novels and, most likely, in her letters. These were the letters, she argues, that Cassandra Austen destroyed or edited.

3. As Claudia Johnson states, Austen scholarship "has always been preceded by very definite ideas about what it would find there" (xix).

4. Moers refused to include the portrait of Austen in *Literary Women*. She says that "there is no acceptable Jane Austen portrait" and uses a drawing of Austen's niece Fanny Knight instead (see her plate 1).

5. Many scholars have commented on reading letters as narratives. See, for instance, Bossis; Goldsmith vii–xii; Hileman; and Spacks, *Gossip* 76–78.

6. There is hardly room to name them all here, but a few deserve particular notice. See Brown; Gilbert and Gubar; Johnson; Kirkham, *Jane Austen*; Smith; Sulloway; and Thompson.

7. See Gooneratne, esp. 16–30; Juhasz; and Kaplan. Kaplan's essay describes nineteenth-century society as comprising two separate cultures, "a general male-dominated culture and . . . a women's culture," each with its own set of values and worldviews. Jane Austen, says Kaplan, lived with a "cultural doubleness" that was expressed in her letters (211–12).

8. Thompson provides a particularly useful discussion of money and fashion in Austen's time; see esp. 27–32.

9. In *Pride and Prejudice*, for example, Elizabeth Bennet "had set her heart on seeing the Lakes" but is told by her Aunt Gardiner that Mr. Gardiner's business would prevent their traveling so far. While she was "excessively disappointed," Elizabeth knew "it was her business to be satisfied" (239).

10. In addition to Edward, Austen had five other brothers, one of whom, George, was an invalid all his life. Two brothers, Francis and Charles, joined the navy, and both became admirals. James, her oldest brother, followed their father's example and became a clergyman. Henry, the brother who became most involved in the publication of Austen's novels, made money in the militia and then started a banking firm in London—Austen, Maunde and Tilson. He also established branches in smaller towns including Alton, a mile from Chawton where Jane Austen lived. In 1816 Henry's bank failed. In order to repay some of his debts, Henry took clerical orders that same year. See Honan, esp. 375–78.

11. See Kaplan for a discussion of the stylistic differences between the discourse of women's culture and the discourse of male-dominated culture.

WORKS CITED

Austen, Henry. "Biographical Notice." *The Oxford Illustrated Jane Austen.* Ed. R. W. Chapman. 3d ed. 5 vols. London: Oxford UP, 1933. 5: 3–9.

Austen, Jane. *Jane Austen's Letters to Her Sister Cassandra and Others.* Ed. R. W. Chapman. 2 vols. Oxford: Clarendon, 1932.

———. *Northanger Abbey and Persuasion.* Vol. 5 of *The Oxford Illustrated Jane Austen.* Ed. R. W. Chapman. 3d ed. London: Oxford UP, 1933.

———. *Pride and Prejudice.* Vol. 2 of *The Oxford Illustrated Jane Austen.* Ed. R. W. Chapman. 3d ed. London: Oxford UP, 1933.

Austen-Leigh, James Edward. *Memoirs of Jane Austen.* Ed. R. W. Chapman. Oxford: Oxford UP, 1926.

Bossis, Mireille. "Methodological Journeys through Correspondences." Trans. Karen McPherson. *Yale French Studies* 71 (1986): 63–75.

Brown, Lloyd W. "Jane Austen and the Feminist Tradition." *Nineteenth-Century Fiction* 28 (1973–74): 321–38.

Chapman, R. W. *Jane Austen: Facts and Problems*. Oxford: Clarendon, 1948.

[Forster, E. M.] "Miss Austen and Jane Austen." Review of *Jane Austen's Letters to Her Sister Cassandra and Others*, ed. R. W. Chapman. *Times Literary Supplement*, Nov. 10, 1932, pp. 821–22.

Gilbert, Sandra M., and Susan Gubar. *The Madwoman in the Attic: The Woman Writer and the Nineteenth-Century Literary Imagination*. New Haven: Yale UP, 1979.

Goldsmith, Elizabeth C. *Writing the Female Voice: Essay on Epistolary Literature*. Boston: Northeastern UP, 1989.

Gooneratne, Yasmine. *Jane Austen*. Cambridge: Cambridge UP, 1970.

Hileman, Sharon. "Autobiographical Narrative in the Letters of Jane Carlyle." *a/b:Auto/Biography* 4 (1988): 107–17.

Honan, Park. *Jane Austen: Her Life*. New York: Ballantine, 1987.

Johnson, Claudia. *Jane Austen: Women, Politics, and the Novel*. Chicago: U of Chicago P, 1988.

Juhasz, Suzanne. "Bonnets and Balls: Reading Jane Austen's Letters." *The Centennial Review* 31.1 (1987): 84–104.

Kaplan, Deborah. "Representing Two Cultures: Jane Austen's Letters." *The Private Self: Theory and Practice of Women's Autobiographical Writings*. Ed. Shari Benstock. Chapel Hill: U of North Carolina P, 1988. 211–29.

Kirkham, Margaret. "The Austen Portraits and the Received Biography." *Women and Literature* ns 3 (1980): 29–38.

———. *Jane Austen, Feminism and Fiction*. Totowa, N.J.: Barnes, 1983.

Modert, Jo, ed. *Jane Austen's Manuscript Letters in Facsimile*. By Jane Austen. Carbondale: Southern Illinois UP, 1990.

Moers, Ellen. *Literary Women*. New York: Doubleday, 1976.

Smith, LeRoy W. *Jane Austen and the Drama of Woman*. London: Macmillan, 1983.

Spacks, Patricia Meyer. *The Female Imagination*. New York: Knopf, 1975.

———. *Gossip*. Chicago: U of Chicago P, 1986.

Sulloway, Alison G. *Jane Austen and the Province of Womanhood*. Philadelphia: U of Pennsylvania P, 1989.

Thompson, James. *Between Self and World: The Novels of Jane Austen*. University Park: Pennsylvania State UP, 1988.

Todd, Janet. *Women's Friendship in Literature*. New York: Columbia UP, 1980.

POSTSCRIPT

Epistolary Acts and Literary Careers in the Eighteenth Century: Permutations of Public Sphere and Private Persona among Writers

Janet Gurkin Altman

In 1967 in an article in *Studies on Voltaire and the Eighteenth Century*, Georges May wryly raised the question, "Does epistolary literature date from the eighteenth century?" His query was prompted by the emergence in the 1950s and 1960s of a series of monumental critical editions of Enlightenment writers' correspondences. Although May's article focused on the voluminous editions of Voltaire, Diderot, and Rousseau undertaken respectively by Theodore Besterman, Georges Roth, and Ralph Leigh, we could add to this list a considerable number of other eighteenth-century writers whose extant correspondences have only recently found worthy editors.

May's question is both quip and query. Letter writing obviously has a long history of being practiced as "literature," as an art that has its own theory and models, or at least as a craft whose outstanding examples have often been anthologized as literature. In what sense could epistolary literature "date from" the eighteenth century in France, where the letter achieved preeminence as a literary genre in the seventeenth century? Georges May's point in his article, however, was that eighteenth-century correspondences differ radically from the epistolary literature of the French classical period because they are more closely allied with two literary genres that emerged in their modern form in the Enlightenment, even though these genres were still rejected by neoclassical aesthetics as literature—the novel and autobiography. May suggested that the reason that eighteenth-century correspondences, novels, and autobiographies have entered the literary curriculum only in the twentieth century is that our era has perhaps "come back to a concept of the literary phenomenon that is closer to that of the eighteenth century than the concept of literature that dominated intervening periods." May concluded with a call for historians and critics to take full advantage of the splendid critical editions of correspondence made available recently, to do careful "study of these correspondences . . . which are in general read with too much superficiality" (843–44; my translation).

Relatively few literary critics have taken up Georges May's call for more study of French Enlightenment correspondences.[1] Numerous studies of British literary correspondences have emerged since the 1950s, however, including volumes cited frequently in the preceding essays: book-length syntheses by Irving (1955) and Redford (1986), and the collection of articles edited by Anderson, Daghlian, and Ehrenpreis (1966). Within British studies, in fact, the "familiar letter" has long attracted interest as a genre, and there has been widespread consensus that the eighteenth century was the "very palmiest day of the art," as George Saintsbury wrote in 1922 (21). For this reason, perhaps, it has been relatively easy for British studies to embrace eighteenth-century writers' correspondence as a literary genre to be studied on its own terms, like autobiography, the novel, drama, or poetry. In French studies, however, where the missive letter was canonized earlier as a literary genre, the canon of epistolary literature is still largely confined to seventeenth-century writers, and there has been little attempt to synthesize study beyond the seventeenth century.

How *did* eighteenth-century literary figures use the letter? Georges May's basic question about the historical specificity of a cultural practice is a pertinent one to raise again, over twenty years later, now that there is an even larger body of correspondences available for consideration. Modern critical editions—with their commitment to textual completeness and accuracy, their widely shared principle of printing all extant letters and providing critical apparatus to explain variants, allusions, and context—have created both new opportunities to read letters from the past and increasingly sophisticated ways of reading them. The essays in the present collection provide an opportunity to reflect in a special way upon the eighteenth-century writer's use of the letter. Each essay offers two complete, dated letters (one gives three), enabling us to focus on the letter as *a rhetorical entity* (a literary artifact) and as *an act in the life of the writer* (a historical document). These two qualities of the missive letter are as inseparable as they are complex. The letter's literarity (as a "complete work" of writing with particular formal constraints) and its historicity (as a human act implicated in ongoing actions) require historical as well as literary knowledge for interpretation.

This collection offers us the privilege of reading the best-available, most complete text of representative letters with readers who are experts on the writer, the correspondence as a whole, and the contemporary context of the letter writing. Each essay encourages us to open the writer's surviving correspondence and provides signposts for reading it. Readers of this volume will doubtless have preferences that will lead them back to specific correspondences represented here. Since the introduction provides a good orientation to the general study of correspondences, this afterword will comment upon the particular itinerary and openings that the volume as a whole suggests.

Epistolary Confidentiality

Daniel Defoe in 1705–1706 and Jane Austen in 1813:
Epistolary Narrative in the Public and Private Spheres

The seventeen individual letters that form the backbone of this volume span a century of letter writing. Their chronological arrangement permits us to range from Daniel Defoe's eyewitness political reports of 1705 and 1706 to Jane Austen's domestic accounts of November 1813. To move from Defoe to Austen as letter writers is to move from the "spy" to the "domestic" genre, from political science to home economics, from the freewheeling traveler to the homebound observer. Ever the ironist, even in her letters, Austen summarizes the narrative of her daily life as "they came & they sat & they went" (November 6, 1813), a pointed parody of *veni, vidi, vici*.

By coincidence or design, novelists open and close this collection, but the letters chosen by these contributors offer a snapshot of the letter writer before he or she achieved fame as a novelist. Although in 1705 Defoe was already close to forty-five years old, he had just begun his career as a writer, at the dawn of the new century and the beginning of Queen Anne's reign.

After being pilloried for *The Shortest Way with Dissenters* (1702), he deployed
his writing talent as political agent for his rescuer, Secretary of State Robert
Harley, while simultaneously launching a career with the *Review* (1704–13)
that would lead many to consider him the father of modern journalism.
Defoe was nearly sixty when he turned to writing novels, with the publication of *Robinson Crusoe* in 1719. Most of his surviving letters predate the
novels and were addressed to Harley. As Paula Backscheider points out,
Defoe's strategies in his extant letters are much more closely related to
his strategies as journalist than as novelist. Backscheider therefore takes
Defoe's relationship to Robert Harley (their shared opinions and writerly
styles) and the innovative subtleties of Defoe's investigative reporting as
the best context for reading Defoe's available letters.

Defoe covers a great deal of political and geographic territory in his reports to Harley. As secret agent revealing the bases of public opinion for his
secretary of state, Defoe creates an epistolary space that mixes the public
and private spheres in the particular way that his age would have defined
them. The public sphere from which his letters emanate are the committee
rooms, the pubs, the meetinghouses, and most especially the coffeehouses
that Habermas and others have described as crucial new centers for the
development of public opinion in Defoe's era. Defoe's private sphere is not
the personal interior life that Defoe is too restrained to share with Harley
(like most epistolarians from the early eighteenth century). His privacy is
rather the secrecy of a writer who knows how to remain a private detective,
traveling incognito, protecting his letters against interception, disguising
his signature and even his handwriting, in order to safeguard a private space
from which he can articulate political positions.

Backscheider notes that as Defoe developed his distinctive style as a
journalist, he used material from his reports to Harley with increasing
effectiveness and subtlety in his own periodical, bringing the material he
gathered for Harley into public purview in the *Review*, while retaining
his secret screen as Harley's political agent. This readdressing of epistolary material originally sent to a single reader may explain why Defoe's
letters to Harley were the primary Defoe letters preserved; ultimately they
were released to a public domain for which their political thrust was intended all along. As a writer hired by Harley, Defoe remained a politically
engaged journalist writing letters for a wider audience: an audience reach-
able through Harley as a statesman or more directly addressed through the
Review.

Paula Backscheider points out that the letters to Harley, written to describe the unfolding of a historical event, display some of the narrative qualities of a periodical Defoe described as "history writing by inches." If we turn to the only other set of narrative letters in this collection, Jane Austen's letters to her sister Cassandra in 1813, we likewise find "history writing by inches." Here the focus is on daily domestic and family life, rather than on political figures and public events, but the same essential quality of epistolary narrative obtains: an account written as events unfold, by a reporter who introduces a contemporaneous subjectivity as witness and reactor. Defoe, in keeping with his assignment as fast-traveling reporter, synthesizes multiple days at a time, sketches portraits and political projects of "strange and Unaccountable people" (September 10, 1705), summarizes the leaning of entire communities and social groups, and introduces his own subjectivity overtly in the form of advice to Harley. Defoe's letters belong doubly to political history because they both narrate it and attempt to influence its course. In Defoe's letters we see the private writer acting in the public sphere.

In Austen's letters, on the other hand, we see a published (but not public) writer acting in the private sphere. In 1813, the thirty-eight-year-old Austen had just published two novels, *Sense and Sensibility* (1811) and *Pride and Prejudice* (1813), both written prior to 1800, before she was twenty-five years old. Her name did not appear on the title pages of the works printed prior to her death in 1817. Although her friends knew of her authorship, she received little public recognition in her lifetime. The Austen letters that Susan Whealler has selected display a different kind of writer's incognito from that of Defoe's letters. After publication of his first works, Defoe was already so notorious as a writer in 1705 that he could be physically recognized at a distance from London, as is clear from his letter of September 10, 1705. Austen's letters of November 1813, on the other hand, show the extent to which she delighted in being known through her works but not in person ("I am read & admired in Ireland. . . . I am not known to her by *name*"). Austen has avoided the portraiture that makes acclaimed writers known to the public, as well as the pillory display that made Defoe's face famous. Signature and portraiture, which would bring Austen into the public sphere, are not part of her literary persona.

Instead Austen reserves published literature for private pleasure, shared with family and friends. Both of the letters reproduced here develop Austen's preference for literary privacy in the only two passages that contain extended literary references. The first passage consists of eleven consecutive sentences embedded near the end of the long paragraph that constitutes the bulk of Austen's letter of November 3. The eleven sentences seemingly jump from one topic to another, in Austen's stream-of-consciousness style, but they are all connected by literary concerns that crop up rarely in her surviving correspondence. The passage in question begins as Austen describes William to her sister Cassandra, through a succinct analogy with well-known literary figures: "He has more of Cowper than of Johnson in him, fonder of Tame Hares & Blank verse than of the full tide of human Existence at Charing Cross." That Cassandra would appreciate this reference shows the literary bond that existed privately between two sisters, who did not circulate in more public literary clubs and circles. Austen's epistolary space remains resolutely private, even in the way she conveys her own identity as public writer. Her awareness of an audience for her works derives from limited networks of friends of friends—chains of letters and conversation that maintain personal ties while protecting Austen's privacy ("There is a Mrs. Fletcher . . . who is all curiosity to know about me. . . . This comes through Mrs. Carrick, not through Mrs. Gore"). Austen jokes next about the alternatives that could bring her private self into more public display, through an exhibit of writers' portraits or the kind of publicity involved in marriage: "I do not despair of having my picture in the Exhibition at last—all white & red, with my Head on one Side;—or perhaps I may marry young Mr. D'arblay." Shifting wryly back to her own preference, Austen hopes instead that Mrs. Fletcher, as well as others like her, will "indulge herself with S & S," so that her readers' private pleasure will assure a little more financial independence for Austen.

Austen's letters of November 3 and 6 are only three days apart, but in the intervening time her second edition of *Sense and Sensibility* has "stared" her "in the face." This face-to-face encounter with her book results in no mirrored reflection upon self, no Rousseauean sense of the book as a metonymy for the author, no anxious investment of the ego in the book. It occasions only a humorous reiteration of hope for sales and a brief indulgence of pleasure at the novel's being "very much admired at Cheltenham." The book released to the world is free to lead its own life, circulating independently of its author, whose life is pursued separately from the book. In the November 6 letter, Austen's allusion to her literary career occupies only seven consecutive sentences. It is hidden in a paragraph devoted to other comings and goings of the last two days, as if the book's arrival in Austen's home and its reception at Cheltenham were no more significant than the other comings and goings that fill Austen's letter. Indeed, Austen implies that she has mentioned the success of her novel to Cassandra only because Cassandra shares her private pleasure in her writerly identity ("I cannot tire *you* I am sure on this subject, or I would apologise"). *Pleasure* is the word that recurs elsewhere when Austen discusses her writing, but the pleasure remains private: "Your tidings of S & S. give me pleasure. I have never seen it advertised" (November 3, 1813).

Both Austen and Defoe report minutiae that are unintelligible to us without guidance, because the details belong to the shared world of the letter writer and intended reader. The minutiae of Austen's letters, however, have consistently been dismissed by latter-day readers as trivialities, and even Austen shows concern in her letters about becoming "too minute." In her essay, Susan Whealler clears the ground for a different reading of Austen's letters. If Austen's correspondence has disappointed scholars looking for commentary on her own novels, public events, and general topics, Susan Whealler reminds us that to criticize Austen's letters for not discussing war, religion, and politics, as E. M. Forster did, is simply to ignore the subject matter that Austen did choose. Whealler shows us the very real interest of Austen's letters as writing that dignifies the details of everyday life. Through close analysis of the way Austen treats her most frequent topics—travel and money—Whealler argues that Austen subversively "conveys her understanding of the location and application of public power in her society" and exercises "private power" over her own life through particular letter-writing strategies.

Since Austen's letters were published in 1932, moreover, our appreciation has grown for the narrative of everyday life, in novels and history as well as correspondences. As epistolary narrative, Austen's letters to Cassandra—like Defoe's letters to Harley—compose history by inches, but with a marked difference in the logical organization of temporal experience as well as the subject of the narrative. Defoe's journalistic organization of multiple days' experience by political topic (in the epistolary tradition of Marana's popular 1694 *Turkish Spy*) has given way to a diaristic writing to the moment, which traces the letter writer's experience temporally throughout her day. Between Defoe and Austen, Richardson had obviously intervened with influential models for epistolary narrative. Austen's writing to the moment, however, differs radically from Richardson's, even though Austen—like Pamela—marks the interruptions for dinner in her letters and comments upon her problems with pen and ink. Austen's style of free association and her use of dashes, as well as her subject matter, are much closer to the modern novel, or to the patter of post-Chekhovian dialogue, than to Richardson's suspenseful staging of events and dramatic dialogue in his novels. Austen described her novelistic art as that of the miniaturist, and the same could be said of her letters. Her correspondence will doubtless receive more sensitive readings like Susan Whealler's as we seek to understand the experiences of everyday life articulated by writers confined to the private sphere.

Epistolary Diplomacy and Epistolary Pedagogy

Courtly Uses of the Letter: The Case of Lord Chesterfield, 1694–1773

To move from Austen or Defoe as letter writers to Philip Dormer Stanhope, fourth earl of Chesterfield, is to make a quantum leap in prose style, epistolary traditions, and social milieu. Defoe in 1705 was a merchant turned writer, employed by his secretary of state for his remarkable talent as a political observer. Professionally Defoe would remain a publishing writer, achieving literary recognition as a journalist, political satirist, and novelist—not as an epistolarian. Austen, like Defoe, would not be acclaimed as an epistolarian but rather as a highly original novelist, although she pursued her literary career anonymously. Chesterfield, on the other hand, was by class an aristocrat and by occupation a statesman (serving in both houses of Parliament, as viceroy of Ireland, special ambassador to The Hague, and secretary of state). He nonetheless achieved literary fame in the eighteenth century as an epistolarian, with the posthumous publication in 1774 of his letters to his son. Indeed, Chesterfield is the only writer examined in this volume whose literary reputation rests primarily upon his letters.

Chesterfield's literary career is not an isolated case, however. His contemporary, Lady Mary Wortley Montagu (1689–1762), achieved fame as a writer through her highly descriptive Turkish embassy letters—published, like Chesterfield's, one year after her death.[2] Like Chesterfield, Lady Mary moved in diplomatic milieux (as wife of an ambassador). She is one of the few women in the eighteenth century who dared to travel widely, even independently, and to write about her travels.[3] Her social class, intelligence, and atypical mobility as a woman enabled her to create an epistolary space of unusual range—geographically, stylistically, and intellectually.

With Mary Wortley Montagu and Philip Dormer Stanhope, epistolary art springs from an acknowledged literary tradition and the obligations of class, as well as from a very real personal talent. The literary tradition behind Chesterfield is that of courtly "civility," inculcated broadly as a courtly art in manuals from the Renaissance on and illustrated by writers like Malherbe, Guez de Balzac, Voiture, and Bussy-Rabutin, who influenced the course of French prose in the seventeenth century more through the missive letters they published between 1618 and 1697 than through their membership in the Académie Française (see Altman, "Letter Book"). French writers' letters were frequently published in the seventeenth century, largely through efforts of members of the Académie Française, and served as models for letter writing in England as well as France.

The tradition behind Montagu, however, is one that should not be conflated with the largely male model of epistolary civility bequeathed by French classicism. Madame de Sévigné's letters, when they were first published in 1725, inspired Mary Wortley Montagu to rival Sévigné as a writer.[4] It is important to see Sévigné as a writer not recognized or appropriated until the Enlightenment (see Altman, "Politics"). Sévigné's letters shocked readers when they were first published—by their familiarity, intimacy, and political freedom of speech, which differed radically from the court-serving model letters published under Louis XIV. Sévigné's letters are journalistic, and journalism was precisely what had been eliminated from model epistolary civility in seventeenth-century France. Bruce Redford's sensitive analysis of Montagu's correspondence stresses the extent to which Montagu consciously sought to differ from Sévigné in her letter writing, through a Senecan style that held emotions in check, in accordance with Montagu's Stoic philosophy (19–48). Sévigné's epistolary freedom in her reportage nonetheless set an important example for both Montagu and Voltaire, both of whom consciously rivaled her as epistolarians after 1726.

Montagu arguably wrote her letters with publication in mind, whereas Chesterfield did not. Both wrote, however, with an awareness of the classical traditions of epistolary publication, including the published letters of their contemporary Alexander Pope.[5] What Montagu and Chesterfield share as epistolarians—although their style, topics, and modes of organization differ significantly—is a sense of civic obligation and literary elegance as members of a ruling class, writing from one center of government (or exile from that center) to another, passing on their accumulated knowledge to the generation that will replace them. Both are concerned with

the public and private spheres of government in their letters; both have
bequeathed us commentary on political institutions as well as pedagogical
letters to their children. Their epistolary space is defined largely in relation
to courtly politics or the retreat from it.[6]

Chesterfield is more closely aligned with the traditions of courtesy
writing than Montagu. As Alan McKenzie points out, however, Chesterfield makes an important distinction between "civility" and "ceremony."
Although Chesterfield inherited the French tradition of epistolary civility,
he did not have to bear the French burden of "ceremony" and respect for
absolutist authority, which Voltaire started mocking in Chesterfield's time.
Indeed, Chesterfield emblematizes an aspect of English life that Voltaire
discovered, admired, and described so effectively in the 1730s in his *Lettres
philosophiques* (*Letters Concerning the English Nation*): the lack of separation
between literary and political life in England. In France, where writers remained cut off from political power throughout the early Enlightenment,
published letters continued to illustrate courtly ceremony and hierarchy or
suffered from censorship if they did not.[7]

Chesterfield, on the other hand, is a statesman of the type that would
emerge in France with Turgot—the writerly, courtly, but empowered politician. Alan McKenzie's subtle analysis of letters written to three quite
different recipients illustrates the wit, knowledge, and diplomacy that won
admiration for Chesterfield as friend (the forty-year-long correspondence
with Henrietta Howard), diplomat (the "business letters" that he knew
how to compose in "layers" for their likely audiences), and mentor (the
well-known letters to his son). To read Chesterfield's letters to his son—
known since the eighteenth century—in the light of his other letters is to
appreciate the extent to which Chesterfield was theorizing his own practice
as epistolarian and as statesman. In a sense, these letters are Chesterfield's
political testament in the age of pedagogy. They are an Enlightenment
analogue for Richelieu's written legacy to his king—Chesterfield's version
of *Télémaque*, *Emile*, and *The Spirit of the Laws*, written "inch by inch" in
epistolary form. Even if many of the lessons were lost on the original recipient of the letters, their publication in 1773 brought Chesterfield's private
legacy as public servant into the public domain as epistolary pedagogy.

Epistolary Eloquence

Well-Wrought Urns and Dashed-off Letters:
Christopher Smart and Charles Burney

Christopher Smart (1722–71) is less known than two poets of his generation, Thomas Gray (1716–71) and William Cowper (1731–1800), whose talent as both poets and epistolarians has long been acknowledged. Thanks to recent efforts, however, we now have Karina Williamson's collection of Smart's poetry and an edition of his letters that has been carefully annotated by Betty Rizzo and Robert Mahony. Betty Rizzo's essay on Smart's correspondence raises a number of important general questions about the poet's use of the letter, the preservation of letters in particular milieux, and the editing of eighteenth-century correspondences.

Rizzo and other contributors to this volume remind us with considerable precision that the literary correspondences we are able to read today are often only a small portion—and perhaps an unrepresentative sample—of the letters a writer composed and sent. If we are to read surviving correspondences with sensitivity and avoid the errors of the blind man with the elephant, it is important to know as much as possible about letters that were not preserved and the possible reasons for the preservation, destruction, or disappearance of a correspondence. The history over time of what kinds of letters a society exchanges, destroys, preserves, and publishes is in itself part of that society's cultural history.

In Smart's case, where only twenty-five letters survive, Betty Rizzo speculates that this paucity may result from "the view people then took of mental derangement. It was generally regarded with horror and without that scientific curiosity otherwise so characteristic of the educated." Although Smart was admired as a precocious genius early in his poetic career, his incarcerations for madness in 1756–63 left the poet in a public purgatory for the rest of his life and well beyond it, until his rediscovery by Robert Browning in 1887. Thus even though Smart was producing his greatest, most rhetorically controlled poetry between 1763 and 1771—after his release from the madhouse—both he and his works suffered contempt and neglect during this period, and he had difficulty publishing his work. Rizzo makes a compelling case that the letters that had been preserved by family and friends prior to Smart's incarcerations, as well as the ones he wrote during and after those incarcerations, were likely discarded after his bouts with insanity. We can only speculate on these matters, of course, but the detail that Betty Rizzo offers in this particular case encourages further research, including a comparison with Cowper. Cowper's poems and letters were better preserved, in spite of periods of insanity coinciding, like Smart's, with religious conversion—perhaps because Cowper's country refuge protected him more against adverse publicity, perhaps because Cowper's pastoral themes and painterly style were more to the taste of the time. In any event, the disappearance of Smart's letters is an anomaly in an age when writers' correspondences tended to be preserved and published.[8]

Rizzo discusses two examples that represent Smart's chief uses of the letter in the surviving correspondence: the belletristic letter (illustrated here by an elegant Latin fragment in the "rake" tradition, rich in trope and allusion) and the business letter, by and large soliciting money or assistance. Rizzo argues that Smart conceived his letters and poems as complementary parts of his writing cycle and that his published correspondence ought ideally to include most of his poems. The poems confer honor and praise in epistolary fashion and are conceived as balancing the letters asking for benefits. Poems addressed as gifts are to convey benefaction back upon the benefactor in what Rizzo calls "a perfect state of reciprocal generosity."

Betty Rizzo raises another question apropos of the two types of letters we find in Smart's correspondence. They divide neatly into formal and informal communication (literary set piece or casual letter) through a simple index—punctuation. Whereas the classically educated Smart respected established punctuation rules for his formally constructed letters, he did not hesitate to use the ill-reputed dash in his other letters. When Rizzo discusses the rules regarding punctuation marks for stops in the eighteenth century—conceived with precision for length of pause, like musical annotation—she reminds us of the extent to which the rules for oratory still governed the grammar of writing. Rizzo suggests that writing that carefully followed these punctuation rules was expected to be read aloud. She points out that we have come to premature conclusions about the use of the dash among male and female writers from this period and that we should stop editing dashes out of letters when we publish them. We may need to revise earlier assumptions that the dash characterizes chiefly the writing of women, too poorly educated to know other forms of punctuation. Instead, the dash may tell us something about the extent to which writers who used it conceived their prose as writing that was not to be read aloud, at least not in a formal context of public speaking. If Rizzo is correct, we may need also to look more closely at the relationship between orality and literacy, as well as intended audience, apropos of the letter.

The dash, which entered Johnson's *Dictionary* through common usage rather than grammatical prescription, is used systematically in letters by Christopher Smart, Charles Burney, and Jane Austen that are printed above. In each case, Rizzo's observations apropos of Smart apply: the dash most often represents a transition to a new subject, typically when the subject is not developed into paragraphs. In this instance, as Rizzo puts it, "the informal, unliterary letter seems once again to approximate and to substitute for conversation, while the literary set piece has the additional function of serving as art."

Let us consider, for example, the two letters by Charles Burney that Alvaro Ribeiro has selected for discussion. Neither letter appears to be a literary set piece. Indeed, Ribeiro emphasizes that these letters were never intended for publication and were conceived simply as a substitute for conversation. Yet Ribeiro's subtle analysis of chiasmus, echo, and allusion shows how Burney used classical rhetorical devices to create controlled symmetry in the five-part structure of both letters. The "business" part of each letter is embedded at the center, between "carefully plumped cushions of courtesy," which echo each other symmetrically in an $a\ b\ c\ b'\ a'$ structure. Ribeiro's point is that if we subjected eighteenth-century writers' correspondences to this kind of analysis, they might prove more highly composed than we realize and that Burney's seemingly "artless" composition is precisely what rhetoricians like Hugh Blair meant when they called for letters to be "well conducted" as an "easy and familiar . . . conversation carried on upon paper, between two friends at a distance."

One of the problems, however, with the letter-conversation analogy as it is used by Blair and others is that it conflates important differences. Alvaro Ribeiro's analysis of chiasmus in Burney's two letters, for example, is predicated on a paragraph structure that is not normally inherent to familiar conversation. Indeed, many readers of Burney's two letters will appreciate Ribeiro's analysis of their structure visually, as readers, not orally, as listeners. This "conversation carried on upon paper" is marked by the medium of writing that conveys it and enables it to be literally seen, as art. The "speaking voice" that we hear in these letters, moreover, is formed by traditions of oratory and eloquence that have been handed down and inculcated through writing.

We need to distinguish between oratory and conversation as models for

letter writing in the eighteenth century. William Irving conflated two quite
different traditions when he considered a "speech" to be the same thing as
a conversation: "Letters should be written, as a speech should be made, on
the basis of rhetorical rules . . . and the test of success [according to early
English treatises on letters] was the sound they made when read aloud. . . .
Hence the continued emphasis on the idea of conversation. A friend is
talking to a friend" (6–7). In describing early English treatises on letters,
Irving slides too easily from the art of public speaking to "the idea of conversation." We have only to recall the notion of conversation as "gossip"
and move to Jane Austen's letters to recognize that the simple "idea of conversation" is a fuzzy, inadequate concept for describing epistolary style and
structure (see Spacks, esp. 69–78). Conversation has always taken multiple
forms, and we know even less about conversational theory and practice in
the eighteenth century than about oratory and epistolary art during that
period.[9]

Yet letter writers take liberties with the rules of eloquence in familiar
letters, and their use of the dash calls attention to those liberties. Thus
if we look again at Burney's two letters, with their rhetorical similarity
in mind, we note that the dash is absent from the more formal letter to
Samuel Johnson (1755), but it appears seven times in the letter to Hester
Thrale (1778). A dash interrupts the unity of the first paragraph to set off
a sentence fragment introduced as an aside: "—And then our good, great,
& dear Doctor." It intrudes in Burney's fourth paragraph to cut off a se-
quence of anxious thoughts about his son's future: "—But, why do I talk
of things beyond my Ken?" Likewise, a dash interrupts the last paragraph
with a playful self-reprimand: "—But I forget that I am writing, & my
Pen prattles away your Time." Whereas the letter to Johnson divides easily
into five parts corresponding to five paragraphs, dashes interrupt paragraph unity in the letter to Thrale. They communicate the meandering of
thoughts that resist such structure. In these sentences set off by dashes we
are much closer to Austen's style than to the classical eloquence maintained
consistently in the letter to Johnson.

Ribeiro's illuminating analysis shows that the letter to Thrale is just
as "composed" as the letter to Johnson and that both letters are "acts of
intimacy," drawing Burney closer to his correspondents as he gracefully
conducts what could have been awkward business with them. Nonetheless,
if we look at sentence structure, vocabulary, and punctuation in the letters,
we see two quite different styles. The lengthy, complex, balanced sentences

of the letter to Johnson yield to shorter, paratactic sentence chains, exclamations, and even a fragment in the letter to Thrale. To Johnson, Burney speaks of "windows at their breasts" and "Philosophy." To Thrale he speaks of his "Stomach" and darts with vivid detail from one topic to another, from his "Dicky-Bird" to Queeney's education, to ideas about a "Language of Music" that are dear to him.

The two Burney letters illustrate beautifully the shift from public forms of letter writing to more private ones, by a writer who shows keen awareness of shades of publicity and privacy in the letters themselves. The discreet encomium to Samuel Johnson won Johnson's interest for the "elegance" of its "civilities," and it shows Burney's mastery of an epistolary eloquence influenced by oratory. Although not intended for publication, this letter is very much in the tradition of public speaking, its "business" is Johnson's publications, and it is designed to gain admission to a circle of publishing writers. The letter to Thrale is more influenced by conversational style than the letter to Johnson but is also a more private, intimate letter. In it Charles Burney's "voice" speaks in asides and veers toward interior monologue, while remaining aware of the "Badinage" necessary to keep conversations going in public. At the center of Burney's letter to Thrale is a prayer for more privacy in his pedagogy, neatly separated from his description of "Public" teaching by a dash: "It is neither pleasant to a Pupil to hear, nor a Preceptor to tell Faults, in *Public*—Pray, if you can, let us fight our A, B, C-Battles in private, next Time." Dashes may well signal a move to private communication. Paradoxically, the letters that are the most "conversational" may be the letters that are least intended to be read aloud.

Epistolary Quarrels in the Literary Public Sphere

Robert Dodsley and the Art of Repartee

The republic of letters in the eighteenth century, even more than in previous centuries, was forged and maintained by networks of copious correspondence. These dyads and networks were known to the eighteenth century as well as ours, since correspondences between major writers were often published during their lives or shortly after their deaths. The correspondence of Pope and the Scriblerians (Swift, Bolingbroke, Gay, Arbuthnot, and others), which occasionally took the form of joint letters, reinforced this literary circle's identity, not only for themselves but also in the eyes of a public interested in reading their communications with each other.[10]

The publication of contemporary writers' letters in England did not become a major enterprise until the eighteenth century, but it took a quite different turn from the tradition established earlier in France. As the French classical tradition was forged in the seventeenth century, each generation hailed a new model epistolarian, from Malherbe at the turn of the century to Guez de Balzac in the 1630s and Voiture in the 1650s. The overriding principle guiding publication in France was a judicious selection of letters that could serve as models for writing. The private life of the writer was edited out or simply was never conceived as representable. Through letters organized around the conventions of court and salon life, these writers set the tone for an aristocratic society called to live in these two centers of public life. Published letters displayed the courtesy system and reinforced the image of the writer as a loyal servant of the French monarchy and aristocracy. Publication of writers' letters thus served to maintain the public sphere as one of "representative publicness" (*repräsentative Öffentlichkeit*), as Jürgen Habermas has described it (8): that is, the display of inherent spiritual power or dignity through insignia, dress, demeanor (form of greeting and pose), and rhetoric (forms of address and formal discourse in general).

In England, on the other hand, the widespread publication of writers' letters began later than in France and coincided with the rise of an interest in biography. It appealed to an audience that sought less a model for writing letters themselves and more some insight into the writer's thoughts and life. The letters of William Temple, which Swift helped prepare for publication in 1700–1703, and the letters of John Locke, first published in 1708, illustrate the "tendency to unlock cabinets of the great" that ushered in an accelerated publication of "lives and letters" in the eighteenth century (Irving 141). This opening up of a public figure's private communications for public scrutiny was conducted with much emphasis on the division between the private and the public. Pope's well-known metaphor of the letter as a "window in the bosom" emblematizes the renewed vision of the letter as a communication of private inner thoughts.

In this sense, the publication of writers' letters in England contributed to the transformation of an aristocratic "representative publicness" (*repräsentative Öffentlichkeit*), which eliminated the private sphere from representation and relied upon feudal "aura" for authority, into what Habermas describes as the "bourgeois public sphere" (*bürgerliche Öffentlichkeit*), which relied upon rational discussion and reintroduced the distinction between private and public. The "bourgeois public sphere," which developed first in England and then in France in the eighteenth century, is one in which "a public passionately concerned with itself sought agreement and enlightenment through the rational-critical *public* debate of *private* persons with one another" (Habermas 43, my emphasis). Habermas discusses how the middle class's "privateness oriented to an audience" became institutionalized through changes in family life, economic organization, architectural design, the development of political journalism, and the rise of the bourgeois novel (43–51).

For Habermas, the Enlightenment's development of a "literary public sphere" (*literarische Öffentlichkeit*) "as an authority to which appeal could be made" played a crucial role in the transformation of an assembly of estates into a modern parliament, as it took place in England during the hundred years following the Glorious Revolution (57). The two letters by Robert Dodsley that James Tierney discusses illustrate quite clearly this new function of the literary public sphere in the minds of eighteenth-century writers.

The two quarrels we glimpse in Dodsley's letters of January 6, 1756, and December 5, 1758, took place privately. They never became the object of general public debate, like the better-known quarrels that had begun in France in the fall of 1755, when Rousseau penned responses to letters from Voltaire and Charles Bonnet attacking his *Discourse on Inequality*.[11] As Tierney points out, however, by 1756 Dodsley had already taken public risks championing democratic causes as both a writer and a publisher, and it is not surprising that he would soon be publishing Rousseau's *Second Discourse* (1762). If we look closely at Dodsley's exchanges with both William Warburton and David Garrick, we can note that whether these letters were intended for publication or not, they were written with the awareness that they might be published.

David Garrick filed copies of his letters and Dodsley's response with endorsements that frame their unity as a quarrel. These endorsements underline Garrick's Olympian refusal to carry on a correspondence with Dodsley, even though Dodsley had written to him about *Cleone* in 1757: "My first letter to Dodsley" (December 3, 1758), "Dodsley's Answer" (December 5, 1758), and "My Answer to Master Rob' Dodsley" (December 6, 1758). Garrick's letters are designed to look good in public according to the courtesy system, which also permits him to put Dodsley in his place. Thus his first letter follows standard form for congratulation (first sentence), correction of rumor (second sentence), and invitation (last sentence). This veneer of public courtesy permits Garrick to patronize Dodsley, as James Tierney points out, and ultimately to seal their rupture with a condescending letter reminding "Master Robert Dodsley" of his lowly background. Garrick also evades discussion of his attempts to undermine the staging of *Cleone*. His letters maintain a hierarchy of "houses" predicated upon the superiority of his Drury Lane theater to Covent Garden, where Dodsley's *Cleone* has played. As "lord" of Drury Lane, Garrick, with *noblesse oblige,* sends a letter to the commoner who had aspired to Garrick's house of lords through his first tragedy but who must content himself with acclamation in Covent Garden. Garrick's letters rely upon aura for authority rather than open discussion.

Dodsley's "thank you for your Compliments" letter, on the other hand, politely alludes, point by point, to the injuries that Garrick refuses to acknowledge and gracefully explains why Dodsley has seen no ground thus far for a cordial relationship with Garrick. Although Dodsley's response cuts off discussion, it is structured as a summary rebuttal. Effectively their time for discussion of *Cleone* has passed. Dodsley's response to Garrick records the moment when Dodsley abandons appeals to the deaf "tyrant" and rests his case with public opinion—that is, with the audience of spectators and readers who would ultimately guarantee the success of his first tragedy.

In the case of the exchange with William Warburton, Dodsley's rebuttal is more developed and is as carefully structured as a lawyer's argument. In this instance, however, Dodsley's adversary has entered the arena of public discussion with him. Warburton's letter of December 26, 1755, is structured as a string of logically connected points submitted for reasoned judgment according to the laws of "justice." It closes, moreover, with a request that Dodsley make this letter available to the rival bookseller Andrew Millar. The letter is to represent Warburton's exact truth, in case Dodsley has "said any thing contrary to these contents." In the letter, Warburton clarifies his intention to sell shares of his "property in Pope" only to persons of his own choosing, who will continue to respect him as "Master" of the property. Warburton conceives his letter as a signed testimony, assuring his control over the posthumous edition of Pope. Dodsley's response refutes charges carefully and eloquently, one by one, in a letter that does him honor. Ultimately, however, sensing Warburton's unremedied disdain, he closes with an appeal to "the opinions of all who best know me" and to "the public in general" as recognizing the merits that Warburton has rejected.

Dodsley's exchanges with Warburton and Garrick, which James Tierney has elucidated through his careful research, illustrate the way in which the literary public sphere in the Enlightenment encouraged discussion across opposing political lines, much as it would take place in Parliament.[12] As Tierney argues, these letters reveal a democrat confronting autocrats. Both parties address their opponents directly and conceive their letters as a performance that can be submitted to public opinion. Whereas the famous literary quarrels of French classicism were restricted to matters of language and literary convention and took place within a relatively restricted reading public, the literary quarrels of the Enlightenment introduce issues of economic property, clear divisions in political philosophy, and an appeal to broad bases of public opinion. The early development of political parties in England and the engagement of writers like Defoe, Swift, and Bolingbroke on their behalf gave writers access to political life earlier than in France. Epistolary communication in this context, as Dodsley's correspondence illustrates, reflects writers' awareness of themselves as politically engaged correspondents, appealing to an expanded reading public as judge of their differences.

Epistolary Mentors in the Literary Public Sphere

Samuel Johnson and Denis Diderot

Many of the letters in this collection are from one major literary figure to another, and they capture different moments in literary relations. Dodsley's letters take us into the literary marketplace with one of England's most important publishers and enact a moment when literary relations are ruptured. The desired partnerships with David Garrick and William Warburton abort in the letters themselves. Charles Burney's 1755 letter to Samuel Johnson shows us the epistolary act through which Burney introduced himself to Samuel Johnson and his literary circle in London, while his 1778 letter to Hester Thrale shows Burney maintaining his warm relations with the Johnson-Thrale circle now comfortably housed at Streatham.

The essays by Lance Wilcox and Emita Hill, on Johnson's letters to Boswell and Diderot's letters to a young actress, reveal a role that certain writers in England and France began to play in the second half of the eighteenth century—that of personal mentor for the general public. The reading public that was touched by the moral message of certain writers sought the writer out in person, by letter or a visit, for literary and moral edification. Rousseau's and Voltaire's correspondences testify to this cult. Robert Darnton and others have pointed out that what was new in the phenomenal reader response to Rousseau was the desire of readers to communicate with the writer himself and to take him as their personal director of conscience. Voltaire functioned similarly as patriarch of Ferney, as did Doctor Johnson in London.

Samuel Johnson's magnetic power as writer and conversationalist drew a circle of young persons toward him. James Boswell, like Charles Burney, was deeply moved by Johnson's *Rambler* essays as he was starting out in life. The Johnson letters that Lance Wilcox presents (1763 and 1782) capture two moments parallel to the Burney letters (1755 and 1778): the initiation of a young writer's epistolary relationship with Johnson through "first" letters, and the maturation of communications within the Johnson circle. Lance Wilcox emphasizes the extent to which James Boswell was, in fact, already the "implied reader" of Johnson's *Rambler* and *Rasselas*, so that Johnson and Boswell played out the roles of Sage Counselor and Young Dog that Johnson had developed in his writing. Wilcox draws a suggestive comparison between these two character types, as Johnson developed them, and the distinction that Kierkegaard would later draw between the ethical and the aesthetic life in *Either/Or*.

By Wilcox's analysis, the full range of letters to Boswell shows Johnson moving from the oratorical style of public mentor developed in the *Rambler*—most visible in Johnson's early correspondence with Boswell, when he speaks "man-to-boy"—to a more conversational, private, allusive style after their shared Scottish journey of 1773, as Boswell matures. The death of Boswell's father in 1782, when Johnson himself was ill, occasioned a return to the "marmoreal prose" of Johnson's "vintage *Rambler* style." The September 1782 letter, however, as Wilcox shows, uses Johnson's *vox celeste* purposefully as a "ventriloquism," since Johnson moves through other styles in the rest of the letter, including ordinary prose and social chitchat.

The informal style of Johnson's private persona surprised his eighteenth-century audience when they read the letters to Hester Thrale that she published in her edition of 1788. Bruce Redford notes that the gap between public and private persona among major eighteenth-century letter writers is at its greatest in these letters. Johnson's letters to Thrale exemplify "the far end of the spectrum, the widest possible divorce between *ex cathedra* and *sub rosa* selves" (206). Lance Wilcox's analysis complements recent work done on the letters to Thrale by showing how Johnson put both his public and his private styles to work in the letters guiding Boswell.

Denis Diderot never assumed the role of public moral guide that Johnson and Rousseau played so effectively. In his best-known writings Diderot does not cultivate the voice of a pedagogue prescribing or advising courses of action. On the contrary, quintessential Diderotian style is dialogue that raises controversial questions and explores multiple aspects of moral issues without resolution. We see this dialogical style at work in his best-known correspondences as well, in the letters to peers in his cultural circle— Falconet, Grimm, and Sophie Volland. Diderot was not sought out by admiring readers as a personal adviser, in the way that Rousseau, Voltaire, and Samuel Johnson were, for another compelling reason. In Enlightenment France, although Diderot became publicly known and satirized as *le philosophe* during his work on the *Encyclopédie*, his need to write clandestinely kept most of his writing anonymous or unpublished until well after his death.

The letters that Emita Hill has selected from Denis Diderot's correspondence, however, display a moment when Diderot used what was perhaps his most publicly "authorized" voice. This was the voice that he had developed, published, and officially signed as author during his foray into the most public of literary genres—the theater. In 1765, when Diderot initiated the correspondence with Mademoiselle Jodin, he had seen his *drame bourgeois, Le Père de famille*, staged in Marseille (1760) and at the Comédie-Française (1761). Between 1755 and 1761 he had reflected deeply upon theater and had published enough theory and examples of bourgeois drama to exert a decisive influence on Lessing (*Le Fils naturel* and the *Entretiens avec Dorval* in 1757, *Le Père de famille* and *De la poésie dramatique* in 1758). Thus when Diderot took up his pen in August 1765 to inform a friend's daughter of the dire straits in which a burglary had left her mother, both the mother's situation and the daughter's profession summon up Diderot's theatrical voices. Diderot addresses the young actress, Marie-Magdeleine Jodin, with the paternal concern and authority of the fathers in his dramas, and he narrates the burglary episode with melodramatic flair. He offers detailed advice for theatrical performance based on the ideas he developed in his discourse *On Dramatic Poetry*. For both his advice on morals and his advice on acting Diderot indulges in prescriptive address: do this, do not do that. The parameters that govern his advice are similar to those underlying Johnson's admonishments to Boswell: to choose the ethical (read "virtuous") life over the aesthetic (read "libertine").

As Emita Hill points out, Diderot's advice to Mademoiselle Jodin as an actress contradicts the well-known theory of acting as cold, distanced control that Diderot would later develop in *Le Paradoxe sur le comédien*. To a certain extent, I think, this is because Diderot is still closer to the more prescriptive ideas on acting that appear in the discourse *On Dramatic Poetry*. The letters to Mademoiselle Jodin enabled him to address these ideas specifically to an aspiring actress. Emita Hill suggests, however, another compelling reason: a double standard skews advice to the actress, as Diderot urges her to remain emotionally sensitive and morally virtuous and to take direction from a male protector.

Unlike the actor, the actress remains subject to male tutelage, just as the actress's career expectations in the eighteenth century would not extend to becoming director of a troupe and a theater. An actress seeking economic and literary independence would do better to become a novelist, as did Marie-Jeanne Riccoboni.

The Eighteenth-Century Writer's Use of the Letter

The letters and essays in this volume span a century during which writers moved from dependence on patronage to dependence on the marketplace.[13] The first three essays illustrate quite different paths that epistolary talent took during the early part of this transition. Defoe's letters to Harley (1705 and 1706) represent what Arnold Hauser has characterized as an "exceptionally favourable situation for authors" in England. During the period between the Glorious Revolution and the appointment of Walpole in 1721, "the role of court circles as patrons of literature is taken over by the political parties and the government, which is now dependent on public opinion" (3: 47). Defoe's letters show how a writer was able to earn his living and participate in political life by defending the interests of a party that represented his own convictions. Chesterfield's letters (1728, 1745, and 1749), on the other hand, illustrate the diplomacy of an aristocrat who did not have to live by his pen but who chose to employ his writing talents as a public servant and statesman. The letters of Christopher Smart (1753 and

1766) open onto a more troublesome moment of this transition, the plight of a *poète maudit* in a market economy. They show us the way Smart solicited benefactors through epistolary poems and supplications. These letters hark back to an earlier conception of the literary work as a present rather than a product, even though the benefactors to whom Smart writes are part of a market economy of printing and subscriptions.

Of the three groups, Defoe's letters represent an innovation of the eighteenth century: the break with the older, courtly forms and the political empowerment of the letter writer. Chesterfield and Smart as epistolarians represent an aspect of letter writing that was still important in the eighteenth century but would decline significantly in the nineteenth century: a sense of writerly production as a gift rather than a commodity. With the clarification of copyright laws, even letters would be clearly defined as property, whose ownership and circulation were regulated by law. This privatization of ownership had as consequences the development of an intensified privacy in epistolary communication that the eighteenth century did not know.[14]

The letters presented in the first three essays are the very medium through which writers pursue their living, be it a livelihood (Defoe and Smart) or a life (Chesterfield). In the next three, on the other hand, letters are the means through which writers forge literary relations or rupture them. The selections of letters by Charles Burney (1755 and 1778), Robert Dodsley (1756 and 1758), and Samuel Johnson (1763 and 1782) display the epistolary acts through which distant writers drew close, cemented and dissolved partnerships, and formed younger writers in an era when writers had achieved significant political and economic independence. Epistolary communication took place in a more private sphere, as literary figures moved into their own "houses"—publishing houses, theaters, and private homes. In private residences like Streatham, literary circles gathered to share more informal, daily-living activities than in the earlier clubs or salons or coffeehouses. The self-conscious mix of private and public voices that we find in these letters shows writers' awareness that both private life and public performance have become equally displayable in novels, dramas, and published letters. Johnson's and Burney's letters trace the move from an eloquence influenced by public speaking to a modulation of voices adjusted for conversation with people with whom one lives. Dodsley's letters show how a private quarrel is conducted in language designed for public display. The forensic art of repartee in the Dodsley exchanges shows writers appealing to the same general public opinion that was assuming political importance as the "bourgeois public sphere" described by Habermas.

Finally, Diderot's letters to Mademoiselle Jodin in 1765 and Jane Austen's letters to Cassandra in 1813 remind us that the bourgeois public sphere that gave expanded power and control to men often had a double standard for women. Emita Hill points out how "the paradox of the actress" differs from "the paradox of the actor" and serves to keep the actress under tutelage to a male director. The impact of the double standard in the bourgeois public sphere would become clear only after the French Revolution had settled the debates over women's rights in the negative. Jane Austen, whose writing career began after the Revolution, embraces the private sphere to which she has been relegated with a mix of pleasure and irony in her letters. She uses privacy to creative advantage while poking fun at the limitations of her confinement.

The letters reproduced and discussed in the preceding essays are an infinitesimal fraction of the correspondence bequeathed to us by writers from the British and French eighteenth century. Nonetheless, like the passages that Erich Auerbach selected for his *Mimesis*, these letters—when closely and knowledgeably read—illuminate the larger cultural context from which they came. Each of the foregoing essays describes the complex ways in which literary figures appropriated the letter during a period when epistolary communication took on expanded literary and political possibilities as a private act. In these letters, among many other phenomena, we see writers move from public forms of art to more private forms that find their language during this period. We see male writers take on expanded public power in the service of political parties and as public mentors for private persons, while the female epistolarian develops an acute awareness of women's exile from the public sphere. At the same time that the Enlightenment was defining new roles for writers, both men and women remained attached to courtesy writing and epistolary networking, older forms of sociability and publicity that could not imagine a writer working in isolation. The cult of complete privacy in letter and diary writing would not be possible until the nineteenth century.

NOTES

1. Isolated articles on individual letter writers have appeared, but no book-length collections or efforts at synthesis on eighteenth-century French correspon-

dences. In fact, more books and articles on French Enlightenment correspondences appeared before Georges May's 1967 article than since. A major effort has gone into editing these voluminous correspondences, however, so that some of the most interesting analyses are those supplied by the editors, in anthologies like J. A. Dainard, *Editing Correspondence* (New York: Garland, 1979), as well as in editorial introductions.

Georges May provides a good summary of literary studies prior to 1967. For a sampling of more recent literary approaches to French Enlightenment correspondences, see MacArthur on the Walpole–du Deffand correspondence, Carrell on Julie de Lespinasse, Melançon on Diderot, Mervaud on Voltaire, and Launay on Rousseau. See also the chapters by Showalter on Graffigny in *Men/Women of Letters* and *L'Epistolarité à travers les siècles*.

2. Publication of a model epistolarian before or shortly after death was a tradition under French classicism. François Malherbe (1555–1628) contributed to letter anthologies published before he died as part of an effort to reform the French language, and he helped prepare his letters for their posthumous publication in 1630 and 1645. Jean-Louis Guez de Balzac (1595–1654) published his first volume of letters in 1624; at age twenty-nine he had inherited Malherbe's mantle as leading epistolarian. Vincent Voiture (1597–1648) was a member of Guez de Balzac's generation, but his epistolary style was not revealed to the general public until two years after his death, in 1650. Bussy-Rabutin (1618–1693) became the leading epistolarian of the next generation of academicians; his four-volume letter collection was published in 1697, four years after his death.

3. The letters for which Lady Mary is best known are often called the Turkish embassy letters. The full title of the three-volume 1763 edition, however, reveals the broader frame in which these travel letters were presented to the reading public: *Letters of the Right Honourable Lady M——y W——y M——e: written during travels in Europe, Asia and Africa, to persons of distinction, men of letters &c in different parts of Europe: which contain, among other curious relations, accounts of the policy and manners of the Turks, drawn from sources that have been inaccessible to other travellers.* The travel genre, particularly letters describing political and social institutions of foreign cultures, had been illustrated by very few women prior to Montagu.

4. After reading the first edition of Sévigné's letters with great pleasure, Lady Mary wrote to Lady Mar in June 1726: "I assert, without the least vanity, that mine will be full as entertaining 40 years hence. I advise you therefore to put none of 'em to the use of Wast paper"; Montagu 2: 66.

5. Pope (1688–1744), Montagu (1689–1762), and Chesterfield (1694–1773) were born within five years of each other. Pope published his letters during his lifetime (1737 and 1741), whereas Montagu's and Chesterfield's were published a year after their deaths.

6. Montagu organizes her letters to her daughter, Lady Bute, concerning the

upbringing of her granddaughters around the principle of resignation to women's exile from public life: "My only Design is to point out to my Grand Daughters the method of being contented with that retreat to which probably their circumstances will oblige them, and which is perhaps preferable to all the show of public Life" (3: 27, letter of March 6, 1753).

7. At midcentury, in the *Encyclopédie*, Jaucourt lamented the insipidness of modern writers' letters and alluded to censorship as its cause: "Nos lettres modernes . . . ne sont que frivoles complimens de gens qui veulent se tromper. . . . [Elles] roulent rarement sur de grands intérêts, sur de véritables sentiments. . . . Quant à nos *lettres* de correspondance dans les pays étrangers, elles ne regardent presque que des affaires de Commerce; & cependant . . . les ministres qui ont l'intendance des postes, prennent le soin de les décacheter & de les lire avant nous" (S.V. "Lettres des modernes").

8. Irving discusses the role of Grub Street booksellers like Edmund Curll in promoting publication of correspondences at the beginning of the eighteenth century (138–63). He notes that by the middle of the century an edition of letters became "quite the expected thing with the death of any person of the mildest distinction" (287).

9. See Dieter A. Berger, *Die Konversationskunst in England, 1660–1740: Ein Sprechphänomen und seine literarische Gestaltung* (Munich: Fink, 1978).

10. Pope, who arranged for so many joint publications of the Scriblerians, envisaged these as a group portrait, conveying a specific image to the public. In 1727, shortly after their *Miscellanies* were printed, Pope wrote Swift: "I am prodigiously pleas'd with this joint-volume, in which methinks we look like friends, side by side, serious and merry by turns, conversing interchangeably, and walking down hand in hand to posterity; not in the stiff forms of learned Authors . . . but in a free, un-important, natural, easy manner; diverting others just as we diverted our selves"; *The Correspondence of Jonathan Swift*, ed. Harold Williams, 5 vols. (Oxford: Clarendon, 1963–65), 3: 201. The letter collections Pope published in the 1730s and 1740s, especially the 1741 edition of his own correspondence, are conceived along similar lines, as a group portrait of the Scriblerians. In the passage just quoted, Pope's vision for this portrait of a select circle contrasts significantly with the French tradition of publishing the *Lettres choisies de Messieurs de l'Académie Française* to illustrate proper epistolary forms and language reforms. If the Scriblerians in many respects assumed the Académie Française's function of correcting the literary world, they chose satire as a vehicle and the informality of "merry conversation" for their group portrait. The Scriblerians present letters, moreover, as exchanges conducted over time ("conversing interchangeably, walking down hand in hand to posterity"). Whereas Académie Française letters were organized by type of letter and by author, Pope's 1741 edition is organized by exchanges ("Letters to

and from Mr. Gay, to and from Dr. Swift"). Pope's description suggests a conscious desire to differ from the tradition of presenting "stiff forms of learned Authors."

11. In August 1755, when the first copies of Rousseau's *Discours sur l'origine . . . de l'inégalité* appeared in France, Voltaire wrote Rousseau a barb-ridden letter beginning, "J'ai reçu, Monsieur, votre nouveau livre contre le genre humain" (Aug. 30, 1755). Rousseau quickly responded by a respectful, reasoned defense on September 10, 1755. In October the naturalist Charles Bonnet published another attack in the *Mercure*, written as a "Lettre de Philopolis, citoyen de Genève," to which Rousseau likewise responded by letter.

12. Although Parliament tried to guarantee the secrecy of its proceedings, the press found numerous ways to expose its deliberations to the public. Habermas sees the century-long evolution toward "full publicity of the parliamentary deliberations" in England as a crucial transformation of a "public authority now being called before the forum of the public" (60–61).

13. For a good summary of this history, even though it represents an earlier stage of research, see Hauser 3: 3–84. Hauser concluded that "after the middle of the century, patronage comes to an absolute end, and round about the year 1780 no writer any longer counts on private support" (52).

14. See Michelle Perrot, "Le Secret de la correspondance au XIX siècle," in *L'Epistolarité à travers les siècles*, 184–88.

WORKS CITED

Altman, Janet Gurkin. "The Letter Book as a Literary Institution, 1539–1789: Toward a Cultural History of Published Correspondences in France." *Men/ Women of Letters* 17–62.

———. "The Politics of Epistolary Art." *A New History of French Literature.* Ed. Denis Hollier. Cambridge: Harvard UP, 1989. 415–21.

Anderson, Howard, Philip B. Daghlian, and Irvin Ehrenpreis, eds. *The Familiar Letter in the Eighteenth Century.* Lawrence: UP of Kansas, 1966.

Auerbach, Erich. *Mimesis: The Representation of Reality in Western Literature.* Trans. Willard Trask. 1946. New York: Doubleday, 1957.

Carrell, Susan Lee. *Le Soliloque de la passion féminine ou le dialogue illusoire: Etude d'une formule monophonique de la littérature épistolaire.* Paris: J.-M. Place, 1982.

Darnton, Robert. "Readers Respond to Rousseau." *The Great Cat Massacre and Other Episodes in French Cultural History.* New York: Basic, 1984. 214–56.

L'Epistolarité à travers les siècles: Geste de communication et/ou d'écriture. Ed. Mireille Bossis. Colloque de Cerisy. Zeitschrift für französische Sprache und Literatur 18. Stuttgart: Franz Steiner Verlag, 1990.

Habermas, Jürgen. *The Structural Transformation of the Public Sphere: An Inquiry into a Category of Bourgeois Society*. Trans. Thomas Burger, with Frederick Lawrence. Cambridge: MIT P. 1989. Originally published as *Strukturwandel der Öffentlichkeit*. Darmstadt: Hermann Luchterhand Verlag, 1962.

Hauser, Arnold. *The Social History of Art*. 4 vols. New York: Vintage, 1958.

Irving, William Henry. *The Providence of Wit in the English Letter Writers*. Durham, N.C.: Duke UP, 1955.

Launay, Michel. "Aspects socio-linguistiques d'une enquête sur la correspondance de J. J. Rousseau." *Revue des Sciences Humaines* ns 161 (1976): 63–81.

MacArthur, Elizabeth J. "Plotting a Metonymical Life Story: The Correspondence of Madame du Deffand and Horace Walpole." In *Extravagant Narratives*. Princeton: Princeton UP, 1990.

May, Georges. "La Littérature épistolaire date-t-elle du XVIIIe siècle?" *Studies on Voltaire and the Eighteenth Century* 56 (1967): 823–44.

Melançon, Benoît. "Etat présent des études sur la correspondance de Diderot." *Recherches sur Diderot et l'Encyclopédie*, no. 6 (April 1989): 131–46.

Men/Women of Letters. Ed. Charles A. Porter. *Yale French Studies* 71 (1986).

Mervaud, Suzanne. "Voltaire et Frédéric II: une dramaturgie des Lumières, 1736–1778." *Studies on Voltaire and the Eighteenth Century* 234.

Montagu, Lady Mary. *The Complete Letters of Lady Mary Wortley Montagu*. Ed. Robert Halsband. 3 vols. Oxford: Clarendon, 1965–67.

Redford, Bruce. *The Converse of the Pen: Acts of Intimacy in the Eighteenth-Century Familiar Letter*. Chicago: U of Chicago P, 1986.

Saintsbury, George. *A Letter Book: Selected with an Introduction on the History and Art of Letter-Writing*. London: G. Bell, 1922.

Spacks, Patricia Meyer. *Gossip*. Chicago: U of Chicago P, 1986.

CONTRIBUTORS

JANET GURKIN ALTMAN, professor of French at the University of Iowa, is the author of *Epistolarity: Approaches to a Form* (Columbus: Ohio State UP, 1982), among other important works on correspondence.

PAULA R. BACKSCHEIDER, the Pepperell-Philpott Eminent Scholar, Auburn University, is the author of *Daniel Defoe: His Life* (Baltimore: Johns Hopkins UP, 1989). She has just completed a book on power, politics, and the rise of mass culture in early modern England.

EMITA B. HILL, chancellor at Indiana University at Kokomo and professor of romance languages and member of the graduate faculty at Indiana University, edited the correspondence between Diderot and Falconet, volume 15 of Diderot's *Oeuvres complètes* (Paris: Hermann, 1986).

ALAN T. MCKENZIE, professor of English and director of Graduate Studies at Purdue University, is the author of *Certain Lively Episodes: The Articulation of Passion in Eighteenth-Century Prose* (Athens: U of Georgia P, 1990) and the Chesterfield entry in the *Dictionary of Literary Biography*, volume 104.

ALVARO RIBEIRO, S.J., assistant professor of English at Georgetown University, coedited with René Wellek *Evidence in Literary Scholarship: Essays in Memory of James Marshall Osborn* (Oxford: Clarendon, 1979) and has edited the first volume of *The Letters of Dr Charles Burney* (Oxford: Clarendon, 1991).

BETTY RIZZO, professor of English at the City College of the City University of New York, is the coeditor of *The Annotated Letters of Christopher Smart* (Carbondale: Southern Illinois UP, 1991).

JAMES E. TIERNEY, professor of English at the University of Missouri–St. Louis, is the editor of *The Correspondence of Robert Dodsley, 1733–1764* (Cambridge: Cambridge UP, 1988).

SUSAN C. WHEALLER, associate dean of Academic Affairs and associate professor of English at Rockford College, is at work on an article on art, accomplishment, and Jane Austen.

LANCE E. WILCOX, assistant professor of English at Elmhurst College, is the author of articles on Johnson, Law, Gibbon, and Shakespeare.

INDEX